Smalltalk-80

Bits of History, Words of Advice

Glenn Krasner, Editor

Xerox Palo Alto Research Center

 Addison-Wesley Publishing Company
Reading, Massachusetts • Menlo Park, California
London • Amsterdam • Don Mills, Ontario • Sydney

D1523457

This book is in the
Addison-Wesley series in Computer Science
MICHAEL A. HARRISON
CONSULTING EDITOR

Cartoons drawn by Jean Depoian

Library of Congress Cataloging in Publication Data

Main entry under title:

Smalltalk-80 : bits of history, words of advice.

Bibliography: p.
Includes index.
1. Smalltalk-80 (Computer system) I. Krasner,
Glenn. II. Title: Smalltalk-eighty.
QA76.8.S635S58   1983   001.64'.25   83-5985
ISBN 0-201-11669-3

Reprinted with corrections, June 1984

ISBN 0-201-11669-3
   CDEFGHIJ-AL-8987654

Preface

The Software Concepts Group of Xerox Palo Alto Research Center (PARC) has been working on the problem of how to give users access to large amounts of computing power. We have concentrated our efforts on the study of software systems, rather than on the creation of specific hardware packages. Our method has been to develop a software system called Smalltalk, to create applications in that system, and then, based on our experiences developing the applications, to design the next system. We have developed and used three major Smalltalk systems over the last 10 years, as well as a few minor variations.

We have documented and released the latest of these systems, the Smalltalk-80 system. We published a description of the system and a complete specification of its implementation in the book, *Smalltalk-80: The Language and Its Implementation*. This first book, however, does not cover the use of the system or programming style for writing large applications in the system. These topics are covered in the forthcoming books *Smalltalk-80: The Interactive Programming Environment* and *Smalltalk-80: Creating a User Interface and Graphical Applications*. Nor does the first book discuss implementation techniques beyond the formal specification, which is the subject of this book, *Smalltalk-80: Bits of History, Words of Advice*.

To check the accuracy and the clarity of the first book, we invited a number of groups outside of Xerox to build implementations of the Smalltalk-80 system. Those groups uncovered problems with the written description, and with the system itself, which we then corrected. They also formed the beginning of a community of Smalltalk implementors with whom we can discuss our ideas, and from whom we can learn about successful and less successful implementation experiences. Paul McCullough of Tektronix suggested that all the implementors submit papers describing their experiences to a software engineering journal or to collect papers from each group into book form. This book, then, is the outcome of that suggestion.

The papers in this book should be of value to other Smalltalk-80 implementors. To implement the Smalltalk-80 system, one has to match the specification with his or her own hardware environment. Each of the groups represented in this book had different experiences with this problem. In addition, some of the groups tested (or speculated about) various schemes for better Smalltalk-80 virtual machine implementations.

In addition to Smalltalk-80 implementors, software engineers should be interested in the papers in this book. Although they are written in the context of Smalltalk-80 implementations, the papers cover the general software engineering topics of managing large software projects, virtual memory design and implementation, software caching mechanisms, and mapping software needs onto hardware design.

The papers in this book raise more issues than they resolve. Smalltalk is still quite young—the Smalltalk-80 system is just a snapshot of research in progress. There are many other issues that need to be raised and many ideas that need to be tested before some of the resolutions can be found. It is our hope that this collection of works will get other implementors thinking about key issues in Smalltalk implementations.

Part One of this book is a collection of papers that provide some background and history of the Smalltalk-80 implementation. The first paper is by Adele Goldberg, manager of the Xerox PARC Software Concepts Group (SCG); it describes the history of releasing the Smalltalk-80 system to the non-Xerox world. Dan Ingalls, who has been the chief architect of the many Smalltalk implementations, tells how the previous systems led up to the Smalltalk-80 system. Glenn Krasner, also of SCG, presents the design of the format of files that are used for sharing Smalltalk-80 code among implementations. The last paper in this section is by Allen Wirfs-Brock of Tektronix, and explores the various design decisions that Smalltalk-80 implementors may face.

In Part Two we present papers that describe the experiences four implementors had in bringing their systems to life. Paul McCullough writes about the process they went through at Tektronix, including a step-by-step description taken directly from their logs. His paper points out how valuable the outside implementors were at discovering problems with the system and its documentation. Joe Falcone and Jim Stinger describe the experience they had at Hewlett-Packard bringing up a couple of implementations. Peter Deutsch, of Xerox SCG, gives some details of how he took advantage of hardware architecture to increase the performance of his Smalltalk-80 implementation. Stoney Ballard and Steve Shirron describe an implementation they made at Digital Equipment Corp., which differs radically from the suggested implementation of the storage manager, in order to provide improved performance.

Descriptions of implementation experiences help others make their design choices; actual measurements and analyses provide additional concrete help. Part Three is a collection of measurements made by the implementation groups. The first paper, by Kim McCall of Xerox SCG, describes a set of benchmarks that is provided in the Smalltalk-80 system to help measure the performance of an implementation. All the implementation groups were willing to run these benchmarks, and a comparison of their results is included in the paper. This gives a number of implementations against which new implementors can measure their progress. Rick Meyers and Dave Casseres of Apple Computer provide an interesting set of analyses of their MC68000-based implementation. David Ungar and David Patterson of the University of California Berkeley give a before-and-after description of the process of measuring an implementation, optimizing the time-consuming parts, and measuring the effects of the optimizations. Joe Falcone made measurements of the Hewlett-Packard implementation that compare static properties with dynamic properties of the system. Finally, Tom Conroy and Ed Pelegri-Llopart of UC Berkeley present an analytic model for measuring the potential performance gains of a particular cache scheme for Smalltalk-80 implementations.

In Part Four we present papers that look toward the future of Smalltalk systems and propose ideas for extending the Smalltalk-80 system beyond its initial form. The first paper is a description by Ted Kaehler and Glenn Krasner of Xerox SCG of an object-oriented virtual memory design. Steve Putz, also of SCG, presents a solution to the problem of coordinating changes made by many people to an evolving Smalltalk-80 system. Jason Penney describes his implementation of a file system at Tektronix, and discusses the use of the Smalltalk-80 system for programming. From the University of Washington, Guy Almes, Alan Borning, and Eli Messinger, present an analysis of the potential for implementing the Smalltalk-80 system on the Intel iAPX432 microprocessor. Although they did not actually implement the system, their paper provides a good analysis of how to match an object-oriented system to object-oriented hardware. Applying compiler technology, Robert Hagmann of the University of California, Berkeley, proposes ways to increase the performance of a Smalltalk-80 implementation. The last paper, by Scott Baden of the University of California, Berkeley, proposes hardware architecture support that would enhance the performance of implementations.

**Acknowledg-
ments**

We would like to thank the authors, their co-workers, and their organizations for their contributions to this book, for their diligence during the release and review process, and for their willingness to be open about the strengths and weaknesses of their Smalltalk-80 implementations. We would also like to thank the Xerox Research management for allowing us to release the Smalltalk-80 system, thus widening the community of Smalltalk implementors with whom we can share experiences and insights.

Many people contributed to the production of this book. Each author also acted as an editor of an early draft of another author's paper. Janet Moreland helped coordinate this swapping with copying and mailing. Doug Carothers answered legal questions. Ted Kaehler provided other bits of help, and Frank Zdybel added some words of his own. Dave Robson built the translator that allowed us to deliver manuscripts electronically. Eileen Colahan of the International Computaprint Corporation was extremely cooperative and flexible in turning these electronic manuscripts into print. The cartoons in the book are by Ted Kaehler, redrawn by Addison-Wesley artist Jean Depoian. Adele Goldberg merged the images into the cover design with help from Rebecca Cannara. Particular thanks go to production editor Fran Fulton for her cooperation and patience, and to Jim DeWolf and Cheryl Wurzbacher of Addison-Wesley.

Registered trademarks mentioned in this book are: AED-512, Advanced Electronic Design, Inc.; UNIX, Bell Laboratories; DEC, DECSYSTEM, DECSYSTEM20, UNIBUS and VAX, Digital Equipment Corporation; HP-IB, Hewlett-Packard; GPIB, National Instruments; BitPadOne, Summagraphics Corporation; and Smalltalk-80, Xerox Corporation.

Palo Alto, California   G. E. K.
June 1983

Contents

PART ONE

Background

DEBUGGING AFTER A
SMALLTALK CRASH

1

The Smalltalk-80 System
Release Process

Adele Goldberg
Manager, Software Concepts Group
Xerox Palo Alto Research Center
Palo Alto, California

Introduction

The Smalltalk-80 system has its roots in the Xerox Palo Alto Research Center starting more than 10 years ago. During a decade of research, three major systems were designed, implemented, and tested with a variety of users. The systems were named for the year in which they were designed. The first two were Smalltalk-72 and Smalltalk-76. The latest version, called the Smalltalk-80 system, was developed to be adaptable for implementation on a large number and variety of computers.

The Smalltalk research efforts focus on increasing the support that computing systems can provide to users who are not computer scientists by profession. These efforts are centered on the visual impact of bitmapped graphics, on highly interactive user interfaces, and on increased flexibility in terms of user programmability. Among the outcomes of this work were the basic concepts of windows, menus (textual and iconic), and scroll bars. Implementations of these concepts are used to expand the virtual space of a display screen; they typically emphasize the use of pointing devices rather than keyboards for selecting objects (documents, devices) and operations on objects (commands).

In 1979 and 1980, requests and clearances were agreed upon within the Xerox Corporation to permit the dissemination of the Smalltalk-80 system to the non-Xerox world. The stated purposes of this dissemination were to:

1. expand the community of Smalltalk programmers in order to gain more general experience with how people can use the language;

2. expand the community of programming language researchers who study aspects of the Smalltalk style of programming;

3. influence hardware designers to consider ways in which to provide increased performance for the Smalltalk style of interaction; and

4. establish a standard for Smalltalk as an object-oriented programming language and a graphics-based, interactive program development environment.

The dissemination was planned in three parts: a series of introductory articles, a book giving detailed system specifications, and a magnetic tape containing the system itself. The series of articles would provide an early and less formal introduction to the Smalltalk-80 system. Ultimately, these articles were published in the August 1981 special issue of *Byte* magazine. The system specification was divided into two major components—the Virtual Machine and the Virtual Image. The Virtual Machine for a particular hardware system consists of an interpreter, a storage manager, and primitives for handling the input/output devices. The Virtual Image is a collection of objects that make up descriptions of classes providing basic data structures (including numbers), basic graphics and text, compiler, decompiler, debugger, and viewing and user interface support. The Virtual Image contains approximately 10,000 objects. The proposed book would contain the formal specifications for the implementation of the Virtual Machine, as well as a description of the language and the interfaces to the objects in the Virtual Image. The proposed tape would contain a digital representation of the Virtual Image that could be loaded into a hardware system on which the Virtual Machine had been implemented.

All systems running the Smalltalk-80 system would therefore look the same; each would have to support bitmapped graphics and a pointing device for controlling a cursor on the graphics display. The issue of protecting the software was resolved by copyrighting the Virtual Image and publicly disclosing the Virtual Machine; licensing under copyright grants the licensee the right to reproduce the Image only for incorporation into a hardware product of the licensee. Any unincorporated reproduction and distribution is prohibited. The modular approach to the Smalltalk design made this form of protection feasible.

An initial attempt to produce a book about the Smalltalk system described the design of an unfinished system that was to be called Smalltalk-80. Chapters of the book were written in the spring and summer of 1979. Since much of this written material described how to implement the system, an appropriate review of the material required following the specifications and actually implementing the Virtual Machine. This was accomplished by involving members of software groups of several computer manufacturers in the process of review and implementation. Although the Smalltalk systems had received a great deal of publicity since Smalltalk-72 was first designed, few people outside Xerox's research centers had actually used them before this review.

The cautious invitation issued to six companies was to read the book material in order to understand the nature of the system. Reviewers were also invited to visit the Xerox Palo Alto Research Center in order to see a live demonstration of the system. If they were still interested in the system after reading the written material and participating in a demonstration, they were invited to enter the second phase of review— an actual implementation. A company could only accept the invitation if it had (1) the required hardware (at least a 16-bit processor, a bitmapped display, and a way of indicating locations on the display), and (2) a software team on the project that consisted of regular employees only.

Only four of those invited were able to enter the second phase of the review, Apple Computer, Digital Equipment Corporation, Hewlett-Packard, and Tektronix. These four companies agreed to share in debugging the formal specification of the Virtual Machine. Problems encountered and general design advice would be exchanged with all participants. Besides assisting in completing a book about the system, this review process would test the ability of these manufacturers to successfully create a full implementation of the Smalltalk-80 system based on the information provided in the book. Success would be measured by each manufacturer's ability to "read and adopt" the Virtual Image; a more subjective measurement would be the actual performance of the system on each manufacturer's hardware.

By 1982, the review process was complete enough that a revision of the book was possible. Actually, the written material was treated much the way the Smalltalk software had been treated over the decade of research—it was thrown away, with the exception of the (now debugged) formal specification of the Virtual Machine. All of the chapters were rewritten. Because of the volume of material that was to be disseminated, the book became three books—one for the programmer and language designer (*Smalltalk-80: The Language and Its Implementation*), one for the user and programming environments designer (*Smalltalk-80: The Interactive Programming Environment*), and one for the applications designer (*Smalltalk-80: Creating a User Interface and Graphical Applications*).

For their participation in the review process, each manufacturer received a right to use the Smalltalk-80 Virtual Image in their research and in their developed hardware products. Thus the Virtual Machine has been provided outside Xerox without obligation, while the Virtual Image for use in conjunction with the Machine has been licensed under the auspices of copyright. That is, the reproduction and redistribution of the Virtual Image or portions of the Virtual Image are permitted only as incorporated into a product of these manufacturers/licensees.

The Review Process

The first tape containing a Virtual Image was delivered February 17, 1981. The image file contained 328 records, 512 bytes per record. The purpose of this tape was to debug the image file format, and to get the reviewers started loading in and running a version of Smalltalk. The image had two deficiencies: the source code for the class hierarchy was primarily a subset of the system, and the primitives called from each class had only preliminary class/method and number assignments. The reviewers were also provided a detailed memo instructing them how to read the image file format and summarizing the information provided in the book on formats for object pointers, object space, contexts, compiled methods, and classes.

As part of the agreement, telephone consultation was available to the implementors. Any major bugs or discrepancies in the specifications were reported via telephone and logged. It was possible to monitor each implementor's progress with respect to their discovery of or compensation for the bugs. The process of revising the system image itself was carried out at Xerox with the aid of electronic mail: bug reports, bug fixes, status reports, and new ideas were typically communicated electronically. Eventually these communications evolved into a Smalltalk-80 subsystem called the Version Manager which supported (re-)configuration of new system releases.

The second tape was delivered on July 24, 1981. In addition to the image file (this time 589 records long), the tape contained a file of the source code, a file into which the system writes its "audit trail" of changes, and three files containing traces generated by the Smalltalk-80 simulator as it executes the first bytecodes in the Virtual Image. The traces were made by running the formal specification of the interpreter written in Smalltalk-80 code (the code is included in the chapters of the book).

The three traces, provided in all subsequent tape releases, show decreasing levels of detail over increasing durations.

1. The first trace shows all memory references, allocations, bytecodes, message transmissions, returns, and primitive invocations for the first 115 bytecodes executed.

2. The second trace shows only the bytecodes, message transmissions, returns, and primitives for the first 409 bytecodes.

3. The third trace shows message transmissions, primitives, and returns for the first 1981 bytecodes.

The traces allow the implementors to compare their system's actual behavior with the "expected" behavior.

This second tape contained a full system according to the specification of the Smalltalk-80 Virtual Machine. All the source code had either been rewritten according to the class hierarchy for Smalltalk-80, or had been translated from the Smalltalk-76 classes into the Smalltalk-80 syntax. However, this translated code was not the definition for the final system.

The third tape was delivered four months later on November 18, 1981. It contained the same kinds of files as were provided on the second tape. By this time, however, the system user interface had been completely rewritten and a great deal of new functionality had been provided in the program development environment. The image file was now 977 records long.

Once again, the Virtual Machine had been changed, in particular, several primitives were added. This time the changes were mostly those discussed and agreed upon by the implementors who attended the "First Ever Smalltalk-80 Implementors' Conference" held September 24-25, 1981, in Palo Alto. Much of the discussion at this conference centered around the uses of reference counting, garbage collecting, and method caches. The Smalltalk-80 system design separates storage management from the Virtual Machine specification. The various implementors were able to try out several storage management schemes, as well as several different approaches to reference counting. Source code management was also discussed, notably the solution of making source code bona fide Smalltalk objects in a virtual memory system, rather than trying to use external text files. Benchmarks for comparing system implementations were specified, and agreement was reached on writing a book on implementation considerations (that is, the book in which this chapter appears).

A fourth tape was later provided in order to distribute a Virtual Image that had been used for some time and in which many bugs had been fixed and some new features added. In particular, the fourth image added a model interface to a file system. The image file was now 1011 records long. The implementors who had been successful in running the third tape were able simply to load and run this fourth tape, without any changes to their Virtual Machine implementation. The goal of distributing system releases as Virtual Images was thus reached and the review process terminated.

Additional Collaborations

Prior to the delivery of the third image, an additional research license was given to the University of California at Berkeley in order to provide material for study by a graduate seminar on computer architecture (taught by Professors David Patterson, John Ousterhout, and Richard Fateman). The students in the seminar obtained an early version of the Hewlett-Packard implementation of the Smalltalk-80 Virtual Machine on which to run the Virtual Image provided by Xerox. After some initial use and study, the students wrote their own implementation in the C language for a VAX/780. The purpose in executing this license was to establish a close collaboration with a group of researchers experienced with the application of state-of-the-art hardware architecture technology to high-level programming languages.

Once the review process was completed, a special collaboration was formulated with the Fairchild Laboratory for Artificial Intelligence Research (FLAIR). Several implementations had been carried out on hardware systems consisting of an MC68000 processor, from which several clever ideas for improving the performance of the interpreter had been devised. The researchers at Xerox and FLAIR felt that by working together they could combine these clever ideas into a MC68000-based system with better performance than so far demonstrated. At the time that this chapter was written, this implementation project was still under way.

A Final Word

The book review process, as envisioned by the research team, satisfied two needs: publication of research results, and setting a standard for a new form of personal computing. Publication took the form of written articles; the quantity of material and the integrated presentation of that material required a full book and a special issue of a magazine. The published system, however, was best appreciated in its dynamic form; publication was best served by distribution of the actual system software. Through this distribution, a shared system base has been created.

2

The Evolution
of the Smalltalk
Virtual Machine

Daniel H. H. Ingalls
Software Concepts Group
Xerox Palo Alto Research Center
Palo Alto, California

Introduction

In this paper we record some history from which the current design of the Smalltalk-80 Virtual Machine springs. Our work over the past decade follows a two- to four-year cycle that can be seen to parallel the scientific method and is shown in Fig. 2.1. The paper appears in two

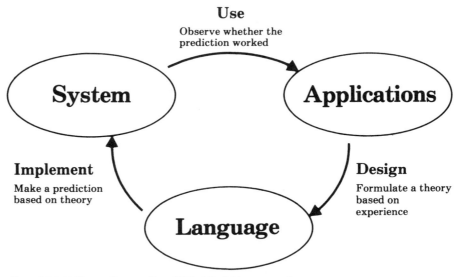

Figure 2.1

sections that are relatively independent of one another. The first section traces the evolution of the current design from the perspective of form following function. It follows the major implementation challenges and our solutions to them. The second section relates some of the *methodology* which evolved in pursuing this cycle of reincarnation. Readers who are less interested in the details of Smalltalk can skip to the second section and interpret our experience relative to other programming languages and systems.

Form Follows Function

From the first Smalltalk interpreter to the definition of the Smalltalk-80 Virtual Machine, the Smalltalk language has been characterized by three principal attributes:

- Data stored as objects which are automatically deallocated,
- Processing effected by sending messages to objects,
- Behavior of objects described in classes.

In spite of other opinions to the contrary, we consider these to be the hallmarks of the "object-oriented" style of computing. In this section we shall trace the evolution of the underlying machinery which has supported language systems in this style over the last ten years. Some of the changes have augmented the power of the language, and some have increased its efficiency. Each change can be seen as an attempt to bring the underlying machinery more into harmony with the day-to-day demands of object-oriented programming.

Smalltalk-72

The very first Smalltalk evaluator was a thousand-line BASIC program which first evaluated 3+4 in October 1972. It was followed in two months by a Nova assembly code implementation which became known as the Smalltalk-72 system[1].

☐ *Storage Management* Objects were allocated from a linked list of free storage using a first-fit strategy. Objects which were no longer accessible were detected by reference-counting. They were then returned to the free storage list, with adjacent entries being automatically coalesced. Since pointers were direct memory addresses, compaction would have been complicated, and was not attempted. Contexts, the suspended stack frames, were managed specially as a stack growing down from high memory while normal allocation grew up from low memory. This separation reduced the tendency to leave "sandbars" when returning values from deep calls, a problem in the absence of compaction.

☐ *Token Representation of Code*   All code was stored in a single tree made up of instances of Array (it was called Vector then), a variable-length array of pointers. The code in this tree represented a pattern description, similar to Meta. Fig. 2.2 presents the Smalltalk-72 definition of a class of dotted-pair objects, followed by a few examples of its use. Responses printed by the system are underlined.

to pair	to *is the defining word, as in LOGO.*
| head tail	| *declares instance variable names.*
(isnew ⇒	isnew *is true if an instance is just created.*
(″ head ← :. ″ tail ← :)	″ *means literally the next token, here the*
⊿ head ⇒	*names* head *and* tail.
(⊿ ← ⇒	← *is a message like any other.*
(″ head ← :)	: *fetches the next value from the incoming.*
↑ head)	*message stream.*
⊿ tail ⇒	⊿ *matches the next literal token*
(⊿ ← ⇒	*like the Smalltalk-80 message*
(″ tail ← :)	peekFor:
↑ tail)	*false* ⇒ (*body*) *does nothing, but*
⊿ print ⇒	*true* ⇒ (*body*) *evaluates the body, and*
(″ [print. head print.	*then leaves the outer scope.*
″ . print.	*In this way several such constructs*
tail print. ″] print))	*work as a CASE statement.*
<u>pair</u>	
″ a ← pair 2 5	*Here a* pair *is created, called* a.
<u>[2.5]</u>	
a tail ← pair 3 7	a *gets its* tail *changed.*
<u>[2.[3.7]]</u>	
b tail head	a*'s tail* (=[3.7]) *gets the message* head.
<u>3</u>	

Figure 2.2

The code was viewed by the interpreter as simply a stream of tokens. The first one encountered was looked up in the dynamic context, to determine the receiver of the subsequent message. The name lookup began with the class dictionary of the current activation. Failing there, it moved to the sender of that activation and so on up the sender chain. When a binding was finally found for the token, its value became the receiver of a new message, and the interpreter activated the code for that object's class.

In the new context, the interpreter would begin executing the receiver's code, matching it with the token stream which followed the original occurrence of the receiver. Various matching operators would select a route through the code which corresponded to the message pattern encountered. The matching vocabulary included matching a literal token, skipping a token, picking up a token literally, and picking up the value of a token. The latter operation invoked the same dynamic lookup described above for the receiver.

☐ *Classes* Most class properties were stored in a single dictionary. Instance variable names were denoted by a special code which included their offset in the instance. Class variables appeared in the same dictionary as normal name/value pairs. Another entry gave the size of instances, and another gave the "code" for the class. When a class was mentioned in code, it would automatically produce a new instance as a value. The unfortunate result of this special behavior was to make classes unable to be treated as ordinary objects.

☐ *Applications* Smalltalk-72 was ported to the Alto[2] as soon as the first machines were built, and it provided a stable environment for experimentation over the next few years. The Alto provided a large bitmap display and a pointing device, and thus made an ideal vehicle for working with graphical user interfaces.

Development of the Smalltalk-72 system began with Textframes and Turtles. Textframes provided text display with independent composition and clipping rectangles; Turtles gave us line drawing capability, modeled after Papert's experiments with turtle geometry[3]. In both cases, Smalltalk's ability to describe multiple instances added considerable leverage to these primitive capabilities. Soon many interesting and useful applications were written, including a mouse-driven program editor, a structured graphics editor, an animation system and a music system. Finally, Smalltalk-72 served as the basis for an experimental curriculum in object-oriented computing for high-school children[4].

☐ *Shortcomings* The Smalltalk-72 system was used heavily by a dozen people for four years. The many practical applications gave us a lot of experience with the power of classes and the message-sending metaphor. In the course of this work, we also became increasingly aware of many limitations in the Smalltalk-72 system.

Dynamic lookup of tokens was both inefficient and unmodular. The dynamic lookup tempted some programmers to write functions which "knew" about their enclosing context. This code would then cause subtle errors when apparently innocent changes were made in the outer level.

The message stream model was complicated and inefficient. One could not tell what a given piece of code meant in isolation. This became a problem as we attempted to build larger systems in which modularity was more of an issue. Also, a considerable amount of time was wasted on execution-time parsing (determining whether the result of a receiver expression should gobble the next token in the execution stream).

As mentioned above, classes were not first-class objects. Also, as our experience increased, we came to realize the need for inheritance. This was felt first in the commonality of behavior of Arrays, Strings, and sub-Arrays. For the time being, we referred to common functions from these similar classes so as to factor the behavior, but it was clear that some sort of inheritance mechanism was needed.

Smalltalk-74

In 1974 we produced a major redesign of the Smalltalk interpreter with the aim of cleaning up its semantics and improving its performance. While the redesign was a mixed success, Smalltalk-74 was the site of several advances which fed into the later systems.

☐ *Message Stream Formalism* We succeeded in formalizing the operation of the interpreter, a step in the direction of simplicity and generality. For instance, we were able to provide a programmer-accessible object which represented the incoming message stream. Thus, not only could all the message stream operations be examined in Smalltalk, but the user could also define his own extensions to the message stream semantics. While this was a local success, it did not solve either of the real problems: token interpretation overhead, and non-modularity of receiver-dependent message parsing.

☐ *Message Dictionaries* Classes were given a message dictionary to allow primary message matching to be done by hashing. This did not do much for execution speed, since the previous interpreter had tight code for its linear scan, but it did help compilation a great deal since a single message could be recompiled without having to recompile all the code for the class. Unfortunately classes were still not able to be treated as normal objects.

☐ *BitBlt* Smalltalk-74 was the first Smalltalk to use BitBlt as its main operation for bitmap graphics. The specification for BitBlt arose out of earlier experience with Turtle graphics, text display, and other screen operations such as scrolling and menu overlays. Our specification of BitBlt has been used by others under the name RasterOp[5]. While the general operation was available to the Smalltalk programmer, much of the system graphics were still done in machine-coded primitives, owing to inadequate performance of the token interpreter.

☐ *OOZE* Smalltalk-74 was the system in which the OOZE ("Object-Oriented Zoned Environment")[6] virtual memory was first implemented. OOZE provided uniform access to 65K objects, or roughly a million words of data. Smalltalk-74 served as the development environment for OOZE, so that when Smalltalk-76 was designed, OOZE was debugged and ready for use.

☐ *Applications* In addition to the previous applications which we had developed, Smalltalk-74 served as host to an information retrieval system and complete window-oriented display interface. Owing to the virtual memory support, it was possible to integrate many functions in a convenient and uniform user interface.

Smalltalk-76

In 1976 we carried out a major redesign of the Smalltalk language and implementation[7]. It addressed most of the problems encountered in the previous four years of experience with Smalltalk:

- Classes and contexts became real objects;
- A class hierarchy provided inheritance;
- A simple yet flexible syntax for messages was introduced;
- The syntax eliminated message stream side-effects and could be compiled;
- A compact and efficient byte-encoded instruction set was introduced;
- A microcode emulator for this instruction set ran 4 to 100 times faster than previous Smalltalks; and
- OOZE provided storage for 65K objects—roughly the capacity of the Alto hardware.

The design for this system was completed in November of 1976 and seven months later the system was working. This included a full rewrite of all the system class definitions.

Experience with Smalltalk-76

The Smalltalk-76 design stood the test of time well. It was used for four years by 20 people daily and 100 people occasionally. A large portion of the design survives unchanged in the Smalltalk-80 system. However, the Smalltalk-76 design did have some snags which we encountered during our four-year experience.

☐ *Block Contexts* Smalltalk-76 had to provide a mechanism for passing unevaluated code which was compatible with a compiled representation. A syntax was devised which used open-colon keywords for passing unevaluated expressions (the semantics were the same as the square bracket construct in the Smalltalk-80 language). This approach was supported by block contexts which allowed executing code remotely. Since the Smalltalk-76 design had no experience to draw from, it was weak in several areas.

One problem which was discovered in the process of supporting error recovery was that block contexts could not be restarted because they did not include their initial PC as part of their state. This was not normally needed for looping, since all such code fragments ended with a branch back to the beginning. Happily, we were able to fix this by defining a new subclass.

Two other problems were discovered with remote contexts when users began to store them as local procedures. For one thing, there was no check in the interpreter to recover gracefully if such a piece of code executed a return to sender after the originating context had already returned. Also, the system could crash if remote contexts were made to call one another recursively, since they depended on their home context for stack space, rather than having their own stack space.

There were two other weaknesses with remote code. There was an assymmetry due to use of open-colon keywords. For example one would write

newCursor showWhile: [someExpression]

to cause a different cursor to appear during execution of someExpression. But if the code contained a variable, *action*, which was already bound to remote code, one wanted that variable to be passed directly, as with a closed-colon keyword. The only way to handle this without needing a pair of messages with and without evaluation was to write

newCursor showWhile: [action eval].

This would do the right thing, but caused an extra remote evaluation for every level at which this strategy was exercised. Besides being costly, it was just plain ugly.

Another weakness of remote contexts was that, while they acted much like nullary functions, there was no way to extend the family to functions which took arguments.

Finally, there was a question about variable scoping within remote code blocks. Smalltalk-76 had no scoping, whereas most other languages with blocks did.

All of these problems with RemoteContexts were addressed one way or another in the Smalltalk-80 design.

☐ *Compilation Order*   The Smalltalk-76 interpreter assumed that the receiver of a message would be on the top of the execution stack, with arguments below it. The number of arguments was not specified in the "send" instruction, but was determined from the method header after message lookup. From the designer's perspective this seemed natural; the only other reasonable choice would be for the receiver to lie underneath the arguments, as in the Smalltalk-80 system. In this case it seemed necessary to determine the number of arguments from the selector in order to find the receiver in the stack, and this looked both complex and costly to do at run time. There were two problems with having the receiver on the top of the stack. First the compiler had to save the code for the receiver while it put out the code for the arguments. This was no problem for three of the compilers which we built, but one particularly simple compiler design foundered on this detail. The second problem with post-evaluation of receivers was that the order of evaluation differed from the order of appearance in the code. Although one should not write Smalltalk code which depends on such ordering, it did happen occasionally, and programmers were confused by the Smalltalk-76 evaluation scheme.

☐ *Instruction Set Limitations*   The Smalltalk-76 instruction set was originally limited to accessing 16 instance variables, 32 temps, and 48 literals. These limits were both a strain on applications and on the instruction set. A year later we added extended instructions which relieved these limits. This was important for applications, and it also took pressure off the future of the instruction set. With extended codes available, we had the flexibility to change the instruction set to better reflect measured usage patterns. For example we found that we could get rid of the (non-extended) instructions which accessed literals 33-48, because their usage was so low. Such measurements led us eventually to the present Smalltalk-80 instruction set.

Experience with OOZE

☐ *Address Encoding*   In OOZE, object pointers encoded class information in the high 9 bits of each pointer. This had the benefit of saving one word per object which would have been needed to point to the class of the object. In fact, it actually saved two words on many objects because classes contained the length of their instances. Variable length objects had separate class-parts for common lengths (0 through 8). However, the address encoding had several weaknesses. It squandered 128 pointers on each class, even though some never had more than a couple of instances. It also set a limit on the number of classes in the system (512). This did not turn out to be a problem, although an earlier limit of 128 did have to be changed. Finally, owing to the encoding, it was not possible to use object pointers as semantic indirection. For this reason, Smalltalk-76 could not support become: (mutation of objects through pointer indirection) as in later Smalltalks.

☐ *Capacity*   While the OOZE limitation of 65K objects is small by today's standards, it served well on the Alto. The Alto has a 2.5 megabyte disk, and with a mean object size of 16 words, OOZE was well matched to this device.

☐ *Interpreter Overhead*   OOZE had a couple of weaknesses in the area of performance, which only became significant after our appetites had increased from several years' experience. One was that the object table required at least one hash probe for every object access, even just to touch a reference count. Another was a design flaw in the management of free storage which required going to the disk to create a new temporary object if its pointer had been previously placed on a free list. We designed a solution to both of these problems. Temporary objects would be treated specially with pointers which were direct indexes into their object table. Freelists would only be consulted when an object "matured" and needed a permanent pointer assigned. Because temporary objects account for many accesses, much of the overhead of probing the permanent object table would be eliminated. Since Smalltalk-76's days seemed numbered, we did not take the time to implement this solution.

Efficiency and Portability: Smalltalk-78

In 1977 we began a project to build a portable computer capable of running the Smalltalk system. Known internally as NoteTaker, it began as a hand-held device for taking notes, but ended up as a suitcase-sized Smalltalk machine. Several factors converged to define this project. We wanted to be able to bring Smalltalk to conferences and meetings to break through the abstractions of verbal presentations. With the Intel 8086 and other 16-bit microprocessors (the Z8000 and MC68000 were coming, but not available yet), we felt that enough computing power would be available to support Smalltalk, even without microcode. Finally, portability seemed to be an essential ingredient for exploring the full potential of personal computing.

The design challenge was significant. We were moving to an environment with less processing power, and the whole system had to fit in 1/4 Mbyte, since there was no swapping medium. Also we faced transporting 32K bytes of machine code which made up the Smalltalk-76 system, and it seemed a shame not to learn something in the process. The result of these forces was the design of Smalltalk-78.

☐ *Cloned Implementation*   The Smalltalk-78 implementation was significant in that it was not built from scratch. We were happy enough with the basic model that we transported the entire Smalltalk level of the system from Smalltalk-76. In order to do this, we used the system tracer (see p. 24) which could write a clone of the entire system onto an image file. This file could then be loaded and executed by the Smalltalk-78 interpreter. The tracer had provisions in it for transmut-

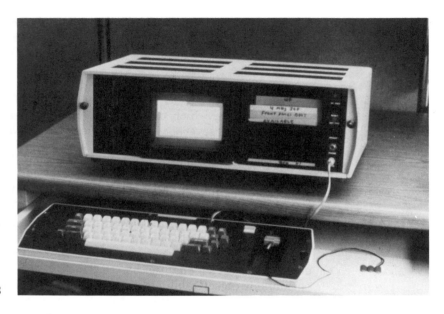

Figure 2.3

ing object formats as necessary, and even for changing the instruction set used in the methods.

☐ *Indexed OT* The Smalltalk-78 design centered around an indexed object table, which is the same design as in the Smalltalk-80 system. This greatly simplified object access and yet retained the indirection which made for easy storage management in Smalltalk-76. Reference counts were stored as one byte of the 4-byte table entry. Given an object pointer in a register, a reference count could be incremented or decremented with a single add-byte instruction with an overflow check.

☐ *Small Integers* Since there would not be room in core for more than 10K objects or so, it was possible to encode small integers (-16384 to 16383) in part of the pointer space. Since object table indices would all be even (on the 8086, they were multiples of 4), we encoded small integers as two's complement integers in the high-order 15 bits, with the low-order bit turned on. With this design, allocation of integer results was trivial, integer literals could be stored efficiently, and integer values did not need to be reference counted.

☐ *In-line Contexts* In order to save time allocating new contexts, and to take advantage of the stack-oriented instructions available in most microprocessors, the representation of contexts was redesigned. Instead of having a separate object for each context, a large object was allocated for each process, in which contexts could be represented as conventional stack frames. This special representation complicated the handling of blocks and the debugger, requiring an interface which referred to the process and an offset within the process.

In addition to reduced allocation time, the time to transfer arguments was eliminated by allowing the contexts to overlap; the top of one context's stack (receiver and arguments) was the base of the next context's frame.

☐ *Reduced Kernel—The Leverage of BitBlt* We have always sought to reduce the size of the Smalltalk kernel. This is not only an aesthetic desideratum; kernel code is inaccessible to the normal user, and we have always tried to minimize the parts of our system which can not be examined and altered by the curious user. In this particular case, we were also moving to a new machine. While writing a certain amount of machine code seemed inevitable, we did not relish the idea of transcribing all 32K bytes of code which comprised the Smalltalk-76 kernel. Fortunately, much of that bulk consisted of various routines to compose and display text, to draw lines and implement Turtle geometry, and to provide various interfaces to bitmap graphics such as moving rectangles, and copying bits to buffers as for restoring the background under menus.

The definition of BitBlt grew out of our experience with text, lines and other bitmap graphics. Now the constraints of the NoteTaker implementation provided the motivation to implement all these capabilities in Smalltalk, leaving only the one primitive BitBlt operation in the kernel. This was a great success in reducing the size of the kernel. The full NoteTaker kernel consisted of around 6K bytes of 8086 code. This figure did not include Ethernet support, real-time clock, nor any significant support for process scheduling.

☐ *Performance* The performance of the NoteTaker was interesting to compare with the Alto. The Smalltalk instruction rate improved by a factor of two, and yet the display of text was much slower (being in Smalltalk, rather than machine code). By adding a small primitive for the inner loop of text display and line drawing, this decrease was largely compensated. User response for such actions as compiling was significantly improved, owing to the faster execution and to the freedom from the swapping delays of OOZE.

☐ *Mutability* Smalltalk-78 used no encoding of object pointers other than for small integers. Class pointers and length fields (for variable-length objects) were stored just as any other fields. It was therefore possible in this design to allow mutation of objects, and this was made available as the primitive method for become:.

☐ *Relevance* We learned a great deal from the NoteTaker challenge, even though only 10 prototypes were built. We made the system much more portable, and had demonstrated that the new generation of microprocessors could indeed support Smalltalk. The decision not to continue the project added motivation to release Smalltalk widely.

TinyTalk

At the same time as the NoteTaker implementation, we performed an experiment[8] to see if a very simple implementation could run on a conventional microprocessor such as a Z80 or 6502. This implementation used marking garbage collection instead of reference-counting, and was able to use simple push and pop operations on the stack as a result. A method cache largely eliminated the overhead in message lookup and, since primitive codes were included in the cache, access to primitives was fast. The system did actually fit in 64K bytes with a little bit of room to spare. Another experiment which was done in conjunction with this implementation was to demonstrate that a special case of BitBlt for characters could run much faster than the general version.

Smalltalk-80

With Smalltalk-78 behind us, few changes were made to the Virtual Machine to produce the Smalltalk-80 Virtual Machine. The main change was an increase in power from allowing blocks with arguments. Beyond this, mostly we cleaned up many details, some of which supported more extensive cleanups in the Smalltalk level of the system.

☐ *Contexts Again* We felt that the optimized contexts of Smalltalk-78 did not justify the loss in clarity which they entailed. So in the Smalltalk-80 language we reverted to Contexts as objects, leaving such optimizations up to implementors clever enough to hide their tricks entirely from Smalltalk. In order to simplify the management of Contexts in the Virtual Machine, we decided to use two sizes of contexts instead of making them truly variable-length. This meant that, if separate free lists were managed for these two lengths, storage for contexts could be allocated and freed with relatively little fragmentation and coalescence overhead.

☐ *Blocks with Arguments* While the syntax changed little in the Smalltalk-80 language (open colon and other non-ASCII selectors were banished), our extended discussions of syntax led to the current description for blocks with arguments. In fact, this required no change to the Virtual Machine, but it had the feel of such a change in the language.

☐ *BlockContexts* We re-engineered BlockContexts in the Smalltalk-80 language. Smalltalk-78 had already handled their recursive application by providing independent stack space for each invocation. Beyond this, mechanisms were defined for checking and diagnosing such anomalous conditions as returning to a context which has already returned.

□ *Compilation Order*   Smalltalk-78 had perpetuated the post-evaluation of receiver expressions so as to avoid delving into the stack to find the receiver. In the Smalltalk-80 language, however, we encoded the number of arguments in the send instruction. This enabled strictly left-to-right evaluation, and no one has since complained about surprising order of evaluation. We suspect that this change will yield further fruit in the future when someone tries to build a very simple compiler.

□ *Instruction Set*   In addition to revamping the send instructions, we made several other improvements to the instruction set. We completed the branch instructions by adding branch-if-true. We put in 2- and 3-byte extensions to retain reasonable compactness without restricting functionality. We also added a few compact codes for returning true and false, and for pop-and-store into temps and fields of the receiver.

□ *Methods*   The encoding of method headers followed the earlier Smalltalk-78 design. In order to simplify the allocation of contexts, a bit was included to indicate whether a large frame was necessary to run the method or not.

Future Directions

While the present Smalltalk design has evolved over a decade now, that does not mean it is finished. As when one climbs a large mountain, the higher reaches are gradually revealed and it seems there is as much to do now as when we started.

□ *Virtual Memory*   An obvious shortcoming of the Smalltalk-80 specification is that it does not include a virtual memory. There are several reasons for this. Our experience with OOZE suggested that object-oriented approaches might be significantly better than simple paging, and we did not want to commit ourselves to one or the other. From our experience with porting the system from one interpreter to another, it was clear to us that implementors could experiment with the virtual memory issue fairly easily, while still working from the Smalltalk-80 image specification. The current object formats allow a simple resident implementation, and yet lend themselves to extension in most of the obvious directions for virtual memory.

□ *Reducing Concepts*   It is always useful to reduce the number of concepts in a language when possible. Smalltalk distinguishes many levels of refinement: subclassing, instantiation, blocks and contexts, to name a few. It is likely that some of these distinctions can be dissolved, and that a cleaner virtual machine design would result.

□ *Typing and Protocols*   While the Smalltalk-80 language is not a typed language in the normal sense, there is nonetheless an implicit notion of variable type in the protocol (full set) of messages which must be understood by a given variable. We have described an experimental system based on this notion of type[9], and a serious treatment of this approach would likely involve changes to the Virtual Machine.

☐ *Multiple Inheritance*   While the Smalltalk-80 system does not provide for multiple inheritance, we have described an experimental system which supports multiple superclasses using the standard Virtual Machine[10]. This is another area in which serious use of the new paradigm might suggest useful changes to the Virtual Machine.

☐ *Tiny Implementations*   While, on one end of the spectrum, we seek to build vastly larger systems, we should not ignore the role of small systems. To this end, there is a great deal of room for experimentation with small systems that provide the essential behavior of the Smalltalk-80 system. Threaded interpreters offer simplicity and speed, and it shouldn't be difficult to capture the essence of message sending in an efficient manner.

Maintaining an Evolving Integrated System

We have had considerable experience maintaining an evolving integrated system. In this section we cover several of the challenges and our solutions which support the Smalltalk approach to software engineering.

Applying the Smalltalk Philosophy

One way of stating the Smalltalk philosophy is to "choose a small number of general principles and apply them uniformly." This approach has somewhat of a recursive thrust, for it implies that once you've built something, you ought to be using it whenever possible. For instance, the conventional approach to altering such kernel code as the text editor of a programming system is to use off-line editing tools and then reload the system with the new code and try it out. By contrast, Smalltalk's incremental compilation and accessibility of kernel code encourages you to make the change while the system is running, a bit like performing an appendectomy on yourself.

The recursive approach offers significant advantages, but it also poses its own special problems. One of the benefits is that system maintainers are always using the system, so they are highly motivated to produce quality. Another benefit is high productivity, deriving from the elimination of conventional loading and system generation cycles. Consistent with the Smalltalk philosophy as articulated above, things are also simpler; the tools and the task are one, so there are fewer versions to worry about. The complementary side of this characteristic is that if the only version is compromised, you are "down the creek without a paddle."

Figure 2.4

The Snapshot Concept

The Alto had a particularly nice characteristic as a personal machine: being based on a removable disk pack, once you had installed your personal pack, any machine you used behaved as your personal machine. When we built the Smalltalk environment, based on an extensible programming language, we arranged the system so that when you terminated a working session, or *quit*, the entire state of your system was saved as a *snapshot* on the disk. This meant that as Smalltalk came to be a stand-alone environment, containing all the capabilities of most operating systems as well as the personal extensions of its owner, any Alto instantly took on that specialized power as soon as you inserted your disk and *resumed* your working session. The snapshot also served as a useful checkpoint in case of fatal errors.

In the later virtual memory systems, OOZE automatically saved a snapshot from time to time, which could subsequently be resumed following catastrophes such as loss of power or fatal programming errors. The robustness of OOZE in this respect was remarkable, but owing to the finite latency period of the checkpointing process, it was necessary to act quickly when fatal errors were recognized, lest they be enshrined forever in the mausoleum of a snapshot. In such circumstances, the alert user would quickly reach around to the rear of the keyboard and press the "boot" button of the Alto before the next automatic snapshot.

Then he could resume his work from a previous state saved a few minutes before. This process was known as "booting and resuming." The term came to be jokingly applied to other situations in life, such as unsuccessful research efforts and other less serious endeavors.

Minimum Kernel for Maximum Flexibility

Most systems are built around a kernel of code which cannot easily be changed. In our Smalltalk systems, the kernel consists of machine code and microcode necessary to implement a virtual Smalltalk machine. You clearly want the kernel to be as small as possible, so that you encounter barriers to change as infrequently as possible. For example, in Smalltalk-72 it was a great improvement when the primitive read routine was supplanted by one written in Smalltalk, since it could then be easily changed to handle such extensions as floating-point constants.

Speed comes into play here, because if the kernel is not fast enough, it will not support certain functions being implemented at a higher level. This was the case for text display in Smalltalk-76. Similarly, generality is important, for the more general the kernel is, the more kernel-like functions can be built at a higher level. For example, the one BitBlt primitive in Smalltalk-80 supports line drawing, text, menus and freehand graphics.

The Fear of Standing Alone

While Smalltalk-72 and -74 were used as long-lived evolving images, the systems as released were always generated from scratch, by reading a set of system definitions into a bootstrap kernel. With the Smalltalk-76 system, we took a bold step and opted to ignore support for system generation. The system was built in two parts: a Virtual Machine was written in microcode and machine code, and a virtual image was cross-compiled from a simulation done in Smalltalk-74. Although this paralleled our previous strategy, we knew that we would soon abandon support for Smalltalk-74, and thus the Smalltalk-76 system would be truly stand-alone. In other words, if a bit were dropped from the system image, or if a reference-count error occurred, there would be no way to recover the state of the system except to backtrack through whatever earlier versions of the system had been saved. As the system became more reliable, we went for days and then weeks without starting over, and finally we realized that Smalltalk-76 was on its own. If this sounds risky to you, think of how we felt!

Standing Alone Without Fear: The System Tracer

While the foregoing approach may seem foolhardy, we actually had a plan: Ted Kaehler said that he would write a Smalltalk program, the *system tracer*, which would run inside of Smalltalk and copy the whole system out to a file while it was running. Considerable attention would have to be paid to the parts of the system which were changing while the process ran. Two months after the launch of Smalltalk-76, Ted's first system tracer ran and produced a clone without errors. While we

Figure 2.5

all breathed a sigh of relief at this point, the full implications only
dawned on us gradually. This truly marked the beginning of an era:
there are many bits in the Smalltalk-80 release of today which are copies of those bits first cloned in 1977.

The system tracer solved our most immediate problem of ensuring
the integrity of the system. It caught and diagnosed inaccurate reference counts, of which there were several during the first few months of
Smalltalk-76. Also, although it took four hours to run, it performed the
function of a garbage collector, reclaiming storage tied up in circular
structures, and reclaiming pointers lost to OOZE's zoning by class. The
essential contribution of the system tracer, however, was to validate our
test-pilot philosophy of living in the system we worked on. From this
point on, we never started from scratch again, but were able to use the
system we knew so well in order to design its follow-ons.

Figure 2.6

Spawning and Mutation

As time passed we found that the system tracer had even more potential than we had imagined. For one thing, it offered an answer to the problem of using a fully integrated system for production applications. This problem manifests itself in several ways: a fully integrated system contains many components which are not needed in production, such as compiler, debugger, and various editing and communications facilities. Also, at a finer grain, much of the symbolic information which is retained for ease of access may be wasteful, or even objectionable (for security reasons) in a production release of the system.

The system tracer could be instructed to *spawn* an application with all unnecessary information removed. This could be done *post facto*, thus freeing application programmers from the integrated/production dichotomy until the final release of a product. In actual fact, since the goal of our research is integration, we never pursued the full potential of the system tracer to drop out such "product" applications. The closest we came was to eliminate unnecessary parts of the system when we were short of space for certain large projects.

The possibility of using the system tracer to produce mutations became evident soon after its creation, and we took full advantage of this. For instance, prior to the Smalltalk-80 release, we wanted to convert from our own private form of floating-point numbers to the standard IEEE format. In this case, we simply included an appropriate transformation in the system tracer and wrote out a cloned image which used the new format. Then we replaced the floating-point routines in the Virtual Machine and started up the new image. Similar transformations have been used to change the instruction set of the Virtual Machine, to change the format of compiled methods, and to change the encoding of small integers. It was in this manner that Smalltalk-78 and -80 were built out of Smalltalk-76.

It is hard to say how far one should take this approach. Sometimes a change is so fundamental that it requires starting again from the ground up, as we did from Smalltalk-74 to -76. Even in such cases though, it seems easiest to simulate the new environment in the old, and then use the simulation to produce the actual new system.

Figure 2.7

The Virtual Image

When we decided to release the Smalltalk-80 system, the question arose as to what form it should take. From the discussion above, it should be clear why we chose the virtual image (a fancier term for snapshot) format. This was the one way in which we could be sure that the release would set a standard. Any implementation, if it worked at all, would look and behave identically, at least in its initial version. At the same time, we tried to decouple the image format as much as possible from such implementation-related details as reference counting versus garbage collection, machine word size, and pointer size. At the time of this writing, implementations exist which vary in all of these parameters. It should be possible to decouple similarly our choice of bitmap display representation, but this project was not of immediate interest to us.

Conclusion

The evolution of the Smalltalk system is a story of good and bad designs alike. We have learned much from our experiences. Probably the greatest factor that keeps us moving forward is that we use the system all the time, and we keep trying to do new things with it. It is this "living-with" which drives us to root out failures, to clean up inconsistencies, and which inspires our occasional innovation.

References

1. Goldberg, Adele, and Kay, Alan, Eds., "Smalltalk-72 Instruction Manual", Xerox PARC Technical Report SSL-76-6, 1976.

2. Thacker, C. P., et al., "Alto: A Personal Computer", in *Computer Structures: Readings and Examples*, 2nd Edition, Eds. Sieworek, Bell, and Newell, McGraw-Hill, New York, 1981; (also Xerox PARC CSL-79-11), Aug. 1979.

3. Papert, Seymour, *Mindstorms*, Basic Books, New York, 1980.

4. Goldberg, Adele, and Kay, Alan, "Teaching Smalltalk", Xerox PARC Technical Report SSL-77-2, June 1977.

5. Newman, William, and Sproull, Robert, Principles of Interactive Computer Graphics, 2nd Edition, McGraw-Hill, New York, 1979.

6. Kaehler, Ted, "Virtual Memory for an Object-Oriented Language", *Byte,* vol. 6, no. 8, Aug. 1981.

7. Ingalls, Daniel H. H., "The Smalltalk-76 Programming System: Design and Implementation", Conference Record, Fifth Annual ACM Symposium on Principles of Programming Languages, 1978.

8. McCall, Kim, "TinyTalk, a Subset of Smalltalk-76 for 64KB Microcomputers", *Sigsmall Newsletter,* Sept. 1980.

9. Borning, Alan H., and Ingalls, Daniel H. H., "A Type Declaration and Inference System for Smalltalk", Ninth Symposium on Principles of Programming Languages, pp. 133–141, Albuquerque, NM, 1982.

10. ―――――――――――――――――――――, "Multiple Inheritance in Smalltalk-80", pp. 234–237, Proceedings at the National Conference on Artificial Intelligence, Pittsburgh, PA, 1982.

3

The Smalltalk-80 Code File Format

Glenn Krasner
Software Concepts Group
Xerox Palo Alto Research Center
Palo Alto, California

Introduction

In the Smalltalk-80 system, programmers define classes and methods incrementally by editing in system browsers. At some point, programmers may want to share their class descriptions with others using different Smalltalk-80 systems. Some means of communication is therefore required. We have chosen to use files as the means of communication, and call such files *code files*.

Code files for the Smalltalk-80 system allow the programmer to communicate source code (class descriptions or parts of class descriptions) between one Smalltalk-80 system and another (possibly the same system, later in time). The format of such files was devised as a result of a number of design considerations:

- Restrictions on the allowable character set,

- Whether to allow the code to be "readable" when printed on conventional printers,

- Whether to retain/allow more than one emphasis of the text (font and face changes),

- Whether to include source code in the system image (core) or to place it on external files,

29

- Whether to allow for executable expressions in addition to source code of methods, and

- Whether to provide for system crash recovery.

The Smalltalk-80 code file format is restricted to contain a common set of characters ("printing" ASCII characters plus a small number of control characters). It gives up the ability to have multiple emphases of text in order to be as good (or as bad) on conventional printers as it would be on more capable printers (raster laser xerographic printers, for example). The approach taken keeps source methods on file storage to minimize the amount of core used, includes intermingling of executable expressions with source code for methods, and provides for some amount of system recovery.

Background

The Smalltalk-80 system is powerful and comprehensible, in part because everything in the system is treated in a uniform way, as an object. However, at the point where the Smalltalk-80 system meets the external world, this uniformity cannot be maintained. The external world does not consist of Smalltalk-80 objects, but rather of disk files, network communication, hardware storage devices, and printers. These define a much more limited structure of information. For example, disk files typically consist of collections of 8-bit bytes; networks define a limited set of data that can be communicated; hardware storage devices define what kinds and, more importantly, how much information can be handled; and printers typically are restricted to a small number of characters as the only data they can handle. If the Smalltalk-80 programmer never had to meet this external world, there would be no problem. Everything he or she dealt with would be within the Smalltalk-80 system. For some programmers, this is sufficient. Most programmers, however, must meet the external world because they want to share information with some other system. The Smalltalk-80 code file format is a format for representing code objects (i.e., source code for methods or expressions), especially for communication via the media of electronic secondary storage and paper.

Constraints and Goals

The constraints and goals for the design of the format consisted of:

- Having a format that would serve as a communications protocol among Smalltalk-80 systems and from a system to paper. We saw the paper version as being used by people not fortunate enough to have display-based browsers and, perhaps more importantly, as one in which algorithms or pieces of code could be published.

- Having a format that could be printed without translation on conventional printers. We are interested in first having the world build Smalltalk engines, with bit-map displays and good pointing devices and lots of computing power. Later, we *expect* them to want to use good printers; we are willing to wait before we require them to do so.

- Having a format that would look satisfactory on paper. Often this means allowing multiple font and type face information, as well as formatting information. However, given the first goals, it means not having extra characters that describe such information cluttering up the printed page.

- Having the source code for the more than 4000 methods in the system take up as little main memory as possible. We expect that reasonable Smalltalk-80 machines will have virtual memories, where space restrictions would not be a problem. However, the number of bytes taken up by the source code alone (more than a million) would preclude most current machines from having *any* resident implementation. Therefore the file format was to serve as a somewhat limited form of virtual memory.

- Having a format that would include executable expressions. Typically what people want to communicate between systems includes method definitions, class descriptions, and class initialization expressions. By providing for executable expressions, all these desires can be met.

- Minimizing the amount of disk space taken up. For example, one would not want an entire disk system to become full of text when only a small percentage of the text is actually needed.

- Allowing a certain amount of recovery from system disasters. The Smalltalk-80 system is one in which it is possible to change almost anything. This provides great power and flexibility, but has the danger that a system change could destroy the system itself. It was desired that code files, since they are somewhat external to the system itself, could provide recovery from such disasters.

The Code File Format

Smalltalk-80 code files are defined as text files that contain only the "printing" ASCII characters, codes 32 (space) through 127 (DEL), plus carriage return, line feed, tab and form feed (codes 13, 10, 9 and 12, respectively). The file is broken into *chunks*, which are sequences of characters terminated by an exclamation point (!), with exclamation points within a chunk doubled. The meanings of chunks will be described in the sections to follow.

Exclamation point was chosen for a number of reasons. It is not used as a Smalltalk-80 selector. It is used in English at the end of sentences, so it is a reasonable terminator. It tends not to appear in code, so it rarely has to be doubled. Also, it is thin, so we felt it would not be too obtrusive on the page.

File Streams

The interface between Smalltalk-80 objects and disk files is encapsulated by the Smalltalk-80 class FileStream. File Streams support sequential and random access of disk files through the following protocol

class name	FileStream
superclass	ExternalStream

opening and closing

openOn: aString
Answer an instance of FileStream representing the disk file named aString.

close
Close the file.

sequential accessing

next
Answer the character in the file after the current position, and update the position.

nextPut: aCharacter
Store aCharacter as the character of the file after the current position, and update the position.

atEnd
Answer true if the current position is at the end of the file, false if it is not.

setToEnd
Set the current position to be the end of the file.

random accessing

position
Answer the current position.

position: anInteger
Set the current position to be anInteger.

Two messages were added to FileStream to deal with chunks, one to read a chunk from the file, and another to write a chunk onto the file fileIn/Out

nextChunk
Answer a string that is the chunk starting at the current position, undoubling embedded exclamation points, and excluding the terminator.

nextChunkPut: aString
Write aString as a chunk starting at the current position, doubling embedded exclamation points, and terminating it with an exclamation point.

Code Files Used for Source Methods

The Smalltalk-80 system relies on the code file format to read and write the source methods of the system. In this way, the files are used to communicate information from the system to itself at a later point in time. Each CompiledMethod in the system keeps a short (3-byte) encoding of the location of its source. This encoding includes which of four file streams contains the chunk of source code for that method and the position, within that file, of the first character of its chunk. A global array called SourceFiles points to the four file streams.

The code for getting the source method in class CompiledMethod could be*

getSource
```
| sourceIndex sourceFile sourcePosition |
sourceIndex ← self sourceIndex.
sourceFile ← SourceFiles at: sourceIndex.
sourcePosition ← self sourcePosition.
sourceFile position: sourcePosition.
↑sourceFile nextChunk
```

Of the four file streams, one, SourceFiles at: 1, is a read-only file stream of source methods. It is known as the *sources file*. Periodically all the source code of the system may be condensed into this file.

The second file stream, SourceFiles at: 2, is a file stream to which every change to the system sources is appended. It is known as the *changes file*. When a method is changed and recompiled, its new source code is appended to this file (and the encoding bytes of the CompiledMethod are changed to point at the new source). Periodically, the changes file may be condensed as well. Since this file grows while a programmer is working, the changes file may want to be condensed much more often than the sources file. The third and fourth file streams are currently unused.

*For implementation efficiency, the code in the Smalltalk-80 system is not actually this, but provides the same function.

The code in class CompiledMethodto store a new source code string could be

storeSourceString: aString

```
| sourceFile sourcePosition |
sourceFile ← SourceFiles at: 2.
sourceFile setToEnd.
sourcePosition ← sourceFile position.
self setSourceIndex: 2
    sourcePosition: sourcePosition.
sourceFile nextChunkPut: aString.
```

Because the changes file is only altered by appending to it, previous versions can always be found. Periodically, a Smalltalk-80 programmer will make a *snapshot* of the state of the system. If the system crashes at a later time, then, when the system is resumed at the point of snapshot, the compiled methods in the snapshot of the system will still point to their place in the files at the time the snapshot was made. The end of the file will contain changes added between the snapshot and the crash, and these can be recovered. For example, suppose a programmer changed the definition of getSource in class CompiledMethod once (version A), then made a snapshot, then changed it twice (versions B and C), and the system crashed because of an error in C. Then the system can be restarted at the snapshot point, the source and compiled method for getSource will be version A, but versions B and C will be near the end of the changes file. The programmer could look at the end of the changes file, copy version B into the browser for compilation, and ignore C. Then the programmer has recovered to the equivalent of just before the C change brought down the system.

To improve recovery, the system also records several other things on the changes file. For example, whenever the user executes an expression in a code editor, the expression is appended as a chunk on the changes file. Also, when the user performs a system snapshot, a chunk consisting of the comment "------SNAPSHOT-----" is appended to the changes file, marking the occurrence of a snapshot.

Code Files Used for Shared Code

Besides storing the system sources, the code file format serves to communicate code and expressions between one system and another. For this we have added a level of syntax and semantics above the chunk level. The syntax and semantics are defined and implemented by the message fileIn in class FileStream,

fileIn
```
| aString sawExclamation |
self position: 0.
[self atEnd]
   whileFalse:
      [sawExclamation ← self peekFor: $!.
      aString ← self nextChunk.
      sawExclamation
         ifFalse: [Compiler evaluate: aString]
         ifTrue: [(Compiler evaluate: aString) fileInFrom: self]]
```
peekFor: aCharacter
```
" Answer true and move past if next = aCharacter "
self next = aCharacter
   ifTrue: [↑true]
   ifFalse: [self position: self position - 1. ↑false]
```

That is, when sent the message fileIn, a file stream looks for an exclamation point. As long as it does not see one, it reads and has class Compiler evaluate the next chunk as a Smalltalk-80 expression. If it did see an exclamation point, then after the expression is evaluated, it hands the stream (itself) to the object that was returned as the value of the expression (see example below).

In particular, the methodsFor: aString message sent to a class will return an instance of ClassCategoryReader that has its instance variable myClass set to the class, and its instance variable myCategory set to the string. The class category reader will respond to the fileInFrom: message by reading chunks from the file stream. Each chunk is presumed to be the source for a method, and, for each chunk, the class category reader has the compiler compile it and install the compiled method in the proper class and category. This continues until an empty chunk is found.

fileInFrom: aFileStream
```
| aString |
[aFileStream atEnd or: [(aString ← aFileStream nextChunk) isEmpty]]
   whileFalse:
      [Compiler compile: aString
             forClass: myClass
             inCategory: myCategory]
↑self
```

For example, the code for fileIn, peekFor: aCharacter, and fileInFrom: aFileStream would appear in a code file as

```
!FileStream methodsFor: 'fileI/O'!
fileIn
    | aString sawExclamation |
    self position: 0.
    [self atEnd]
        whileFalse:
            [sawExclamation ← self peekFor: $!!
            aString ← self nextChunk.
            sawExclamation
                ifFalse: [Compiler evaluate: aString]
                ifTrue: [(Compiler evaluate: aString) fileInFrom: self]]!
peekFor: aCharacter
    "Answer true and move past if next = aCharacter"
    self next = aCharacter
        ifTrue: [↑true]
        ifFalse: [self position: self position - 1. ↑false]!!

!ClassCategoryReader methodsFor: 'fileI/O'!

fileInFrom: aFileStream
    | aString |
    [aFileStream atEnd or: [(aString ← aFileStream nextChunk) isEmpty]]
        whileFalse:
            [Compiler compile: aString
                    forClass: myClass
                    inCategory: myCategory]
    ↑self!!
```

The class category reader created by the expression FileStream
methodsFor: 'fileI/O' will read and compile the methods for fileIn and
peekFor: aCharacter before returning control to the file stream; the
reader created by ClassCategoryReader methodsFor: 'fileI/O' will read
in only the method for fileInFrom: aFileStream.

The example shows a number of visual properties that make it easier
to read code format files when they are printed. Each category is
delimited by a short "methodsFor:" line; it is easy to locate the names
of the class and the category for each. Each method is a visual chunk
with all but its first line indented. This of course, depends on the programmer keeping the convention of including a tab before each line
other than the message pattern. This convention is supported by the
"format" command in the code editor.

In addition to the source code for methods, the code file format and
its interpretation allow any expression to be saved on a file. In particular, one may save an entire class description from a Smalltalk-80 system. That file will consist of an expression defining the class, followed
by an expression setting the global comment of the class, followed

the source code for the methods in the class, in the format described above. When a file stream on such a file, in this or some other system, is told to fileIn, it will recreate the entire class description.

Users could also define their own "readers," objects created with expressions preceded by an exclamation point, just as ClassCategoryReaders are created with the "methodsFor:" expressions. These user-defined readers would be used for creating an object with special external representation, just as class category readers create methods whose external representations are strings of characters formatted for readability.

Note: In addition to this, since many classes have initialization code especially for class variables, if the message initialize is defined in the class, the expression chunk "<class> initialize!" will appear at the end of the file containing the class definition. Then, when the file is told to file in, the initialization code will be executed after the methods are compiled.

Code File Format for Both Source Methods and Shared Code

The conventions for shared code given in the previous section are also followed in the two source code files. That is, the sources file is organized as a sequence of class descriptions in the above format, arranged alphabetically by class name, with form feeds between them. The compiled methods in the system point to the beginning of their chunks. In this way, printing out the sources file will give an alphabetical listing of the system sources with page breaks between each class.

The changes file is a collection of chunks of the form

    !<class name> methodsFor: ' <categoryName> '!
    <source method>!!

The compiled methods in the system that point to the changes file also only point to the beginning of their chunks. The chunks appended to the changes file when the user evaluates an expression are in the executable form

    <expression>!

This means that the sources file could be filed in to redefine the system classes to their state before changes were made, and the changes file could be filed in to redefine the changes and re-execute the expressions made since changes were started. The Smalltalk-80 system provides two ways of looking at the changes file for recovery, to create a view on a file whose contents are the last few thousand characters of the changes file and to create a ChangeList browser to view the changes.

**Matching the
Goals and
Constraints**

The Smalltalk-80 code file format meets most of the goals and satisfies most of the constraints of its design. It serves as a communications format between systems. It is used extensively, not only for source code within a system, but also for exchanging source code between systems. In addition, because it is restricted to the standard ASCII character set, it can be printed on conventional printers as well as on more capable printers.

The code files have a reasonable appearance on paper. Of course, this is a matter of taste. In a few years we will likely no longer consider its appearance reasonable because our opinions of "reasonable appearance" will change. Methods are "chunked" together, and the "methodsFor:" lines separate categories of methods. Except for the single exclamation point at the end of each method, there are no characters to distract the reader. The form feeds between class descriptions also help the readability of the code.

The amount of main memory required to handle sources is quite small, especially compared with the size of the source code itself. It requires only 3 bytes per compiled method, plus the space taken up by the interpretation code (outlined in this paper). Compared with over a million bytes of source code, this is a great savings and considered worth the added complexity.

The format includes executable expressions. The system currently uses this feature sparingly—for class descriptions and initialization, and for recording expressions evaluated by the user. However, the format provides a generality that can be exploited in the future.

Disk space efficiency is a compromise in our design. Having one read-only sources file does help meet this goal since multiple systems can share this file. At Xerox, we often keep this shared file on a remote server, where multiple systems can access it and where it does not take up any local disk space. On the other hand, constantly appending to the changes file consumes disk space. The Smalltalk-80 development style often involves defining and redefining methods many times. Since each definition is appended to the changes file, this causes the file to grow. However, the user can invoke the system's ability to compact the changes file at any time by sending the message compactChanges to Smalltalk, an instance of SystemDictionary.

Although using the changes file in this way is wasteful of disk storage, there is the advantage that a considerable amount of recovery from system crashes is possible. By recording all code changes and many other user events on the changes file, the programmer can recover should the system go down. In particular, if a programmer is experimenting with the user interface code and makes a mistake that renders the interface unusable, there will be a trail of the experiments when the system is restarted.

Other Paths

A couple of other directions in the design of the Smalltalk-80 code file format that we did not take are worth noting. One direction would have been to invent a standard representation for the Smalltalk-80 virtual memory, and insist that everyone's system use it. The advantages with this would have been that the source code would fit in the system and that no special mechanism would be needed to retain system sources. However, it would not solve the communication problem, nor the recovery problem.

Another idea we discussed was to store only comments and temporary variable names on the files; the other pieces of text could be generated by the system, as is currently done by the Decompiler. The benefits here are that fewer characters of disk space are needed and that code would appear in a consistent "pretty-printed" way. We decided that the disadvantages of this approach outweigh its advantages. Although it saves disk space in terms of the number of characters, there would be extra space used (either on disk or in main memory) to describe the mapping between comments and their place in the methods. This mapping would also involve a more complex computation. Another major disadvantage is that the code files would not be human readable. Also, we did not want to give up the flexibility of storing and displaying the code in the way it was typed, rather than in the pretty-printer's format. Keeping the sources "as is" seemed an easier approach than designing a more flexible pretty-printer, and even a flexible pretty printer would not provide that total flexibility.

The Smalltalk-80 system uses only two of the four source file streams provided; it does not exploit the flexibility that four can provide. One could imagine ways to use two more files. For example, one of the files could be used as a read-only version of the condensed changes file, providing a level of system backup between the sources and changes file.

Another direction that we did not pursue was to allow the text stored on the files to have multiple emphases (font and face changes) of the text. The Smalltalk-76 system[1] had two formats that preserved emphases, and produced listings that were easier to read and that allowed programmers to tailor the visual aspects of their code to suit their tastes. Since the Smalltalk-80 principles allow such tailoring in other areas of the system, tailoring source text ought to be allowed as well. Unfortunately, we were unable to design a file format that allowed both emphasis description and direct printing of the file on conventional printers. Solutions to keeping emphasis descriptions always involved using non-ASCII characters or had extra characters which would clutter the page if directly printed. We assume that in the future more printers will be available that print many fonts and faces. When this is the case (or to help make this be the case), we hope that some other standard that preserves emphases will emerge.

Conclusion

The Smalltalk-80 code file format was developed to allow communication between the flexible world of a Smalltalk-80 system and the less flexible world of disks, networks, storage devices and printers. It is used by the system to keep the source code for the methods on disk files, rather than within the memory of a resident system. It is also used to communicate changes between one system and another, and to provide a level of recovery from errors. The format is flexible enough to allow both code (source methods) and executable Smalltalk-80 expressions to be read in and/or evaluated; it also includes a general mechanism to allow objects in the Smalltalk-80 system to read and interpret the files. The format satisfies its design constraints and leaves the door open for several useful extensions.

References

1. Ingalls, Daniel H. H., "The Smalltalk-76 Programming System: Design and Implementation", Conference Record, Fifth Annual ACM Symposium on Principles of Programming Languages, 1978.

4

Design Decisions for Smalltalk-80 Implementors

Allen Wirfs-Brock
Tektronix, Inc.
Beaverton, Oregon

Abstract

The Smalltalk-80 virtual machine specification describes the required behavior of any Smalltalk-80 interpreter. The specification takes the form of a model implementation of a Smalltalk-80 interpreter. An implementor of a Smalltalk-80 interpreter is not required to exactly copy the data structures and algorithms of the model interpreter. The only requirement is that any Smalltalk-80 interpreter exhibit external behavior which is identical to that described by the formal specification. The implementor is free to make design tradeoffs that may increase the performance of the implementation while preserving the required external behavior. This paper identifies some of the design decisions which face a Smalltalk-80 implementor and discusses several design trade-offs.

Introduction

The Smalltalk-80 virtual machine specification as it appears in *Smalltalk-80: The Language and Its Implementation*[1] describes the required low level behavior of any Smalltalk-80 implementation. The specification takes the form of a Smalltalk-80 "program" which exhibits this behavior. One approach to the implementation of a Smalltalk-80 interpreter is to literally translate this program into some appropriate implementation language. While this approach will result in an interpreter which exhibits the required behavior, the performance of the resulting interpreter may be unsatisfactory.

An alternate implementation approach is to construct an interpreter that uses algorithms and data structures which differ from those used in the formal specification. These would be chosen to optimize performance for the host implementation environment. Such an interpreter may achieve higher performance but requires greater implementation effort.

This paper presents an overview of the design decision space which confronts the implementors of Smalltalk-80 interpreters. Specifically, it examines *some* of the potential design trade-offs concerning the host hardware and implementation language, the interpreter data structures, the actual execution of Smalltalk-80 instructions, and the creation and destruction of objects. Even though the design issues are examined assuming an interpreter implementation utilizing a conventional computer or microprocessor as a host, many of the trade-offs should be applicable to a microcoded or hardware implementation.

The Formal Specification

The first part of the Smalltalk-80 virtual machine specification defines the virtual machine architecture. This includes the definition of the primitive data types, the instruction set, and the interface to the object memory manager. The second part describes the internal operation of the object memory manager. An implementation of the Smalltalk-80 virtual machine is commonly referred to as a Smalltalk-80 interpreter. The formal specification completely defines the required behavior of a Smalltalk-80 interpreter.

The formal specification takes the form of a collection of Smalltalk-80 methods which implement a Smalltalk-80 interpreter. It is, in effect, an implementation of a "model interpreter." Within this model the "registers" of the virtual machine are represented as Smalltalk-80 instance variables, the data structures are explicitly defined via constant field offsets and bit masks, and the required semantics of the interpreter are implicit in the behavior of the methods. The model bytecode interpreter implementation can be viewed as the definition of the correct behavior of a Smalltalk-80 implementation.

The specification does not place any particular requirements upon the internal implementation of the object memory manager. Of course, it assumes that any implementation will correctly preserve stored data and that this data will be available to the interpreter when requested. The memory manager implementation chapter may also be viewed as a model for how an object memory manager may be implemented.

An implementor of a Smalltalk-80 interpreter must design and construct an interpreter whose behavior conforms to that defined by the formal specification. One method of accomplishing this is to directly translate the Smalltalk-80 methods of the model implementation into an appropriate implementation language. One might even consider using a program to perform this translation. Figure 4.1 gives an example of a method from the formal specification and Figure 4.2 shows how it might be translated into Pascal.

The principal advantage of the direct translation approach is that it is a simple method of obtaining a semantically correct interpreter. It also is a very good way for an implementor to learn how the interpreter works internally. The principal disadvantage associated with this approach is that the resulting interpreter may exhibit disappointing performance levels. The data structures and algorithms of the book's interpreter were selected to provide a clear definition of the required behavior; they will probably not be optimal for any particular host computer. The challenge for a Smalltalk-80 implementor is to design an interpreter which will yield acceptable performance within some particular host environment. At Tektronix, we utilized the direct translation approach (see Chapter 5) and were able to very quickly build a working (but slow) Smalltalk-80 implementation. Experience gained from this initial implementation enabled us to later design a significantly improved second generation interpreter.

initializeGuaranteedPointers
    " Undefined Object and Booleans "
    nilPointer ← 2.
    falsePointer ← 4.
    truePointer ← 6.
    " and so on ... "

pushConstantBytecode
    currentBytecode = 113 ifTrue: [↑self push: truePointer].
    currentBytecode = 114 ifTrue: [↑self push: falsePointer].
    currentBytecode = 115 ifTrue: [↑self push: nilPointer].
    currentBytecode = 116 ifTrue: [↑self push: minusOnePointer].
    currentBytecode = 117 ifTrue: [↑self push: zeroPointer].
    currentBytecode = 118 ifTrue: [↑self push: onePointer].
    currentBytecode = 119 ifTrue: [↑self push: twoPointer].

Figure 4.1

```
const
    {Undefined Object and Booleans}
    nilPointer = 2;
    falsePointer = 4;
    truePointer = 6;
    {and so on ...}
procedure pushConstantBytecode;
    begin
        case currentBytecode of
            113: push(truePointer);
            114: push(falsePointer);
            115: push(nilPointer);
            116: push(minusOnePointer);
            117: push(zeroPointer);
            118: push(onePointer);
            119: push(twoPointer);
        end {case}
    end {pushConstantBytecode};
```

Figure 4.2

The Host Processor

The first major design decision which will confront a Smalltalk-80 implementor will be the choice of the hardware which will host the implementation. In many situations the implementor will have little freedom in this area. Where the implementor has the freedom to select the host processor, there are a number of considerations which should enter into the decision process.

A processor which is to host a Smalltalk-80 interpreter should be fast. An interpreter which executes 10,000 bytecodes per second may be perceived by a Smalltalk-80 programmer to be quite slow. The original Tektronix implementation, which could execute 3500 bytecodes per second, was considered to be just barely usable. The Xerox Dolphin implementation executes 20,000 bytecodes per second and is considered to have "adequate" performance, while the Xerox Dorado at 400,000 bytecodes per second has excellent performance (see Chapter 9). At 10,000 bytecodes per second the interpreter will have, on the average, only 100 microseconds in which to fetch, decode, and execute each bytecode. At a more acceptable performance level of 100,000 bytecodes per second, the interpreter will have only 10 microseconds for each bytecode.

A Smalltalk-80 host processor architecture must support a large amount of main memory (either real or virtual). The standard Smalltalk-80 virtual image consists of approximately 500,000 bytes of

Smalltalk-80 objects. To this must be added the space for interpreter, the interpreter's data structures, the display bitmap, and additional space to contain objects created dynamically as the system runs. The total requirements of the system will easily approach one million bytes of memory with even a modest application. Although it may be possible to configure a virtual image with fewer features and more modest memory requirements, this can be most easily done utilizing an operational Smalltalk-80 system. For this reason, the implementor will need a development system with at least 1 megabyte of main memory.

By caching a number of variables which represent the execution state of a Smalltalk-80 method in internal registers, an implementation will probably get dramatically improved performance. A good host processor should have sufficient internal registers to allow these values to be cached in its registers. The exact number of registers needed to contain cached values will depend upon the specifics of the interpreter design. However, as a general rule, 8 is probably not enough while 32 is probably more than enough. For example, one of our implementations for the Motorola 68000 processor could have easily made use of several more than the 15 registers which were available.

Smalltalk-80 interpreters frequently look up values in tables and follow indirect references. For this reason it is desirable that the host processor provide good support for indexed addressing and indirection.

Hardware support for the Smalltalk-80 graphics model is another major consideration. Smalltalk-80 graphics is entirely based upon the manipulation of bitmaps. Although some implementations have simulated this model using other display technologies (for example, by using a vector oriented raster terminal), the results have been less than satisfactory (see Chapter 5). Acceptable results will only be achieved if an actual hardware bitmapped display is provided. A frequent concern of new implementors is the performance of BitBlt, the bitmap manipulation operation. One concern is whether specific hardware support will be required for this operation. Our experience with the 68000 was that adequate BitBlt performance was easy to achieve with straightforward coding, while adequate bytecode interpreter performance was very difficult to achieve. This leads us to believe that a host processor capable of achieving adequate performance when interpreting bytecodes will probably perform adequately when BitBlt-ing. In particular, the processor's ability to perform shifting and masking operations will affect the overall performance of BitBlt.

The Implementation Language

The choice of an implementation language for a Smalltalk-80 interpreter is typically a trade-off between the ease of implementation of the interpreter and the final performance of the system. Implementors should consider using a high-level programming language as the first implementation tool. A high-level language based interpreter can be quickly implemented and should be relatively easy to debug. Unfortunately, the final performance of such implementations may be disappointing. This may be the case even if a very good optimizing compiler is used.

It is generally accepted that the code generated for a large program by an optimizing compiler will be "better" than that which a human assembly language programmer would write for the same problem. Conversely, for short code sequences, a human programmer can usually write better code than that generated by an optimizing compiler. Although a Smalltalk-80 interpreter may appear to be a complex piece of software, it is actually a relatively small program. For example, our assembly language implementation for the Motorola 68000 contains approximately 5000 instructions. Furthermore, a large portion of the execution time tends to be spent executing only a few dozen of the instructions. These instruction sequences are short enough that carefully written assembly code can achieve significantly better performance than optimized compiler generated code. Our 68000 bytecode dispatch routine consists of five instructions, while the bodies of many of the push and pop bytecodes consist of only one or two instructions.

A successful Smalltalk-80 interpreter design will consist of an efficient mapping of the virtual machine architecture onto the available resources of the host processor. Such a mapping will include the global allocation of processor resources (registers, preferred memory locations, instruction sequences, etc.) for specific purposes within the interpreter. An assembly language programmer will have complete freedom to make these allocations. Such freedom is typically unavailable to a high-level language programmer who must work within a general purpose resource allocation model chosen by the designers of the compiler.

Object Pointer Formats

The most common form of data manipulated by a Smalltalk-80 interpreter are Object Pointers (commonly referred to as Oops). An Oop represents either an atomic integer value in the range -16,384 to 16,383 or a reference to some particular Smalltalk-80 object. The formal specification uses a standard representation for Oops. This representation defines an Oop to be a 16-bit quantity. The least significant of the 16 bits is used as a tag which indicates how the rest of the bits are to be interpreted. If the tag bit is a 0 then the most significant 15 bits are interpreted as an object reference. If the tag bit is a 1 then the most significant 15 bits are interpreted as a 2's complement integer value.

Note that the size of an Oop determines both the total number of objects which may exist at any time (32,768) and the range of integer values upon which arithmetic is primitively performed.

Because Oops are used so frequently by the interpreter, their format can have a large impact upon the overall performance of the interpreter. The most common operations performed upon Oops by the interpreter are testing the tag bit, accessing the object referenced by an Oop, extracting the integer value from an Oop, and constructing an Oop from an integer.

Even though the standard Oop format pervades the formal specification, use of a different format will not violate the criteria for conformance to the specification. This is possible because the internal format of an Oop is invisible to the Smalltalk-80 programmer.

There are several possible alternative Oop formats which may offer varying performance advantages. One alternative is to change the position of the tag bit.

Placing the tag bit in the least significant bit position (the position in the standard Oop format) is most appropriate for a processor which reflects the value of this bit in its condition codes. This is the case for the Xerox processors[2] upon which the Smalltalk-80 system was originally developed, and for some common microprocessors. Using such a processor, the tag bit is automatically "tested" each time an Oop is accessed. A simple conditional branch instruction can then be used by the interpreter to choose between integer and object reference actions. Processors which lack this feature will require a more complex instruction sequence, shifting the Oop, a masking operation, and comparison to perform the same test.

Placing the tag in the most significant bit position causes the tag to occupy the sign-bit position for 16-bit 2's complement processors. For a processor that has condition codes which reflect the value of the sign bit, a test of the tag becomes a simple branch on positive or negative value.

Other factors which will affect the tag bit position might include the relative performance cost of setting the least significant bit as opposed to the most significant bit (is adding or logical or-ing a 1 less expensive than the same operation involving 32,768) for converting an integer into an Oop, and the relative cost of shifts as opposed to adds for converting Oops into table indices.

The standard format uses a tag bit value of 1 to identify an integer value and a tag bit value of 0 to identify an object identifier. Inverting this interpretation has potentially useful properties, some of which are also dependent upon the choice of tag bit position. For example, if a tag value 0 is used to indicate an integer valued Oop and the tag occupies the least significant bit position, then SmallInteger values are, in effect, 2's complement values which have been scaled by a factor of 2. Such values can be added and subtracted (the most common arithmetic operations) without requiring a conversion from the Oop format and the result will also be a valid SmallInteger Oop. Only one of the operands of a multiplication operation will need to be converted from the Oop format for the operation to yield a valid SmallInteger Oop.

If a tag value of 0 is used to indicate object identifier Oops and the tag occupies the most significant bit position, then object identifier Oops can serve as direct indices into a table of 8-bit values on byte addressable processors. This would allow reference counting to be implemented using an independent table of 8-bit reference-count values which is directly indexed using Oops. For a word addressed processor, the standard format allows Oops to be used to directly index a 2 word per entry object table.

The Object Memory

The object memory implementation described in the formal specification views the object memory as being physically divided into 16 physical segments, each containing 64K 16-bit words. Individual objects occupy space within a single segment. Object reference Oops are translated into memory addresses using a data structure known as the Object Table. The object table contains one 32-bit entry for each of the 32K possible object referencing Oops. Each object table entry has the following format:

Bits 0-15 (lsb):	The word offset of the object within its segment
Bits 16-19:	The number of the segment which contains the object
Bit 20:	Reserved
Bit 21:	Set if the Oop associated with this entry is unused
Bit 22:	Set if the fields of this object contain Oops
Bit 23:	Set if object contains an odd number of 8 bit fields
Bits 24-31 (msb):	This object's reference count

For each segment there is a set of linked lists which locate all free space within the segment. In addition there is a single list which links all unassigned Oops and object table entries. Objects are linked using Oop references.

The above design includes several implicit assumptions about the memory organization of the host processor. It assumes that the unit of memory addressability is a 16-bit word. It assumes that the processor uses a segmented address space and that each segment contains 64K words. Finally, it assumes that at most 1024K words (16 segments) are addressable. This organization may be considerably different from that of an actual host processor. Many processors support a large, byte addressable, linear address space. Although the formal specification's design can be mapped onto such a memory organization, such a mapping will result in reduced interpreter performance if it is carried out dynamically.

An object memory design will consist of two inter-related elements, the organization of the actual object space and the format of the object table. The goal of the design will usually be to minimize the time required to access the fields of an object when given an Oop. However, if main memory is limited, the goal of the design may be to limit the size of the object table. A performance oriented object table will usually be represented as an array which is directly indexed by Oops (or a simple function on Oops). A hash table might be used for a space efficient object table representation[3].

The most important component of an object table entry is the field which contains the actual address of the associated object within the object space. Ideally this field should contain the physical memory address of the object represented so that it may be used without any masking or shifting operations. Such a format will permit the contents to be used to directly address the associated object, either by loading the field into a processor base register or by some type of indirect addressing mechanism. In this case, the size of the address field will be the size of a physical processor address.

If the host processor's physical address is larger than the 20-bits used in the formal specification, the size of an object table entry will have to be increased beyond 32-bits or the size of the reference count and flag bits will have to be decreased. Since Oops are typically used as scaled indexes into the object table, it is desirable that the size of an object table entry be a power-of-two multiple of the processor's addressable word size so that object table offsets may be computed by shifting instead of multiplication. For most conventional processors, 64-bits (8 bytes, four 16-bit words, two 32-bit words) would be the next available size. However, a 64-bit object table entry will require 256K bytes and will probably contain many unused bits. An alternate approach is to use separate parallel arrays to hold the address fields and the reference count/flag fields of each entry. This results in an effective entry size which is greater than 32-bits without requiring a full 64-bit entry. Decreasing the size of the reference-count field is another valid alternative. Since most reference count values are either very small (8 or less) or have reached the overflow value where they stick[4], a reference-count field size of 3 or 4 bits should be adequate. The main consideration will be whether the host processor can efficiently access such a field.

The Bytecode Interpreter

The bytecode interpreter performs the task of fetching and executing individual Smalltalk-80 bytecodes (virtual machine instructions). Before examining the actual functioning of the bytecode interpreter, we will consider the general question of time/space trade-offs within Smalltalk-80 implementations. A complete, operational Smalltalk-80 system requires approximately one million bytes of storage to operate. The actual interpreter will occupy only a small fraction of this. (Our first implementation, which was very bulky, required approximately 128K bytes for the interpreter. A later assembly language implementation for the same host needed less than 25K bytes.) Since Smalltalk-80 interpreters seem to strain the computational resources of conventional processors, most interpreter designs will tend towards reducing execution time at the expense of increasing the total size of the implementation.

The model implementation in the formal specification takes an algorithmic approach to interpretation. The interpreter fetches a bytecode, shifts and masks it to extract the operation code and parameter fields, and uses conditional statements to select the particular operation to be performed. While this approach is quite effective for illustrating the encoding of the bytecodes it is often not suitable for a production interpreter because of the computation required to decode each bytecode. A more efficient implementation technique for the bytecode dispatch operation may be to use the bytecode as an index into a 256-way dispatch table which contains the addresses of the individual routines for each bytecode. For example, rather than using one routine, as in the example in Fig. 3.1, there could be seven individual routines, each one optimized for pushing a particular constant value.

The model implementation exhibits a high degree of modularity. This is particularly true in the area of the interface between the bytecode interpreter and the object memory manager. The bytecode interpreter makes explicit calls to object memory routines for each memory access. The performance of a production implementation can, however, be improved by incorporating intimate knowledge of the object memory implementation into the bytecode interpreter. Many object memory accesses may be performed directly by the interpreter without actually invoking separate routines within the object memory manager.

As mentioned earlier, the selection of which interpreter state values to cache is a critical design decision for the bytecode interpreter. The designer must evaluate the cost of maintaining the cached values (loading the values when a context is activated and storing some of the values back into the context when it is deactivated) relative to the actual performance gains from using the cached values. The evaluation should consider the average duration of an activation. Our observations indicate that most activations span a small number of bytecodes (less than

10). Caching too much of the active context can thus lead to situations where considerable execution time is spent caching values that are not used over the span of the activation.

The model implementation caches the actual Oop values of several context fields. This implies that these values must be decoded into real memory addresses (performing an object table lookup or conversion from SmallInteger format) each time they are used. An alternative is to decode these values when they are fetched from the active context and to cache the addresses. This means that the cached program counter would be the actual address of the next bytecode and that the cached stack pointer would be the actual address of the top element of the active context's stack. If this technique is used, care must be taken that the cached values are correctly updated, e.g., when the memory manager changes the physical location of objects (performs a segment compression). It is also essential that the values of the stack pointer and program counter field get updated when the active context changes.

The Smalltalk-80 system's required support for multiple processes, when implemented in an obvious manner, can impose an overhead upon each bytecode. The formal specification requires that a process switch may occur before each bytecode is fetched. An obvious way to implement this requirement is to have a global boolean flag which indicates that a process switch is pending, and to test this flag before fetching each bytecode. This technique has the disadvantage that the overhead of testing this flag occurs for each bytecode executed even though actual process switches are infrequent. Since the number of instructions required to implement most bytecodes is relatively small, this test can be a significant overhead. Alternative implementations techniques can avoid this overhead. For example, the address of the bytecode dispatcher might be stored in a processor register. Routines which implement bytecodes would then terminate by branching to the address contained in the registers. A pending process switch could then be signaled by changing the address in the register to the address of the routine which performs process switches. When the current bytecode finishes, control would therefore be transferred to the process switcher.

Memory Management

The routines of the formal specification's object memory manager may be grouped into two categories. The first category consists of those routines which support accesses to objects. The second category consists of those routines which support the allocation and deallocation of objects.

The access routines (such as fetchPointer:ofObject: and storeByte:ofObject:withValue:) are used by the bytecode interpreter to store and retrieve the information contained in the fields of objects. In many implementations of the bytecode interpreter, these functions will not be performed by independent routines, but will be implicitly performed by inline code sequences within the routines of the interpreter. The object allocation and deallocation routines form the bulk of the memory manager.

Collectively, the memory management routines will probably comprise the most complex part of a Smalltalk-80 interpreter implementation. In addition, unless great care is taken in their design, the percentage of execution time spent in these routines can easily dominate the time spent in all other parts of the interpreter. Our initial implementation was found to be spending 70% of its time within memory management routines (see Chapter 5).

Object Allocation

The bytecode interpreter normally requests the allocation of an object in two circumstances. The first circumstance is the execution of a primitive method (most commonly the primitive new or new:) which explicitly calls for the creation of a new object. The second circumstance is the activation of a new method. This implicitly requires the creation of a context object to represent the state of the activation. The formal specification provides a single generalized set of routines which handle both types of allocation requests. These routines perform the following actions. First they must assign an Oop which will be used to refer to the new object. Second they must find an area of free storage within the object memory, large enough to contain the requested object. Next they must initialize any internal data structures (for example an object table entry or object length field) used to represent the object. Finally, they must initialize the fields of the object with a null value.

Observation of actual Smalltalk-80 implementations indicates that the vast majority of allocation requests are for the creation of context objects (see Chapter 11). In addition, most of these requests are for the smaller of the two possible context sizes. A memory manager design which optimizes the creation of a small context object should thus yield better performance.

There are a number of possible approaches to achieving such an optimization. A memory manager might have a dedicated list of available contexts. These available contexts might be preinitialized and have preassigned Oops associated with them. If the memory manager attempts to ensure that this list will not be empty (perhaps by using a background process to maintain the list), then a context could usually be allocated by simply removing the first element from the list.

A memory manager might choose to dedicate a memory segment to the allocation of contexts. Since such a segment would only contain objects of a single size, the actual allocation and deallocation process should be simplified.

Any scheme to optimize context allocation must, of course, conform to the formal specification's requirement that a context behaves as a normal Smalltalk-80 object. The representation of activation records (contexts) as objects contributes much to the power of Smalltalk-80 (it allows programs such as the Smalltalk-80 debugger to be implemented) but requires a large amount of system overhead to support. A major challenge to Smalltalk-80 implementors is to develop techniques to reduce this overhead while preserving the inherent power of context objects.

Storage Reclamation

Storage reclamation is the second major function of the Smalltalk-80 memory manager. While the Smalltalk-80 storage model allows a program to explicitly request the creation of an object, it does not require a program to explicitly request that an object be deallocated. Once an object has been allocated it must remain in existence as long as it is accessible from any other object. An object may only be deallocated if no references to it exist. It is the memory manager's responsibility to automatically deallocate all inaccessible objects. This process is commonly referred to as garbage collection[5]. The classical method (called mark/ sweep) of performing garbage collection is to periodically halt processing, identify all inaccessible objects, and then deallocate them. This is commonly done as a two-phase process. First all accessible objects are marked. This requires starting at some root object and traversing all accessible pointers in the system. Second, all unmarked objects are deallocated. With a large object memory, such a process may consume a considerable period of time (ranging from several seconds to several minutes). Because of the interactive nature of the Smalltalk-80 system, such delays are unacceptable. Instead, a garbage collection technique which distributes the storage reclamation overhead over the entire computation is required. The most commonly known technique for achieving this is reference counting. This is the technique used by the formal specification's model implementation.

Reference counting requires that each object have associated with it a count of the number of pointers to it which exist in the system. Each time an Oop is stored into a field the reference count of the object associated with the Oop is incremented. Since storing an Oop into a field must overwrite the previous contents of the field, the reference count associated with the old value is decremented. When the reference count of an object reaches zero, the object is deallocated. The deallocation of an object invalidates any object references contained in it and hence will decrement their reference counts. This may recursively cause other objects to be deallocated.

Although reference counting eliminates the long delays characteristic of mark/sweep collection, it introduces considerable overhead into the normal operations of the system. We have found that for our host processor (a Motorola 68000), the code sequences that implement simple bytecodes such as the push and pop operations using reference counting are several times longer than the equivalent routines without reference counting. A Smalltalk-80 interpreter design that can decrease this overhead should have greatly improved performance.

There are several possible approaches to achieving this improved performance. One technique which reduces the actual counting overhead is called deferred reference counting[6]. It is based upon the observations that the most frequent and most dynamic object references occur from context objects and that many of these references are quite transitory. For example, assigning an object to a variable causes the object's reference count to be first increased by one as it is pushed onto the context's stack, then decreased by one as it is popped from the stack, and finally increased by one as it is stored into the variable. Our measurements show that "store instance variable" bytecodes (the most common means of creating an object reference from a non-context object) account for less than 4% percent of the dynamically executed bytecodes. If the need to perform reference counting for references contained within contexts is eliminated, then almost all of the reference counting overhead will have been eliminated.

A Second Generation Design

The first Tektronix Smalltalk-80 interpreter was implemented in Pascal on a Motorola 68000 (see Chapter 5). Even though the performance of this implementation was so poor that it was only marginally useful, the experience gained from this effort enabled us to design a new interpreter which exhibits much better performance. In developing this second generation interpreter we encountered many of the design tradeoffs mentioned in the previous sections of this paper. The new interpreter was designed and implemented by the author over a period of approximately nine months.

We choose to continue using a 68000 as the host for the new interpreter but component advances enabled us to use a 10 Mhz processor with one memory wait state instead of an 8 Mhz processor with two wait states. We choose to implement the interpreter in assembly language. In addition, great care was taken in choosing the code sequences for all of the frequently executed portions of the interpreter. The common byte codes are all open coded with separate routines for each possible instruction parameter.

The active context's stack pointer, instruction pointer, and home context pointer are cached in 68000 base registers as 68000 addresses. The stack pointer representation was chosen such that 68000 stack-oriented addressing modes could be used to access the active context stack. Other registers are dedicated to global resources such as addressing the object table and accessing free context objects.

The Oop format chosen requires only a simple add instruction to convert an Oop into an object table index. Object table entries can be directly loaded into base registers for accessing objects. A separate reference-count table is used. Deferred reference counting is used to limit the reference-counting overhead and to streamline the code sequences for push/pop bytecodes. Complete context objects are not created for leaves of the message send tree. Context objects are only created if a method references the active context or causes another new context to be activated.

The initial (before any tuning and without some optional primitives) performance benchmarks of our second generation interpreter (see Chapter 9) show that it is between five and eight times faster than our original implementation. We feel that these results demonstrate that it is feasible to build usable microprocessor based Smalltalk-80 implementations.

Summary and Conclusions

For any given host processor, its performance as a Smalltalk-80 host can potentially vary widely depending upon how the Smalltalk-80 interpreter is implemented. The goal of a Smalltalk-80 implementor should be to achieve the best possible mapping of the Smalltalk-80 virtual machine specification onto the chosen host computer. To accomplish this, the implementor will need to intimately understand both the internal dynamic behavior of the Smalltalk-80 virtual machine and the idiosyncrasies of the host processor. We would recommend that an implementor gain an understanding of the behavior of the virtual machine by first using a high-level language to implement the interpreter as described by the formal specification. This implementation can then be used to study the actual behavior of the Smalltalk-80 system and explore design alternatives. Finally, a new implementation should be designed which takes maximum advantage of the characteristics of the host processor. We have presented a few of the design alternatives which should be considered by Smalltalk-80 implementors as they develop their interpreters.

References

1. Goldberg, Adele, and Robson, David, *Smalltalk-80: The Language and Its Implementation,* Addison-Wesley, Reading, MA, 1983.

2. Lampson, Butler W., "The Dorado: A High Performance Personal Computer," Xerox PARC Technical Report CSL-81-1, Jan. 1981.

3. Kaehler, Ted, "Virtual Memory for an Object-Oriented Language," *Byte* vol. 6, no. 8, pp. 378–387, Aug. 1981.

4. Baden, Scott, "Architectural Enhancements for an Object-Based Memory System," CS-292R Class Report, Computer Science Div., Dept. of E.E.C.S., University of California, Berkeley, CA, Fall 1981.

5. Cohen, Jacques; "Garbage Collection of Linked Data Structures", *ACM Computing Surveys* vol. 13, no. 3, pp. 341–367, Sept. 1981.

6. Deutsch, L. Peter, and Bobrow Daniel G., "An Efficient Incremental Automatic Garbage Collector," *Communications of the ACM* vol. 19, no. 9, pp. 522–526, Sept. 1976.

PART TWO

Experiences Implementing the Smalltalk-80 System

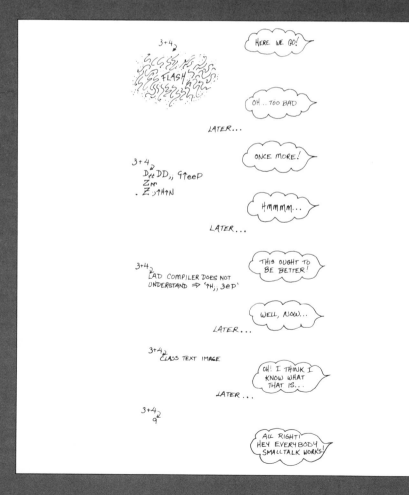

5

Implementing the Smalltalk-80 System: The Tektronix Experience

Paul L. McCullough *
Tektronix, Inc.
Beaverton, Oregon

Introduction

The Tektronix Smalltalk-80 implementation went through a number of hardware and software phases. Our experience will probably prove to be similar to that of other research and prototype groups desiring to implement the Smalltalk-80 system. At best, we will point out some mistakes to avoid; at the very least we can provide an entertaining view of our successes and follies.

This paper gives an overview of our initial hardware and software environments and our initial implementation design. We then present a fairly detailed account of debugging our first system. Next, we describe the evolution of our hardware, software, and development tools. We conclude with some observations and conclusions about the Smalltalk-80 system and its implications for the future.

Readers should note that we were debugging both our implementation and the formal specification. Although we detected a number of errors in the formal specification, these errors have since been corrected and are discussed herein to provide historical perspective.

*Mr. McCullough is currently employed by Xerox Palo Alto Research Center, Palo Alto, California.

Initial Goals

Initially we had four goals for our Smalltalk-80 work:

- Learn about the Smalltalk-80 system, in particular the implementation of the virtual machine,
- Learn about programming in the Smalltalk-80 language,
- Report on errors in the book draft, and
- Implement the virtual machine, realizing that it would not be our final implementation.

Tektronix had no previous experience with object-oriented software, so we were very interested in having a system with which we could interactively program in the Smalltalk-80 language, and in studying the Smalltalk-80 virtual machine. As part of our agreement with Xerox, we were to use our implementation as a means to detect errors in the book draft and to identify ways in which the book might be made clearer. We realized that our initial implementation would suffer from performance problems, but felt that a timely implementation was more desirable than a high performance one.

Initial Hardware

Our initial hardware consisted of:

- Motorola 68000 processor (8 MHz)
- 4 MHz proprietary bus
- 768 Kbytes of RAM
- Tektronix 4025 terminal
- A microprocessor development system, used as a file server

The choice of hardware was based on the availability of a Tektronix designed 68000-based system, along with the need for a large, preferably linear, address space. We also wanted to use a processor amenable to the construction of personal workstations. The Tektronix 4025 terminal is a raster graphics terminal, primarily oriented toward drawing vectors. While our bitmapped display was being designed, the 4025 served as an interim display device. Because the initial Smalltalk-80 virtual image did not depend on the use of a file system, we only used the microprocessor development system as a file server to load and store virtual images.

Software Development Environment

Our virtual machine was developed in a cross-compilation environment using a DECSYSTEM-20. The bulk of the virtual machine was written in a dialect of the proposed ISO Standard Pascal. This particular dialect of Pascal supports the independent compilation of modules and produces assembly language files which are assembled and linked. The resulting executable file is downloaded to the 68000-based system over a 1200 baud serial line. Though the 1200 baud line was an obvious bottleneck, the Pascal software already existed on the DECSYSTEM-20 and we had no desire to port it.

Initial Software

According to Dan Ingalls: "an operating system is a collection of things that don't fit into a language. There shouldn't be one"[1]. Taking those words to heart, we chose to implement our virtual machine on a system that had no operating system. This choice meant that we could not rely on runtime services normally provided by an operating system and had to write those portions that we needed, such as routines to handle input/output to an RS-232 port and perform IEEE 32-bit floating point arithmetic.

Our software implementation team consisted of three software engineers. We chose to partition the programming task into three distinct parts:

- Object Memory Manager
- Interpreter and Primitives
- BitBlt

Object Memory Manager

The initial object memory manager was, for the most part, a strict translation from Smalltalk-80 to Pascal of the methods presented in the formal specification. During the translation phase, we noted four minor typographical errors in the draft of the book involving improper bit masks, or incorrect variable, constant, or method names. We chose to implement the reference-counting garbage collector. Later, because the image creates circular garbage, we added a simple, recursive, mark-sweep collector. The translation process took less than one week and resulted in a working memory manager that maintained a very clear boundary between itself and the rest of the virtual machine. As discussed below, this clear differentiation is both a blessing and a curse.

With minor changes due to different dialects of Pascal, we were able to run programs that tested the object memory manager on the DECSYSTEM-20 with its more sophisticated debugging and performance monitoring software. The test programs read the virtual image, then made calls to the various entry points in the memory manager. Then, with Pascal write statements and the debugger, we were able to examine the state of the object space and determine whether the memory manager was working correctly. These tests indicated several errors in the book's methods: for example, the method that determined where to find the last pointer of an object was incorrect for CompiledMethods, and the recursive freer needed an extra guard to prevent SmallIntegers from being passed off to the pointerBitOf: routine.

At this point, we were able to run test programs that created instances of classes, stored object pointers in other objects, destroyed such links and thus invoked the deallocation of objects, and performed compactions of the object space. Further testing demonstrated that the book's method for swapPointersOf:and: was also incorrect.

In order to speed up the performance of the deallocation portions of the memory manager, we modified the countDown: routine to call forAllObjectsAccessibleFrom:suchThatDo: only when the object's reference count was going to drop to zero, thus saving a procedure activation that was usually unnecessary.

A few other minor changes provided us with a memory manager that was tested on the DECSYSTEM-20. Thus, we had a great deal of assurance that the memory manager would perform correctly on the 68000-based system. Also, we felt that when problems were encountered in our implementation of the virtual machine, we could concentrate on looking for the problem in the bytecode interpreter or primitives, and could ignore the memory manager. In actual practice we made many, many runs of the virtual machine before any problems were found in the memory manager. We heartily recommend having a trustworthy memory manager.

Interpreter and Primitives

In parallel with the development of the object memory manager, we coded the bytecode interpreter and primitives. The interpreter and many of the primitives were written in Pascal. The arithmetic primitives were coded in assembly language in order to simplify the maintenance of the small integer tag bit.

The outer block of the interpreter consists of a call to an initialization routine and a loop containing a very large case statement that acts as the bytecode dispatcher. While the memory manager was a fairly literal translation of the book's methods, much greater care was exercised in the construction of the interpreter. Code that in the book was several message sends was often collapsed into a single Pascal statement. We included in our interpreter the capability of producing traces which duplicate those supplied with the virtual image by Xerox.

In order to give the reader a measure of the complexity of implementing an interpreter (in Pascal), we present the lengths (in printer pages at 60 lines per page) of some of the major routines. These figures include the length of tracing code:

- Looking up a message, including the perform: primitive: two and one-half pages

- Sending a message (including cache lookup): one and one-half pages

- Executing the current method, including the primitives written in Pascal: twelve pages

- Returning a value from the active context: one and one-half pages

- The scan characters primitive (used for text composition): three and one-half pages

- Large integer primitives: four pages

- Process primitives: five pages

We strongly recommend that the first implementation of an interpreter be in a high-level language. By writing the virtual machine in a high-level language, implementors gain a more thorough understanding of the virtual machine as well as a much more quickly completed implementation.

BitBlt

The BitBlt primitive handles all graphics in the Smalltalk-80 system. Due to its importance, we decided to have one person concentrate on its implementation. The routines to implement BitBlt were written in assembly language and closely reflect the structure of the BitBlt methods in the book. To assist in the debugging of BitBlt, there are many conditionally assembled calls to the Pascal runtime print routines. The main BitBlt routine accepts one argument, the address of a Pascal record containing the various BitBlt parameters. When called, the routines perform the following actions:

- Clip the source parameters to the physical size of the source form

- Clip the clipping rectangle to the true size of the destination form

- Clip and adjust the source origin

- Compute the masks necessary for the logical operations

- Check for possible overlap of the source and destination forms

- Calculate the offsets for the starting and ending words

- Copy the bits as appropriate

Certain optimizations are performed for the special cases of clearing, setting, or complementing the destination forms. BitBlt is approximately 2 Kbytes of assembly code.

Summary of Runs

We maintained a fairly detailed log of our attempts to get the virtual machine up and running. The comments we made for each of these runs may be helpful to future implementors of the virtual machine. This summary should provide a sense of the types of errors and problems one should expect when implementing the virtual machine.

1. Reached the first send, then encountered an error in a debugging routine we had written.

2. Reached the first send again, encountered another error in a debugging routine.

3. Encountered a Pascal compiler bug.

4. Reached first send of the @ selector, and discovered that we had transcribed the constant for class SmallInteger incorrectly.

5. The method specified in the book for initializing the stack pointer of a new context was incorrect.

6. We forgot to initialize the sender field when creating a context.

7. In the book, the method returnValue:to: caused the reference count of the sender context to go to zero (thereby making the sender garbage) just before returning to that context. We had to explicitly increase the reference count of the sender context, perform the return, then explicitly decrement the reference count.

8. We had decided to implement the "common selector" bytecodes using full message lookup. Unfortunately, the method header for selector == in class Object did not specify the execution of a primitive. We patched the image to specify the correct primitive number.

9. The first conditional branch we encountered failed because we did not advance the instruction pointer past the second byte of the instruction.

10. We discovered that the source code for SmallInteger < did not specify a primitive, resulting in an infinite recursion. We patched the image again.

11. Discovered that other methods of class SmallInteger did not have primitives specified. We retrenched to executing the following selectors without lookup: class, ==, arithmetics, relationals.

12. Selector at: failed. Our fault, in the routine positive16BitValueOf: a " > " should have been a " < ".

13. Multiply primitive failed due to an assembly language coding error.

14. All relational primitives written in assembly language had an incorrect (and uninitialized) register specified.

15. Made it through the first trace. (Listings of four traces of the interpreter's internal operations were included with the first distribution of the virtual image. Subsequent distributions included three traces.)

16. The book's method for the primitive value: caused the stack to be off-by-one.

17. Once again, we found an error initializing the stack pointer of new contexts.

18. Again, the stack pointer is off. These three errors were caused by an incorrect constant in the book draft.

19. A message selector was not found. Another run is necessary to determine what happened.

20. At the beginning of execution for a block, the cached stack pointer is one too large. In the past, message sends and returns have worked because the routine that stored the stack pointer decremented it.

21. We had coded the at:put: primitive incorrectly: we forgot to have it return anything, hence the stack was off-by-one.

22. We incorrectly coded the at:put: primitive with an uninitialized variable.

23. The at:put: primitive had a > that should have been a > =.

24. The SmallInteger bitShift: primitive added in the SmallInteger bit, but should have Or'ed it in.

25. Interpreting lots of bytecodes, unfortunately not the correct ones. Apparently, we took a bad branch somewhere.

26. We found that the book's methods for the bytecode "push self" did not necessarily work for block contexts.

27. Almost through the fourth trace when the SmallInteger division primitive failed to clear the high-order half of a register. The error was detected by a Pascal runtime check.

28. Through the fourth trace when Sensor primMousePoint dies because of a clash between the interpreter and the Pascal runtimes.

29. We are well beyond the fourth trace when we discover that the method frame:window:para:style:printing: has a MethodHeader extension that specifies primitive number 0. We had assumed that an extension always specified a valid primitive number, but find that it may also be used to specify a method with more than four arguments.

30. We have changed all unimplemented primitives so that they fail, and now correctly handle primitive 0 in MethodHeader extensions. By now, we should have something up on the 4025 display, but do not. Investigating, we find that the book says that the bitmap for a Form is the first field, whereas the sources say it is the second field.

31. We are halftoning the display. We have to make a few adjustments to prevent overrunning the display. Halftoning will take a long time, approximately two hours. After a while, a runtime exception was raised by a Pascal support routine that contained a bug.

32. The "T" for the TopView window title tab is present on the display. Interpreter stopped after sending copyTo: to a SmallInteger.

33. We have disabled halftoning to the 4025, continuing with the study of the problem of sending copyTo: to a SmallInteger.

34. The problem is that the BitBlt primitive, copyBits did not return anything, thus forcing the stack off by one. Similarly, beDisplay, and beCursor did not return anything. We have added more display memory to the 4025.

35. Hurray! "Top View" window title tab is on the screen. Pascal runtime checks detected an out-of-range scalar while setting up arguments for copyBits. We have always assumed that BitBlt arguments are unsigned, but that is not so. We were told that BitBlt should do source clipping, so we will add that to BitBlt.

36. The entire "Top View" window is on the display, then erased. We eventually crashed because we are out of object space, but unsure why.

37. We are out of object space because the book's methods for superclass send was incorrect: another level of indirection is necessary.

38. We now have "Top View" window, Browser, and Transcript window on the display. Interpreter stopped when the mouseButtons primitive failed.

39. We turned on halftoning to see what would happen. This was a mistake because windows are halftoned black and then white. We decided to reload and try again without halftoning.

40. We have reached the idle loop, checking if the mouse is in any window. We changed the position of the mouse (by altering two memory locations) and placed it within the browser. The browser awoke and refreshed four of its panes. The fifth pane (code pane) caused an interpreter crash with a Pascal out-of-range error due to a minor bug in the mod primitive.

41. Great excitement! We have refreshed the window containing a "Congratulations!!" message. Eventually we crashed because the Float < primitive fails. The system tried to put up a Notify window, but had difficulty because of other primitive failures. However, it was able to put up messages in the Transcript window. For a system that is not yet fully implemented, it is amazingly robust. We noticed that certain BitBlt operations seem to put up incorrect information, then erase it. For example, putting up the "Top View" title tab, the text reads "Top Vijkl" for a short time, and the incorrect part is then repainted. Investigation showed the method computeMasks to have a < selector that should have been a < =, an error carried over from the book.

42. Generally poking around with the system. We have found that we need floating point primitives in order for scroll bars to work, so we have implemented all but the fractionalPart primitive. Rather than develop an IEEE Floating Point package, we acquired one from another group at Tektronix. We have also speeded up BitBlt by using 4010-style graphics commands with the 4025.

43. We have implemented object memory statistics to report the number of fetchPointers, storePointers, etc. performed. We have also added a lookup cache for faster message send processing. A clerical error in the caching routines crashes the virtual machine.

44. An uninitialized variable causes the cache to misbehave.

45. The cache is functioning well. Our initial algorithm is to exclusive-or the Oops of the receiver's class and the method, then extract bits 3-7 and index a 256 element array of 8 byte entries. The interpreter definitely runs faster with the cache. The cache consists of the Oop of the selector, Oop of the receiver's class, Oop of the method, the most significant byte of the method header, and one byte indicating either the primitive index or 0.

46. Tried a new hash function, shifting two bits to the left before the exclusive-or because we observed that the Oops of different selectors in the same class are very similar to one another. Some speedup was noted.

47. Another hash function, this time adding the Oops rather than exclusive-oring them. No noticeable change. We did move the mouse to the first pane of the Browser and crashed the system when the interpreter passed a SmallInteger to the memory manager.

48. Further examination of the previous problem shows that we did not cut the stack back far enough after a value: message. This bug was carried over into our code from the book, but only appears when sending value: within an iterative loop.

49. We have fixed value:, now we need to write the perform: primitive.

50. We have installed perform:, but get an infinite recursion because the floating point package is *not* IEEE format. We will write one in Pascal.

51. With the new floating point code, we can now cut text, pop up menus, and so on. This is great!

At this point, we added some simple performance monitoring code. We counted the number and type of object memory references, the number of bytecodes executed, and information concerning the performance of the lookup cache. For each bytecode executed, an average of just under 10 object memory references were made. The majority were calls to fetchPointer:, then storePointer:, fetchByte:, and fetchClass:. The various lookup cache algorithms were found to perform either fairly well (50 to 70% hit rate) or very poorly (20% or worse hit rate). Evidently, caching algorithms either perform quite well or miserably.

Summary of Initial Software

We feel that we were able to implement a relatively complex piece of software in less than six weeks (that is, from nothing to a working system) in less than 60 runs for several reasons:

- We were fortunate to have very good software engineers.

- We had a well-defined task.

- Because it took so long to load the virtual image (about 10 minutes) from the file server and so long (again, 10 minutes) to download our virtual machine from the host, we were very careful in coding and in analyzing crashes. We were also sharing the hardware with another group, so we made good use of our time on the machine.

- The specification, though not without error, was well written.

The Second Virtual Image

About this time, we received the second virtual image from Xerox Palo Alto Research Center (PARC). With this image, the handling of primitive methods was much cleaner, access to BitBlt was improved, the kernel classes were rewritten, and a source code management system was added. Several significant changes to the virtual machine specification were made, with the intention that these would be the final modifications. The second image also made use of the process primitives, while the first image did not.

Because a general cleanup of our interpreter seemed a good idea, and because a fair amount of the interpreter needed to be changed to support processes and new primitive numbers, we rewrote much of it. A history of our runs for the second virtual image follows:

1. We got our "Initializing . . ." message, and the system crashed because we were trying to initialize the cursor frame buffer. Since our bitmap display was not yet available, the presence of this code was premature.

2. We are through one-third of the first trace, but a conditional branch bytecode branched the wrong way.

3. Several problems noted:

   • Metaclass names no longer print properly on our traces.

   • We encountered off-by-one errors in stack operations while handling bytecode 187 because we forgot to adjust the stack index.

   • We encountered off-by-one errors in stack operation for SmallInteger //.

   • Our trace does not print operands for SmallInteger * properly.

   • We need to carefully check the code for all stack operations.

4. M68000 stack overflow causes parity errors.

5. We are through trace 1, and three-quarters through trace 2 when Pascal detects an out-of-range scalar because the routine returnValue:to: returned to a deallocated block context. We had failed to increase a reference count.

6. We are almost halfway through trace 3 when we hit an unimplemented process primitive. We also noticed the primitive return of an instance variable did not pop the receiver, thus causing the stack to be off-by-one.

7. We are about 60% through trace 3 when we try to add nil to an instance of class Rectangle. Caused by our coding error: when a direct execution send fails, we fail to tidy up the stack pointer.

8. We find that we need to implement the process primitives.

9. BitBlt fails to clear the high-order bits of a register causing a crash on the 21380th message sent.

10. Sending the selector + to an Array fails. Stack is off-by-one because the copyBits primitive failed to return self.

11. We find that the resume: primitive does not work due to an uninitialized variable.

12. More problems with resume:, it fails to set a boolean.

13. More problems with the resume: primitive: the process to be resumed has nil as its instruction pointer because the initial instruction pointer is not set in primitiveBlockCopy.

14. The resume: primitive works finally! Unfortunately, the wait primitive does not because of an incorrectly coded branch.

15. The wait primitive works, and we are through the third trace correctly. We forgot to code the setting of the success boolean for primitive become:, so a notify window is created.

16. Fired up the system. We have executed more than 15,000,000 bytecodes and it is still alive!

In order to improve performance, we made many changes to the interpreter and the memory manager. Changes to the interpreter included the caching of absolute addresses in the interpreter, thus employing considerably fewer calls to the memory manager. For example, to extract the fields of a source form, rather than a fetchPointer call to the memory manager for every field, the interpreter merely cached an absolute address and stepped through a range of offsets. Within the memory manager, many procedure calls were replaced with macro calls that were expanded by a macro preprocessor. Not only did this save the overhead of procedure calls, but quite often allowed common subexpression elimination to occur, thus actually decreasing the amount of compiler-generated code.

We also sped up certain parts of the interpreter based on where we believed the interpreter was spending its time. With these optimizations, performance is approximately 470 bytecodes a second.

An observation: Utilizing a raw computer (that is, one without an underlying operating system) to implement a Smalltalk-80 system is a double-edged sword: on the one hand, you can place data structures and code anywhere in the system, and you have complete control of the hardware. On the other hand, the lack of performance monitoring tools and underlying file systems can be a problem because it takes time to implement them, rather than just interfacing to them.

Second Version of the Hardware

At about this time, we added floppy disks to the system, as well as a utility program that could save and restore arbitrary memory locations on the disks, thus freeing us from the microprocessor development system file server. The 10 minute delay for the loading of a virtual image was reduced to about 45 seconds. A more dramatic change to the hardware was the addition of our bitmap display. No longer would we have to translate bitmap operations to vector drawing commands on the 4025, nor wait for a window to be halftoned. We also added a standard Tektronix keyboard and a mouse. In order for the mouse and keyboard (as well as portions of the Smalltalk-80 software) to work, we also added a one millisecond timer interrupt.

As part of another project, a new M68000 processor board was made available to us. Recall that the bus that we were using ran at 4 MHz, which introduced wait states into the M68000. The new processor board used a one longword data cache and a one longword instruction cache to reduce bus requests. This resulted in a 70% speedup in system performance, to approximately 800 bytecodes per second.

The Third Virtual Image

At this point, our goal became to build a virtual machine that was clearly faster (approximately 4000 bytecodes per second), but to do it quickly and at relatively low expense. The method we chose was to develop a performance analysis tool and, using the results of the measurements, to rewrite time consuming portions of the virtual machine in assembly language. The following sections summarize our findings and our techniques for speeding up the virtual machine.

Performance Modeling Tool

To monitor the execution of the virtual machine, we developed a simple analysis tool that was called by the one millisecond timer interrupt routine. Each time it was called, it stored the value of the interrupted

M68000 program counter. By changing a memory location, a routine could be activated to print a histogram showing ranges of program addresses, the number of times the program counter was found to be within the range, and the percentage of time spent within the range. The size of the address range for each line of the histogram was selectable by the user. We mapped routine addresses to these ranges so that the histogram showed time spent in each routine. This tool proved to be invaluable in speeding up the virtual machine.

Prior to utilizing this tool, we decided to measure how much time was spent in the interrupt service routine. The Smalltalk-80 virtual machine expects a timer interrupt every millisecond and the routine checks the mouse and keyboard motion registers. If a change has occurred, the routine makes note of the change so that the bytecode dispatch loop can create a Smalltalk-80 event. Like much of our virtual machine, our timer interrupt routine was initially written in Pascal. Because the interrupt routine has many basic blocks, and the optimizer of the Pascal compiler operates only upon one basic block at a time, the interrupt service routine spent a great deal of time reloading registers with previously loaded values. We discovered that an amazing 30% of the M68000 cycles were going to the interrupt service routine! One of the first optimizations that we performed was to take the Pascal compiler-generated code and to perform flow analysis on it. The new interrupt service routine consumed 9% of the M68000 cycles. Future plans call for hardware to track mouse and keyboard events, and for timers to interrupt the M68000 only when necessary (for example, when an instance of class Delay has finished its wait period).

The Results of Performance Monitoring

The performance monitoring tool showed us some statistics that were surprising to us (the percentage figures presented below do not include time spent in the interrupt service routine nor the performance monitoring tool). Approximately 70% of the M68000 cycles were being spent in the memory manager, 20% in the interpreter and primitives, and 10% in BitBlt. The bulk of the time in the memory manager was spent in only a few routines: fetchPointer:ofObject:, storePointer:ofObject:withValue:, fetchClassOf:, countUp:, countDown:, and two sets of routines generally referred to as the recursive freer and the niller. Previous statistics we gathered had indicated that fetchPointer:ofObject: and storePointer:ofObject:withValue: were popular routines, but they were relatively short and (so it seemed) should consume relatively little processor time.

Looking at the Pascal-generated code, we felt that we could do far better with assembly language, and we recoded all memory manager routines that the interpreter and primitives could call directly. Recoding fetchPointer:ofObject: resulted in a 4.5% speedup. Next, we recoded storePointer;ofObject:withValue: and achieved an additional 13% speedup. The major difference between these two routines is in reference counting: when storing pointers, reference counts must be updated; when fetching pointers they do not. Although we had previously concluded that reference counting was an expensive operation, we now had measurements of just how expensive. After recoding in assembly language all the routines callable by the interpreter and primitives, the system was an aggregate 19% faster.

Next, we considered routines that were private to the memory management module. From the histograms, it was obvious that we spent a great deal of time initializing just-instantiated objects to nil pointers (or zeroes for non-pointer objects). This inefficiency again arose from the strict basic block analysis of the Pascal compiler. For the price of a procedure call to an assembly language routine, we were rewarded with a speedup of nearly 10%.

Another major change to the memory manager came in the area of the so-called recursive freer. When an object's reference count drops to zero, this set of routines is activated to decrement the reference counts of the object's referents and, should their counts drop to zero, recursively free them. The first attempt at speeding up this process was done in Pascal and resulted in nearly a 10% speedup. Later on, we rewrote the recursive freer again in assembly language achieving an additional speedup.

The instantiation of objects was also expensive because several procedure calls were made. We rewrote this code (still in Pascal), collapsing several procedures into one. Later, the instantiation routines were rewritten in assembly language.

Changes to the interpreter and primitives were done in an interesting manner. Recall that we had a functioning, albeit slow, interpreter. With the belief that it is far better to change one thing at a time, rather than everything at once, we modified a small portion of the interpreter and tested the change. Once the change was shown to be satisfactory, we changed another part of the interpreter.

Initially, we rewrote the bytecode dispatch routine, but, in keeping with our philosophy of small changes, none of the bytecode interpretation routines. Thus, the assembly language bytecode dispatch routine set a boolean indicating that the assembly language dispatch had failed and that the Pascal routine would have to take over. Then we added bytecode interpretation routines, more or less one at a time. Eventually, we were able to discard the Pascal dispatch loop and bytecode interpreters completely.

Once all the bytecode interpretation routines were completed, we turned our attention to the primitive routines. These changes were accomplished in a similar manner: initially, all assembly language primitives failed, forcing the Pascal-coded primitives to run. We would then select a primitive, code it in assembly language, and test it. Once it was found to be acceptable, we selected another primitive to re-code. Finally, the Pascal primitives were discarded. Rather than call high-frequency primitive routines, we included many of them in-line.

In order to save some procedure calls to the memory manager when instantiating objects, the interpreter first tries to directly acquire the new object off the free lists. If the attempt fails, the interpreter calls the memory manager. Such "fuzzing" of the line between the pieces of the virtual machine seem necessary to achieve acceptable performance on current microprocessors. This demonstrates how a clear boundary between the memory manager and the rest of the virtual machine is both a blessing and a curse.

The changes to the memory manager and interpreter eventually resulted in a 3500 bytecode per second system.

The Third and Fourth Images

Our technique of making incremental changes to the virtual machine enabled us to use a working system and to bring up new virtual images as they were received from Xerox. A log of the attempts to run the third image follows:

1. At Xerox, the display bitmap is simply an object in the object space. In our implementation, the display bitmap lives at a specific address, and we encountered a problem because this image sends the become: primitive to the current display object. We modified our code in the become: routine.

2. We encountered a Pascal subscript-out-of-range error. The routine that returns instance variables was coded incorrectly, due to an error in the book's specification.

3. There are some new primitives related to the Xerox implementation in the image. We modified our interpreter to understand them.

4. A bit of Smalltalk folklore: "If 3 + 4 works, everything works." We typed 3 + 4 into a window and executed it. It did not work because the SmallInteger size message returned the wrong result.

5. Executing "Circle exampleOne" causes infinite recursion because the graphics classes were coded incorrectly by Xerox. They had not noticed this problem because the Xerox implementation of primitive new: did not comply with the formal specification, allowing their code to execute.

6. The system is up and working.

The fourth image was brought up on the first attempt.

Some Observations

If we analyze the coding errors that we encountered in our various implementations, we find that most fall into the following categories:

- Off-by-one errors

- Failing to return the correct object, or failing to return any object (leading to off-by-one errors)

- Conditional branch reversals

- Errors in the specification

Perhaps the most painful part of debugging a virtual machine is finding the off-by-one errors. These errors typically arise in primitive handling and in the stack activation records. Certain primitives may fail, and Smalltalk-80 methods are expected to take over. During the development of the virtual machine, it is quite common to damage the object references on the stack or to misadjust the stack pointer resulting in off-by-one errors. When returning from a procedure call in many stack machines (the M68000 is an example), if the processor's stack has an extra argument or does not have a return value, the correct return address will not be found, and the processor will return to an erroneous location. The typical result is a system crash. In the Smalltalk-80 virtual machine, the return address (actually the sender field) of the activation record (an instance of either class MethodContext or class BlockContext) is always in a known place, and a correct return can always be made and the machine will definitely not crash. Nonetheless, the interpreter (or primitives) may have pushed an incorrect result value or left garbage on the stack. Only later will this type of error manifest itself. These errors can be time-consuming and relatively difficult to find.

Errors resulting from conditional branch reversals are common, and are not further discussed here.

We certainly found our share of errors in the specification of the Smalltalk-80 virtual machine. This statement should not be taken as an affront to the Software Concepts Group at Xerox PARC. They were both developing and documenting two complex software products (the Smalltalk-80 system itself and the underlying virtual machine), and it was our job to point out discrepancies. Indeed, they produced an amazingly well constructed software system, and future implementors should have fewer problems with their own implementations.

We have programmed very few application programs in the Smalltalk-80 language. However, we do have one very definite data point in this area. Our file system (see Chapter 16) was totally developed in the Smalltalk-80 system and in a relatively short time period. All debugging was done using the Smalltalk-80 system: we never used the Pascal or assembly language debugging tools.

A final observation: the routines collectively known as primitives are about one-third to one-half of the implementation effort. Bear this in mind when scheduling an implementation.

Conclusions

Our work with the Smalltalk-80 system has shown it to be a robust, well-engineered piece of software. The initial, albeit incomplete, virtual machine required six weeks of effort by three software engineers, primarily using a high-level language. This resulted in a slow but useable system. By monitoring where the virtual machine spent its time, we were able to construct a system with adequate performance. For first-time implementors, we heartily recommend a similar approach.

Without question, the Smalltalk-80 system will have a strong impact on many areas of computer science, including language design, system architecture, and user interfaces. Perhaps most importantly, the system and language cause the user to think about problems in new ways.

Acknowledgments

Many people contributed to our Smalltalk-80 effort. Allen Wirfs-Brock designed and implemented the Pascal-based interpreters and primitives and the initial assembly language enhancements. Jason Penney designed and implemented BitBlt, the floating point package, the floppy disk driver, and the assembly-enhanced interpreters. Joe Eckardt designed our excellent bitmap display and has made interesting modifications to the Smalltalk-80 code. Tom Kloos and John Theus designed and maintained our M68000 system, as well as the interface to the mouse, keyboard, and floppy disks. Allen Otis graciously shared his hardware with us in the early days of the project and made some of the first measurements of the virtual machine. Larry Katz made many suggestions for the improvement of the book and served as our unofficial kibitzer during the implementation and provided much food for thought. We would like to acknowledge the various managers (Jack Grimes, Don Williams, Dave Heinen, George Rhine, and Sue Grady) who had the foresight and wisdom to allow us to work on the project. Glenn Krasner, of Xerox PARC, provided answers to our questions and provided us with ideas for speeding up our implementation. And, we would like to thank Adele Goldberg and the Software Concepts Group of Xerox PARC for including us in the book review and implementation process. Without them, we would have naught.

References

1. Ingalls, Daniel H. H., "Design Principles Behind Smalltalk", *Byte* vol. 6, no. 8, pp. 286–298, Aug. 1981.

6

The Smalltalk-80 Implementation at Hewlett-Packard

Joseph R. Falcone
James R. Stinger*
Computer Research Center
Hewlett-Packard Laboratories
Palo Alto, California

Introduction

This report describes one of the four test sites for the Smalltalk-80 release process: a personal computing research group at the Computer Research Center of Hewlett-Packard Laboratories in Palo Alto. The following sections present a history of the work at Hewlett-Packard, an overview of our implementation, a description of the development environment, and some conclusions. A comprehensive analysis of the Hewlett-Packard implementation is in the companion paper (see Chapter 12).

Smalltalk-80 Project at Hewlett-Packard

The Smalltalk project at Hewlett-Packard Laboratories received authorization on December 8, 1980. Beginning in November of 1981 the project slowed considerably, and the new year found nearly all development at a halt. The project officially closed on February 22, 1982, though some independent and academic work on the system continues. The im-

*The views expressed herein are those of the authors, and do not necessarily represent the position of Hewlett-Packard or any commitment to products or services. Copyright © Joseph R. Falcone and James R. Stinger, 1982. All rights reserved.

plementation portion of the project produced nine releases on five distinct host architectures. Documentation review and background work took one person-year of our group's time. We produced the first release of HP Smalltalk in two months, and subsequent releases followed coinciding with the availability of new Smalltalk images and new host computers. The analysis of these systems consumed another person-year.

This section describes our experience implementing a Smalltalk-80 system according to the specifications distributed during the test program. When the project began, neither the documentation nor the software was complete, a fact which profoundly influenced the duration, scope, and direction of the project.

Project History

The first three months of the project involved reviewing chapters of the Smalltalk-80 implementation guide and selecting the first host machine for the implementation. The first few chapters covered the underlying philosophy of Smalltalk and set the ground rules for an implementation. As time passed, the chapters concerned with the specifics of implementation began to arrive.

The Smalltalk-80 language itself was the specification language used to describe the implementation. We felt that this hindered our efforts in two ways. First, it forced us to learn Smalltalk before we had our own system, and at a time when Xerox possessed the only Smalltalk-80 engines (and even those were incomplete). Second, it introduced some unwelcome ambiguity into the specification.

Initially we considered the HP 3000 Series 44 for the implementation host because of its stack architecture and position as the fastest HP processor then available (approximately 0.5 MIPS). This strategy seemed appropriate for the Smalltalk-80 virtual machine architecture as we understood it. However, after studying the matter further, we became aware of several implementation obstacles. We determined that Smalltalk would perform significantly better on the Series 44 if we put it directly on the bare machine, instead of layering it on MPE, the HP 3000 operating system. As there is a tight coupling between MPE and the microcode on the Series 44, the Smalltalk-80 virtual machine code on the bare Series 44 would have to satisfy the expectations of the microcode for MPE structures. We also were not sure how Smalltalk would behave in an environment with separate code and data segments (enforced by hardware), as is the case on the Series 44. We explored changing the microcode of the Series 44, but we felt that the task would take too much effort, especially since none of the members of the group had microcoding experience. We also considered modifying the Smalltalk-80 compiler to produce Series 44 machine code, but Xerox advised that this would be difficult without a working Smalltalk system on which to do it. Because of these problems, plus time restrictions, we decided to postpone putting Smalltalk on the HP 3000 Series 44.

Instead, we decided to implement our first Smalltalk-80 system in Pascal under TOPS-20 on a DECSYSTEM-20 mainframe. Our selection of Pascal as the implementation language reflected the investigative nature of the project. We were not sure that a strongly-typed high-level language could implement the Smalltalk-80 virtual machine as specified, and it was an interesting exercise to try to do it and find out for ourselves.

Around the middle of March we felt we had enough information about the Smalltalk-80 virtual machine to begin writing the interpreter. The first test release Smalltalk-80 image also arrived in March. The DEC-20 implementation proved sufficient and useful for the early stages when many subtle implementation points were unclear. In particular, the type and range checking in Pascal exposed many implementation problems as we progressed. Such experimentation with the manner of the implementation continued throughout the project.

By the middle of April, the first version of the object memory manager was operating. This version included dynamic memory management via reference counts. A month later, the interpreter managed to execute up to the first invocation of a primitive method. We had included a monitor which allowed us to observe the operation of the system via a motion picture display (see p. 103 for more details on the development environment). Two weeks later, on June 5, 1981, we reached a project milestone: we ran the first Smalltalk-80 test image successfully. This system on the DEC-20 became the first HP Smalltalk release.

Although the system ran, we did not have graphics capability until the middle of the summer. This used an HP 2647 terminal connected to the DEC-20 system, and unfortunately, it took 50 minutes to display a single Smalltalk screen. We knew from the start that our DEC-20 did not have a suitable graphics device, so as early as April we began to explore different approaches. We had already ordered a Lexidata 3400 bit-mapped graphics system with an HP-IB (IEEE-488) interface for the proposed HP 3000 Series 44 implementation. Using a National Instruments GPIB11-2 IEEE-488 interface, we could connect the Lexidata to the VAX-11/780 UNIX system owned by our department. After much discussion, we adopted this plan. We gained several advantages by transferring our efforts to VAX UNIX. First, it allowed us to use our Lexidata system as the graphics device. Second, it took advantage of the UNIX and C expertise of a team member. Third, and most importantly, it would give us a version of Smalltalk which could be portable across UNIX engines.

In the process of moving from the DEC-20 to the VAX, we converted the entire system from Pascal to C. We developed editor command scripts for the code conversion to automate the process as much as possible. Over the course of the next month, as we completed various parts of the system on the DEC-20, we moved them to the VAX, so that by June 19 we had transferred the entire system.

The object memory was the first part of the system transferred to UNIX. Because of its dependence on the memory architecture of the host machine, the memory manager was almost completely rewritten. A version of it was running during the first week of May. We eventually rewrote about half of the original Pascal code as part of the move to UNIX. The recoding was necessary partly for reasons of efficiency and partly to take advantage of certain VAX features. In addition to rewriting the object memory manager, we redesigned the execution monitor, the memory inspector, and the input/output routines. Most of the small, frequently-called Pascal procedures became macros. The interpreter and primitive routines remained relatively unchanged. We also integrated the object memory inspector into the execution monitor, so that one could switch between them to examine objects during debugging. By the end of the conversion process, the HP Smalltalk-80 system consisted of 7500 lines of C code. Remarkably, it executed a dozen or so instructions after its first successful compilation on UNIX.

Although some work continued on the DEC-20 Smalltalk-80 system, particularly with the graphics interface, most of our effort shifted to the UNIX version. By the end of June we had fast and slow versions of both the object memory manager and the bytecode interpreter. The fast versions coded many of the C procedures of the slow versions as macros. Although the fast versions were indeed faster, they were less useful for debugging since C debugger breakpoints could only be set on the initiation or completion of a macro, leaving the intermediate steps of the expansion inaccessible. In addition, the slow version of object memory performed much error checking which efficiency considerations had eliminated from the fast version. Once the interpreter stabilized, we discarded the slow version of it, primarily to simplify version management.

A prime reason for moving the Smalltalk system to UNIX was to take advantage of certain tools, such as the C profiling facility *prof.* It showed not only where the system was spending its time, but also how fast it was running. Using the information gained from the profiles we were able to improve the performance of the system considerably through the following techniques:

1. We used structure casts overlaying object memory for contexts and other fixed-size objects to reduce access time. After setting up the base address, these casts allow direct access of all elements of the structure.

2. We expanded small procedures with few invocations in-line.

3. We recoded *very* small procedures as macros.

4. We cached frequently accessed information in special variables, including the stack and instruction pointers as absolute addresses, and the current active context and method as base addresses.

When the second image release arrived in June, instead of abandoning the first image and focusing our attention on converting the system to run the new release, we decided to work with the first image until it was fully functional. We felt the effort would pay off when getting the system to work on subsequent image releases. Unfortunately, the purpose of the first image, as stated by Xerox, was merely to provide a vehicle for debugging the Smalltalk-80 virtual machine interpreter. Thus, there was, no documentation available on the user interface for this first image; neither did we have a complete Smalltalk source listing. Also, the Lexidata graphics system was not available until the end of June. To help ease the problem of not having any graphics output before that time, we modified the scanword primitive to display any text on the session terminal that would normally appear on the graphics device. Thus, we saw text output a full two weeks before we saw our first Smalltalk screen.

By the middle of August, keyboard input was working, including an appropriate mapping of the keys into the Smalltalk character set and a keyboard polling scheme that did not cause the system to wait for a character to be typed if none was in the buffer.

In early September we started to convert the system for the second image while finishing the implementation for the first image. After solving a number of very elusive problems, everything except floating point worked. We were able to do 32 factorial in 14 seconds, 100 factorial in 90 seconds, and 200 factorial in 360 seconds. At this point our chief concern was simply getting Smalltalk to work, and the slow operation of the system was the least of our worries.

By the end of September we had recompiled our first method in the browser, run the *Turtle demo* successfully, and managed to get the snapshot facility working. Early in October we discovered how to declare variables which permitted more sophisticated top-level programming. By the middle of October, the floating point primitives were working. One annoying problem with testing the system was that the code which executed after loading a Smalltalk snapshot refreshed all the windows and required some time-consuming reorganization on entry to the first browser pane. To get around this, we constructed *work images* which were snapshots of the system taken after these tasks had concluded. We also generated a version of the system which did not incorporate the object memory inspector or the execution monitor. We used this new sleek version for demonstrations and software development, while we continued to debug with the original system. By this time the original system contained over 10,000 lines of C code. These systems constituted the second release of HP Smalltalk and the first on VAX UNIX.

We began to make the changes necessary to run the second image in the beginning of September. By the first week in October the system executed up to the first invocation of the inputSemaphore primitive.

This was a major accomplishment since the second image had required a significant restructuring of the system. There were changes in input/output handling, primitive invocation, and process management (for multiple processes). We also discovered that some of the class Oops in the second image differed from those in the previous version. This was a recurring problem with each new release and the system would behave somewhat strangely until we remembered to check the class Oops. By the end of the first week in November the system was 95% functional with the second image, and only a few unimplemented primitives remained.

At about this time, Dave Patterson, representing the University of California at Berkeley, obtained a research license from Xerox enabling him to study the Smalltalk-80 system in his graduate seminar on computer architecture. Dave requested a copy of our UNIX Smalltalk system for his studies, and upon receiving clearance from Xerox to do so, we delivered the second release HP system to him. We expended very little effort in porting the system to their VAX; it took them considerably longer to interface their graphics terminal to it. The experiences of the Berkeley Smalltalk group are discussed in Chapter 11.

By early December the system was fully operational with the second image. This system featured an early version of the new Smalltalk-80 user interface, and it became the third release of HP Smalltalk. We provided this release to Berkeley for use in their studies, since it differed significantly from the previous one.

Also in December, Xerox delivered the third Smalltalk-80 image. The system required only minor modifications for this new image, so it was running in a few days. However, there were some minor bugs that needed attention before it was fully functional. More serious were a number of problems with the Smalltalk code itself which made it necessary to revise this image release (see p. 96).

At this point we were ready to consider enhancements to the system. We added a more flexible image handler, a garbage collector, an optimized object memory system, and a method lookup cache. In addition, we implemented the replaceFrom:to:with:startingAt: method as a primitive to speed up string processing. The third image system with these modifications constituted the fourth release of a HP Smalltalk-80 system. The project closed shortly after this release, and there have been no significant structural changes to the system since. All project members went on to new assignments in the research center.

Cancellation was a major, but not fatal, setback as we undauntedly reached another milestone on March 13, 1982 when the system executed the testStandardTests benchmark without error. Nagging object memory allocator problems had thwarted previous attempts to run the complete benchmark for some time. Unfortunately, as the project had been closed for nearly a month, we could only spare a few moments here and there to work on the system. Debugging was usually done in pairs, and we found it particularly difficult to coordinate our schedules now that we were all working on different projects. But we were determined to attain full functionality, and, given our limitations, it was quite an achievement.

Two weeks later, the fourth Smalltalk-80 image arrived from Xerox. Again, the modifications for this image were minor and took only a few days to make. Enhancements to this version of the HP Smalltalk-80 system include an improved object memory inspector, an increase in the speed of drawing lines by implementing the drawLoopX:Y: primitive, and a new hard-copy facility for the Printronix line printer and the Versatec electrostatic plotter. The system also includes a mechanism for displaying Smalltalk screens on HP graphics terminals, at about three minutes per image—an improvement over the previous 50 minutes in the first release.

On April 28, 1982 we released our fifth version of the Smalltalk-80 system, which we call *HP Labs Smalltalk-84* for historical reasons related to our internal release numbering. This version was the first made available for use by staff at Hewlett-Packard Laboratories Computer Research Center.

In parallel with the documentation and analysis of the system, we made a number of modifications to the fifth release. Many of these modifications were a direct result of having to explain our implementation in this and other technical reports. Documenting the system in detail exposed many aspects that we had overlooked in our rush for implementation. In addition, the battery of tests used to generate the statistics in the companion report suggested many subtle ways to improve performance. In tests this revised version of HP Smalltalk-84 executes from 33% to 500% faster than our previous systems. We released this sixth version on September 13, 1982.

Overview of the System

Smalltalk is similar to other language implementations at Xerox Palo Alto Research Center in that it has its own virtual machine. The Smalltalk-80 virtual machine consists of a byte-oriented instruction set or *bytecodes* together with an associated support environment. Porting the Smalltalk-80 system to a new machine involves implementing a Smalltalk-80 virtual machine emulator to execute bytecodes and manage resources such as memory, time, files, and graphics. The distribution format for the Smalltalk-80 system is an *image* or *snapshot*, somewhat analogous to an APL workspace.

The virtual machine is in three parts: the bytecode interpreter, the primitives, and the object memory. The interpreter dispatches and executes the bytecodes. The primitives are the gateway through which the system makes requests to the underlying resource managers. The memory manager maintains a dynamic object store for the system.

Interpreter

The interpreter is the core of the Smalltalk-80 virtual machine emulator. The Smalltalk-80 virtual machine is an abstract architecture designed to execute Smalltalk and is similar to the P-machine of Pascal. It is a stack machine with a byte-oriented instruction set encoded chiefly to conserve space. Its most unusual aspect is the message send facility, roughly analogous to procedure call in conventional architectures. There are no computational instructions as such because message sends perform their function, with special cases to expedite the more popular ones (such as arithmetic and logical operations). The implementations of most bytecodes are only a few lines of code, but certain types of message sends require many lines of code for selector lookup and context activation, since the worst case amounts to a late-binding procedure call.

Our first implementation of the Smalltalk-80 virtual machine interpreter was a literal translation of the specification we were reviewing: each Smalltalk-80 method in the specification became a Pascal procedure in the DEC-20 version. When we moved the system to UNIX, we converted many of these procedures into C parameterized macros and consolidated several sets of interrelated procedures. These changes helped to avoid the substantial overhead of procedure invocation for most simple operations. In fact, often the consolidated code took less time than the original with the embedded procedure call. The parameterized macro facility gave us the best of both worlds—we moved many short procedures into in-line code without sacrificing the documentation value of the calling structure.

We structured the interpreter as a large switch statement encased in an instruction fetch loop. Early on we made several significant performance enhancements:

1. We moved most of the simple bytecode emulation into the switch cases to eliminate procedure call overhead (which is considerable on some hosts).

2. We cached Oops and addresses of the active context and method to speed up the frequent bytecode fetch and stack push/pop operations.

3. We also cached the Smalltalk-80 virtual machine instruction pointer (IP) and stack pointer (SP) in the form of C address pointers, instead of representing them as integer field offsets.

Since the cached IP and SP values change during execution, occasionally it is necessary to synchronize them with their values in object memory. Some of these occasions are:

1. Change of current active context.

2. Access of the current active context (e.g., instVarAt: and instVarAt:put: primitives).

3. Certain object memory management operations (e.g., compaction).

The most complex operation in the interpreter is message selector lookup. A message send enters the interpreter along with the class of its receiver and a selector. The *current class* below is initially the class of the receiver of the message. The algorithm implementing class behavior inheritance is as follows:

1. Search for the selector in the message dictionary of the current class.

2. If the selector is not found and the superclass of the current class is not nil, then set the current class to its superclass and go to (1).

3. If the selector is not found or the search reaches the end of superclass chain, then give a *message not understood* error.

Unfortunately, even though message dictionary access is through a hash function, the inevitability of selector collisions and the attractiveness of behavior inheritance cause a fair amount of *both* linear dictionary searching and superclass chain traversal. We added a simple method cache which eliminated much of the overhead, especially during repetitive tasks. The clumping of both selector and class values required a hash scheme with unusual characteristics. The cache has 509 elements and the hash function is

((selector bitShift: -1) bitXor: (class bitShift: -1) \\ 509) bitShift: 2

Using a large prime for the cache size distributes hashes more evenly and gives performance comparable to caches four times the size. Unfortunately, any time the system changes the object pointer of a compiled method, selector, or class, Smalltalk invalidates the entire cache. A more sophisticated approach to cache management would be a welcome addition.

We have recently modified the interpreter to transfer the receiver and arguments using the fast block move instruction on the VAX. This has significantly reduced the overhead of context initialization.

Primitives

The system primitives are the roots of the Smalltalk-80 virtual machine. One can view the primitives as a collection of system calls, a library of procedures, or a set of very important methods. Primitives exist for two reasons: Smalltalk cannot implement all system functions (e.g., I/O and basic arithmetic), and more important, Smalltalk code often cannot perform well enough for certain special functions (e.g., graphics).

We implemented most of the non-arithmetic primitives with UNIX system subroutines, and added additional software layers to handle error conditions, to interface with other software and hardware components, and/or to simulate particularly unusual operations. In all, a mass of over 100 C procedures implements the more than 80 primitives included in our system.

While it is not possible to code some primitive operations in Smalltalk, not all of them *have* to be implemented underneath the system. Indeed, some primitives begin life as Smalltalk methods and enter native code after careful evaluation of cost and benefit. As a result, some primitives remain as optional native implementation candidates, with backup Smalltalk code in place to execute if the associated primitive routine is absent or fails. An example is the set of primitives which handle arbitrary precision arithmetic, all of which have Smalltalk code to execute if the primitive invocation balks.

The term *primitive* does not refer to the complexity of the routine, though many are simple, straightforward functions. Rather, it describes the level of implementation—the lowest level possible. Our decision to develop the system in portable high-level languages was in direct conflict with this notion. However, since we could not modify the microcode on our VAX, we had no alternative for the prototype system and the performance of the primitives suffered accordingly. We feel that microcoded Smalltalk-80 virtual machine support could have improved performance by an order of magnitude over our existing system.

One of the more unwieldy concepts in the implementation was that of primitive failure: how and where to look for it, and what to do about it. We implemented most primitives with relatively strict runtime checking of the classes and value ranges of receivers, arguments and their fields. The current system probably has too many checks for valid receivers and arguments, but in some cases these were vitally necessary and helped us considerably during the debugging phase. In particular, the copyBits primitive contains a number of such checks. This checking may be stricter than absolutely necessary given the way the Smalltalk-80 code actually uses the primitives. However, we did not feel the specification of the Smalltalk-80 virtual machine was precise enough to rule out the need for these checks.

The addition of primitives for string processing (replaceFrom:to:with:startingAt:) and for line drawing (drawLoopX:Y:) resulted in impressive performance gains for work in those domains. However, we did not implement the arbitrary precision arithmetic and the file system primitives. Currently the arbitrary precision arithmetic primitives default to backup Smalltalk code which is relatively slow. This is not a serious problem since most Smalltalk system arithmetic stays within the signed 15-bit range of immediate small integer objects. Unfortunately, we will have to redesign most of the Smalltalk file support code to incorporate a reasonable interface for sophisticated hierarchical file systems (like UNIX). The file interface supported by Smalltalk is very low level, using too much information about physical disc operation. We do not consider this approach appropriate even for implementations without an underlying file system.

Currently, we use a Lexidata 3400 graphics system connected to a VAX UNIBUS via HP-IB. The physical pointing device, a Summagraphics Bitpad One with a four-button *puck*, operates through the Lexidata graphics processor. The routines for graphics device interaction shield the Smalltalk-80 system from the details of these lower levels. The Lexidata display memory is maintained by tracking the class Bitmap object associated with the current display form. Every time the bit map of the current display form changes, the graphics driver sends a copy of the altered area to the Lexidata. Since the at:put: primitive can potentially change the bit map, it recognizes when the destination is the display bit map and invokes the graphics driver.

The graphics system required much work to get to its present condition. We began with a 1280 x 1024 display optimized for white on black graphics and a track ball with illuminated throw switches. An HP-IB interface was designed especially for the Lexidata under a special contract and this was our pathway into the host machine. As time passed, pieces of the system fell into place. We developed microcode to use the bit pad in place of the track ball. The bit plane logic was reversed to display a white dot when the corresponding bit is *off* for black on white graphics. Other parameters and microcode in the graphics processor were modified to enhance black on white graphics, but there were limits to this. Regardless of mode, we could not use the system at its maximum resolution. We compromised for improved readability by using the graphics processor to double the pixels in both the X and Y dimensions so that a 640 x 480 Smalltalk *screen* neatly occupies the display. We even have room at the bottom of the display for system messages. In short, this experience was a baptism of fire in computer graphics.

We did try to optimize copyBits by implementing the bit copying operations in VAX assembly language. In this experimental version of copyBits we could copy an entire 640 x 480 pixel bit map in 0.08 second (about 10 times faster than the C routine). Unfortunately, the VAX bit operations work in the opposite direction of that needed for bit map manipulation. Our priorities prohibited modifying all of the bit map management code for reverse bit ordering, which now included microcode in the Lexidata graphics processor.

The current implementation of copyBits makes little use of the extended functionality of the graphics processor, such as area fill or polygon moves. The Lexidata system does manage and update the cursor as it tracks the mouse. In addition, having a screen bit map that is separate from CPU memory permits us to continuously display its contents without regard to processor operation. This is not the case with some integrated graphics configurations where display refresh consumes a significant percentage of CPU bandwidth.

The buttons on our mouse conform to the Smalltalk-80 color scheme: red on left, yellow in middle, blue on right. Because we had *four* buttons, we could attach more functions to our mouse. The fourth one, the green or *HP* button, acts as a shift key for the other three buttons. The following extended functions are available on our system:

1. *green + red*   Take a snapshot of the system.

2. *green + yellow*   Stop the system.

3. *green + blue*   Print the screen.

The HP system offers two flavors of snapshot. Besides the standard Smalltalk snapshot, we implemented a *flash freeze* snapshot which saves the image without executing any Smalltalk code. This avoids the rather tedious motions of the standard mechanism, including restoration of the display screen. The user may select this alternative snapshot through a mouse function or a monitor command. Since this facility permits snapshots at arbitrary bytecode boundaries, we must preserve more state information than is strictly necessary for saving an image via the Smalltalk mechanism. For example, the keyboard input buffer would not need to be kept if we had only the Smalltalk facility. The state information falls into three categories:

Monitor State   Bytecode count and current bytecode. Although this information is not needed to resume execution, it is nonetheless useful, especially during debugging. When a system resumes we always know the exact bytecode where it left off.

Cached Objects   Oops of the current display form, the current cursor bit map, the current input semaphore, the clock semaphore, and any new process waiting to be run. In addition, we save the Oops of all semaphores that have been signaled due to the occurrence of an input event. The Oop of the current active context is saved by storing it in the active context field of the current active process prior to taking a snapshot; similarly the cached stack pointer and cached instruction pointer are saved by storing their current values in the current active context.

I/O State   Cursor position, mouse position, last mouse buttons pressed, current sample interval, input polling interval, the time at which to signal the clock semaphore, the keyboard input buffer, and various indices and flags including the state of the link between the mouse and the cursor (linked or unlinked).

The system can print screen images on Printronix line printers, Versatec electrostatic plotters, and Hewlett-Packard graphics terminals in a variety of resolutions and magnifications. Anytime during a session the user may request a copy of the screen via the mouse buttons or monitor. The screen image is sent to a general bit map spooler.

We process external events and manage the input word buffer on a Smalltalk-80 virtual machine bytecode-synchronous basis. The system recognizes external events by (just before executing the next bytecode) explicitly polling the devices to determine whether they have changed state. One UNIX process implements all Smalltalk processes as well as the switching mechanism. The Smalltalk-80 system does not explicitly use the UNIX interrupt mechanism to support multiple processes. The system checks certain I/O queues after executing a fixed number of bytecodes since the last inspection. The user sets this inspection interval at system initialization.

Object Memory

The object memory itself is a simulator underneath the Smalltalk-80 virtual machine emulator, implementing a small-object dynamic storage manager within the large virtual memory of our host machines. As mentioned before, there are two versions of our memory system. The slow or protected version checks field index bounds and operand classes at the interpreter/object memory interface. The fast version does no checking and consists mainly of C macros. The protected version was very useful for detecting memory problems close to their source.

Access to objects in Smalltalk is via object pointers (Oops) which can be either signed 15-bit immediate integers (small integer objects) or 15-bit indexes into tables of state entries and field addresses (indirect object pointers). The 15-bit range of the object pointer (the other bit decides between small integer and indirect pointer objects) limits the number of indirect objects in the system to 32767. This limit was not a factor in our research.

The final Smalltalk-80 image is by no means *small* as it contains over 450 kilobytes of objects and requires at least half a megabyte with its object table. The suggested Xerox implementation uses a 20 bit address into the object space, but our implementation uses 32-bit virtual addresses. This required a reorganization of the object table into separate tables for the state entries and the field addresses, but the results were favorable.

Table 6.1 Hewlett-Packard Smalltalk-84 Image Format	
Word	*Entry*
0-1	number of entries in the object table
2-3	the length of the object space in 16-bit words
4	system state object Oop
5	offset to the first entry in the table (the first offset)
6	object state header of the first active entry in the object table
7	length in 16-bit words of the first active entry in the object table
8	Oop of the Class of the first active entry in the object table
9	offset to the second entry in the table (the second offset)
10-12	the second active entry in the object table
13	offset to the next entry in the table (the third offset)
14-end of entries	the remainder of the object table entries
followed by	the fields of the objects in the table

Because of host machine differences and efficiency considerations, the HP Smalltalk-80 system uses the image format in Table 6.1 which differs from the standard interchange format. The HP format uses a special coding scheme to indicate free entries in the object table, whereas the interchange format does not eliminate the space wasted by these entries. This format is also space efficient and easy to load and save. The first 8 bytes contain the image size parameters as 32-bit unsigned integers. The number of object table entries is followed by the number of 16-bit words in the object fields space. Next, is the Oop of the system state object, used to restore Smalltalk and the support environment to their exact condition before a snapshot.

The object table follows. It is *not* stored as an exact image of the system object table (that would waste space). Each object table entry in the image is preceded by a 16-bit offset from which the next table entry location is derived. For example: if the first active Oops in the system were 12, 16, 18, 26, and 56, then the offset values (in brackets) would be:

$$[12] > 12 + [4] > 16 + [2] > 18 + [8] > 26 + [30] > 56$$

The first of these offsets determines the location of the first used object table entry. Thereafter the offsets are used to skip the unused entries in between the active ones.

The field pointer portion of the object table entry in memory is initialized by cumulatively adding the object lengths to the base address of the memory allocated for the object space. Therefore, each object table entry in the snapshot consumes 8 bytes: 2 for the offset, 2 for the header, 2 for the length, and 2 for the class. After the object table entries are read in, a single mass read brings the object field space into memory.

Saving an image is similar, except that the object field space must be written on an object-by-object basis, since we cannot assume contiguous allocation on a used system.

We convert the image from the standard interchange format into the HP format by the following transformations:

1. Convert the interchange format state entries into the HP layout.

2. Move the class and length from the fields of each object into the object table entry.

3. Swap the bytes of all non-byte objects (our hosts use low-byte/high-byte ordering rather than the high/low of the image interchange format).

4. Convert objects of class Float in the image from IEEE format to VAX format. The ranges are slightly different so the conversion program indicates when it encounters an IEEE floating point number which has no VAX format correspondent.

5. Create the special HP system state objects in which the snapshot process saves relevant details so that the system may continue later from the same state.

The conversion process takes less than a minute and includes a consistency check on the interchange format image.

The implementation of our object memory system differs from that in the Smalltalk-80 virtual machine specification. The system maintains two tables of object information: the first table contains the 16-bit state entries while the second table has the length and class Oops plus the pointer to the object fields for a size of 64-bits. Since the size of the entries in each table is a power of two, access is fairly efficient. Previous single table versions used either 96- or 80-bit entries which required multiplies by three or five for indexing.

Each state entry contains an 8-bit reference count (used fully), and 6 flag bits for the following conditions:

1. Reference-count overflow and exemption.

2. Object is permanent.

3. Object table entry is available.

4. Object contains pointers.

5. Byte object is odd length.

6. Object has a mark (from garbage collector).

The two remaining bits are for future enhancements, such as a code bit for compiled method objects. We moved the length and class Oops from the fields of the object into this table for more efficient access. This change significantly improved performance for the protected version of object memory, and also reduced the load on the dynamic memory allocator by two words per request, but in doing so increased static allocation by 128 kilobytes. With an object table that is three-quarters full, the actual waste from this is 32 kilobytes, which is negligible in a large virtual memory system. The length entry contains the actual number of words allocated to the object fields (not the same plus two for length and class, as suggested). The pointer to the fields is a 32-bit virtual address instead of a 20-bit quantity divided into a 16-bit offset and a 4-bit segment number.

Early in the implementation, we defined the interface through which the interpreter and primitives communicate with the object memory. The strict adherence to this interface permitted an easy transition from the DEC-20 to the VAX even though their memory systems differed considerably. The interface consists of:

1. Instantiate pointer, word, and byte objects.

2. Load and store pointer, word, byte and float values.

3. Get object length and class.

4. Test and convert small integer and pointer objects.

5. Decrement and increment reference counts.

6. Find first and next instance of a class.

7. Swap object pointers.

8. Query memory allocator state.

The memory system initializes all objects upon instantiation. Word and byte objects need to have their fields set to zero, while pointer objects require nil values or 2's, which most architectures cannot do efficiently. The VAX has a block move instruction which, combined with a predefined array of nil values, is an efficient solution to this problem. The cost of using standard memory accesses to store nil in every field is excessive (since the average size is about 18 words).

Reference-count activity dominates the time spent in the memory system. We implemented a straightforward strategy and attempted to reduce the amount of checking necessary to determine whether an object actually must be reference counted. For example, the shortest path for the count decrement operation is

```
check if small integer bit of Oop is set (is object a small integer?).
ifFalse:[ fetch the header of the object pointed to by the Oop.
   check if exempt flag is set (is object free, permanent or overflow?).
   ifFalse:[ decrement reference count.
      check if reference count > zero.
      ifFalse: enter deallocation routine. ] ]
```

The sequence for the count increment operation is

```
check if small integer bit of Oop is set (is object a small integer?).
ifFalse:[ fetch the header of the object pointed to by the Oop.
   check if exempt flag is set (is object free, permanent or overflow?).
   ifFalse:[ increment reference count.
      check if reference count > zero.
         (note: the byte arithmetic wraps around to zero on overflow.)
      ifFalse: set exempt flag in header to overflow ] ]
```

Measurements of our Smalltalk-80 object memory and similar dynamic memory systems indicate that count maintenance consumes from 20% to 40% of execution time. The implementors of the M3L machine[1] demonstrated the performance advantages of special reference-count hardware. Reference-count maintenance is expensive because it congests data paths with extra traffic and requires ALU cycles during every count function. For example, a *store pointer* operation includes both a count down on the Oop at the destination and a count up on the source Oop. The cost of *store pointer* was the motivation behind its reimplementation in assembly language.

The availability of virtual memory on our host machine was an advantage in the early phases of design. Makeshift memory systems could run even while wasting a lot of space or thrashing over lists. Thus a gradual evolution of object memory implementations progressed until the better ones emerged. The current version implements:

1. A set of special allocation pools.

2. A mechanism for coalescing blocks on the general free list.

3. A marking garbage collector.

The special allocation pools were the most significant addition to the system, and they differ considerably from the free lists described in the specification. There are four pools in the system: one for each of the three most popular sizes of pointer objects and a general pool for the rest. The three special pools take advantage of the allocation frequency of small contexts, points, and large contexts. Each special pool is a linked-list of fixed-length pieces of memory allocated at system initialization and permanently residing in that pool. Only transactions requiring pointer fields of the three sizes can use the special pools so there is no fragmentation in the pool. In our standard configuration, 16 kilobytes of memory in the special pools satisfies over 97% of all instantiation requests.

The transaction traffic of the memory system is very different from that of most programming environments. The system allocates, accesses, and just as quickly deallocates megawords of memory in chunks typically less than 20 words. Since the special pools handle nearly all memory traffic, we have fragmentation effects from only 3% of allocations. Our memory allocator continuously coalesces and recycles this space on the general free list, thus preventing most fragmentation problems. In view of these facts, we feel that the actual long term fragmentation is not serious enough to warrant *dynamic* compaction. Compaction does happen whenever we save and reload an image. This scheme suits our view of personal computer usage patterns well—loading an image, working for a while, then saving the results—and since it takes less than 15 seconds to save and reload an image, we see little advantage to having a separate compactor.

Cycles of inaccessible objects occur with reference-counting memory management schemes. Sadly, some of the occasions for cycle creation involve fundamental concepts in the language, such as sending a message with a block as an argument (where the pointer to the block context is in the temporary variable area of the home context). Periodically we run an auxiliary garbage collector to sweep the object table of all derelict objects caught in cycles. The cost of such a collector in CPU time is high, so it is advantageous to avoid running it. Because contexts are most frequently involved in these cycles, the system invokes the collector when either of the two special allocation pools devoted to contexts becomes empty. By setting the sizes of these pools at system boot we can vary garbage collection frequency. The collector also runs whenever the object table becomes full, but this is a far less frequent occurrence. We found it necessary to lock out the garbage collector whenever the reference counts do not accurately reflect the condition of object memory. The current system requires collector lock-out in only a handful of situations.

Implementation Issues

The Smalltalk-80 distribution process proceeded through five test releases. Each new release posed a variety of problems which we usually resolved after a month or so of changes and corrections. Smalltalk proved to be an incredibly robust system—so robust that it could continue to run after bugs had corrupted major sections of data or code. For example, in implementing the primitive methods sometimes we did not push a result on the stack before returning. In spite of this, the system was able to execute many bytecodes before giving any indication that something had gone wrong. Problems such as this were often difficult to diagnose, even with the sophisticated debugging tools at our disposal.

We list here some of the problems and issues faced in implementing the Smalltalk-80 system in the hope that future implementors can benefit from our experience. These problems are in six categories: arithmetic, primitive methods, input/output, object memory, programming, and general problems.

☐ *Arithmetic Problems*   Many of the problems in the arithmetic area were with floating point numbers. One problem was that we were not certain which floating point representation was used in the first test image. In particular, floating point objects in the first image were *three* words or 48-bits, which seemed to contradict the claim that the Smalltalk-80 system used IEEE standard 32-bit single precision format. As it turned out, it was IEEE format and the system simply ignored the third word. But this was bad news—the VAX did not have IEEE standard floating point arithmetic at that time. We had to convert all objects of class Float to VAX floating point format and hope that none would be outside the VAX range. Fortunately, no Smalltalk floating point numbers have exceeded this limit. And after we went through all of this, DEC introduced IEEE floating point support for the VAX.

In another situation, the routine that extracted the fields of floating point numbers treated the fields as small integers (-16384 to 16383), when in fact they have a range of zero to 65535. This problem occurred in several places throughout the system and was the source of many bugs. As a result of these complications, we were well into converting the system for the second image before the floating point primitives went into operation.

Another problem involved the initialization of the fields of LargePositiveInteger objects. When we first installed the special allocation pools in the memory system, we set the fields of all pool objects to nil upon deallocation. The only requirement to request memory from a special pool was to be the appropriate size—there was no pointer object check. Occasionally a large integer happened to be one of the sizes handled by the special pools, and thus had nils in its fields. If one performed bit operations such as bitOr: on a large integer, these nil values could affect the result. Indeed, we found that when one added two large positive integers of certain values there were extraneous 2's in some of the lower digits of the result. The solution was to correct the allocator to ensure that it only initialized pointer objects with nils.

A third arithmetic problem had to do with the // operation. It was not clear from the original documentation for the first image just what the definition of // was. As we began to use the system, occasionally we would get a mysterious error 'Subscript out of bounds:' which did not seem to have any relation to what we were doing. We had spent quite some time searching for the cause when we discovered that the system was using the // operation to compute the index for a table, and because it truncated in the wrong direction, it often produced a negative index. As the corresponding C operator differed from the Smalltalk definition, we had some difficulty implementing the // operation correctly. Because of this confusion, the specification now includes both variants of the operation.

☐ *Problems with Primitive Methods* There was confusion over the extent of error checking to include in the implementation of primitive methods. Because there were no specific guidelines in the documentation, we decided to implement comprehensive checking. We checked the class and range of the receiver and the arguments and their fields. However, we soon encountered problems with class checking. In some cases the receiver or argument need only belong to a specified class or any subclass thereof. The class check in this situation could be time consuming since it involves a traversal of the superclass chain. Rather than endure this overhead, we removed the class check in these cases. In general, we feel that this checking gave us a useful safety net to protect the system from corrupted code and other problems, but it is not clear that such checking would be desirable in a production system.

During testing of the system with the slow version of object memory, we encountered many *load word* and *store word* range errors in the copyBits primitive. Some of these were caused by insufficient clipping of the source and destination forms. We eliminated them by adding more checks for clipping based on the sizes and relative positions of the source and destination forms. Other range errors stemmed from the way the BitBlt algorithm handled the transition from one row of the bit map to the next. When doing a preload on the last word of a bit map row, the next word loaded in computing the destination word comes from the next bit map row instead of the current row. This did no harm except when the last word of the last bit map row was at the end of the bit map. If it was, the next *load word* generated an error. We fixed this by checking whether the second *load word* goes past the end of the bit map. If it reaches the end of the bit map, we substitute zero for the second *load word* value. This is not the most efficient solution to the problem, but it preserved our investment in the copyBits primitive (which no one wanted to rewrite).

Another problem with copyBits on the third test image involved the coordinate arguments. In some instances, these coordinates contained floating point numbers instead of small integers. We had to check for floating point arguments in the makePoint routine. When the arguments to makePoint were instances of class Float, the primitive converted them to integers before making them into a coordinate point. The final image does not suffer from this problem.

There was a rather simple problem with the swapPointersOf primitive. An early implementation swapped the reference counts along with everything else. Since the reference counts must follow the Oop and not the table entry, the system behaved strangely until we realized what had happened and repaired the primitive.

☐ *Input/Output Problems*   We had many problems with keyboard input and character mapping. With each new Smalltalk-80 test release, we modified our keyboard input routine to accept numeric ASCII codes instead of characters in order to determine the appropriate mapping. This process became easier with each new release and particularly after the second release which was the first to use the ASCII character set.

With the second release came more problems as we had to find a way to input control key codes for those not in the ASCII character set (e.g., control-0 to control-9). Since the Smalltalk I/O code could handle either ASCII-encoded or unencoded keyboards, we designated an escape sequence to input unencoded control characters (control-↑ followed by the character). In the final release, the Smalltalk methods for keyboard input interfered with this scheme so we rewrote most of them.

We found it difficult to implement the polling scheme for keyboard input on the first test image. Often the last character in the buffer would not appear on the screen until the user typed another character and it was interminably slow. Finally, after rewriting the keyboard input primitives and maintaining better control of the buffer, the system improved, although it was still slow. With the second test image, keyboard input was to be interrupt-driven and synchronized with semaphores. Initially we simulated this behavior with another polling scheme. The system checks for keystrokes every n bytecodes, and if any are waiting, it places the key codes in an input buffer and signals the input semaphore. Recently we developed a way to eliminate polling for text input using an interrupt scheme based on UNIX intrinsics. This has improved overall system performance by eliminating the terminal buffer count check which was a part of polling.

Our Smalltalk system manages the mouse in a similar manner. Whenever the system polls the keyboard, it also checks the mouse position and mouse buttons for activity since the last poll. If there are any changes, the system generates appropriate event words, places them in the input buffer, and then signals the input semaphore. Various Smalltalk routines also query mouse position directly, posing some question about the need for our system code to do it as well. A series of experiments suggested that the system was more responsive with mouse position polling in both places.

☐ *Object Memory Problems*   The problems with the object memory manager centered around allocation, reference count management, and garbage collection. At one point there was infrequent trashing of some of the fields of method and block contexts. Somehow the memory system was allocating objects that were overlapping contexts. While we never discovered the source of the problem, we solved it for a while by isolating contexts into special allocation pools. The problem reappeared however, when running the interpreter on the final image. Again we redesigned the memory allocator, this time using linked lists for the pools instead of a table of pointers. We have had no problems with object memory since.

During testing of the interpreter on the second image we noticed that the memory system was allocating many small contexts while deallocating only a few through the reference counting mechanism. We later discovered that when performing sends we neglected to nil out the argument fields of the sender after transferring the arguments. This enabled cycles to develop involving block arguments and contexts. The correct transfer mechanism eliminated over 90% of these cycles.

Shortly after investigating these cycles in object memory, we decided to add a marking garbage collector to our system. At the time, our primary motivation was to reduce the size of the special pools from which the system allocated contexts. In the process of implementing the garbage collector we had to determine the root objects from which marking should proceed. We start from all cached object pointers, plus the Oop of the Smalltalk object. We were then faced with the problem of deciding when to activate the collector. Activation would certainly be tied to some sort of low watermark in the allocator, but should the collector proceed directly from there or be postponed to a safe period or a bytecode boundary? There are times when the garbage collector could do much damage, so it is vital to ensure that it cannot run during these periods. For example, sometimes the system temporarily increases the reference count of an object to ensure that it remains through a critical operation. During the interval between the artificial increment and decrement operations the reference count is inconsistent, and intervention by the collector would discard such an artificially protected object. This is because the collector chases pointers to determine the number of references to an object instead of relying on the reference count in the state header. To prevent intrusion during such operations, we devised critical section locks which disable and re-enable the collector. In addition, we make permanent (via a *permanent* bit in our object state header) those objects that are not to go away under any circumstances (e.g., true).

Once our garbage collector was working, we reduced the small context pool size from 8192 to 256 contexts, a saving of nearly 300 kilobytes of memory. Our investigations have shown that garbage collections are relatively infrequent when browsing or text editing, but that at least one occurs when compiling or decompiling a method, reclaiming as many as 500 objects.

☐ *Programming Problems* As with any programming project involving more than one person, we found ourselves confronted with problems of version management, communication among the members of the team, and implications of changes made to the system. We found UNIX tools to be very useful for managing these situations. In most respects, the project was a model of modern software management. All of us had a background of software projects and we placed a heavy emphasis on software tools and techniques. In fact, we considered managing the software effectively to be almost as important as implementing Smalltalk itself. Some of the management tools are described on p. 103.

We had a resource problem in having to share our host machines with other projects, some of which involved signal processing. There were times when the load on the system was so heavy that it was hopeless to attempt debugging the system. For demonstrations we would get the machine all to ourselves for acceptable performance.

Global variables, of which there were many, gave us the usual problems with proper initialization and usage. We tried to localize state variables as much as possible to only those modules that used them. In spite of these precautions, global variables were the source of several bugs in the system.

Macros were also a source of problems in coding the system. Since we tried to optimize code as much as possible by using macros, we sometimes nested them several levels deep. Upon expansion, these macros could get quite large—nearly 900 characters for the *push* macro, for example. Increasing the size of these macros could produce complaints from the C preprocessor in some situations. We also had to parenthesize macro arguments to ensure the proper order of expansion. A significant difference between macros and procedures is that macro arguments are evaluated at each appearance in the definition instead of only once on procedure entry. For example, a macro may use an argument in a number of different places in the definition. If we pass it a function which always returns the same value, the macro will operate properly. However, if we pass a function like *popStack*, then at each appearance of the function in the definition it will return a different result (plus there will be too many stack pops). We used temporary variables within macro definitions to ensure that arguments are evaluated only once.

We encountered an optimization problem with printing hard copy of the Smalltalk screen. The routine for dumping the screen to the printer worked fine until we ran the system through the C code optimizer. After that, the hard copy routine would print only garbage. Later we discovered that the c2 code optimizer for the VAX produced incorrect code for certain bit operations, and unless it has been changed, it still has this bug.

The Smalltalk-80 Implementation at Hewlett-Packard

☐ *General Problems* The biggest general problem was with the incomplete and sometimes erroneous details of the implementation given in the book. The agreement with Xerox made it our task to debug the documentation and image test releases. As we read through the chapters, we found we had many questions and comments. For example, we had difficulty getting nested blocks to work. Our system was not properly initializing the instruction pointer for a nested block. The initial instruction pointer was coming from the home context instead of the active context as it should have been. The documentation did not make this detail clear, and we wasted some time tracking it down.

Another problem was the result of a similar oversight. In early September, many of the methods in the first image were operational, but some still were not working and others gave 'message not understood' errors. There was no pattern to the failures and the cause seemed almost impossible to isolate. We had just about given up when, in a marathon debugging session, we discovered that the Smalltalk compiler was using *byte* stores to set the 16-bit header *word* of new compiled method objects. Because byte ordering on our host machines is the opposite of that on Xerox systems, a method header constructed in this fashion had the bytes in reverse order. As this header encodes the number of literals and temporaries as well as a special method flag, mere chance dictated whether the byte-reversed header would affect the execution of the method. The final system avoids this problem by having primitives for compiled method creation and manipulation.

A fascinating problem cropped up when we ran the Arc example provided with the third release image. The system mysteriously went into an infinite loop and eventually ran out of object table space through the activation of thousands of contexts! By tracing the execution of the interpreter and looking at the Smalltalk source code, we were able to determine the cause of the infinite loop. The method for the Arc example included the following

anArc ← Arc new.

Since Arc class did not understand the message new, it defaulted to the new message understood by Path class, the superclass of Arc class. The method for new in Path class contained the statement

↑super new initializeCollectionOfPoints.

Following the superclass chain, we made the transition from the metaclass to the class hierarchy by passing through Object class into Class and eventually ended up in Behavior. Here the method new had a primitive associated with it. However, since the receiver was an indexable object, the primitive failed and invoked the backup Smalltalk code which included

self isVariable ifTrue: [↑self new: 0].

Since self was Arc class, we now followed a similar path starting at Arc class looking for a new: message. Again we found it in Path class, and the associated method contained

↑super new initializeCollectionOfPoints: anInteger.

The infinite loop now begins, since we were again looking for the new method in the superclass of Path class and so on. This switching back and forth between new and new: continues until memory is exhausted. The final image release avoids this problem by having the new and new: methods in Path class use basicNew instead of new. The method for basicNew in Behavior has backup Smalltalk code which uses basicNew: instead of new:. Since Path class does not understand the basicNew: message, the basicNew: message in class Behavior is executed and it succeeds, avoiding the infinite loop.

We had problems in making the transition of our system from one release of a Xerox Smalltalk image to the next. These problems were generally minor, although annoying. The most extensive changes occurred in going from the first image to the second. In general, there were differences in some class Oops, and sometimes the structures of some objects changed. Unfortunately, in most cases we had to discover these differences ourselves. These should not be problems for future implementors since the documentation has been rewritten and there will be only one Smalltalk image to deal with. This image is the fifth or final one referred to herein.

Development Environment

An extensive collection of development tools complements the Smalltalk system at Hewlett-Packard. These tools compose our software development environment, which consists of the following layers:

1. The Smalltalk-80 system with its debugger.

2. The Smalltalk-80 virtual machine execution monitor and object memory inspector.

3. The UNIX operating system[2], SCCS version controller, *make* system builder, *sdb* symbolic debugger, and *prof* execution profiler.

These levels offer access to different aspects of execution. For example, we have the capability of setting breakpoints at the Smalltalk-80 statement level (Smalltalk debugger), the Smalltalk-80 virtual machine bytecode level (Smalltalk-80 virtual machine monitor), or the C source level (*sdb*). Often we use all three mechanisms to attack a problem from each particular level of detail. The same goes for performance evaluation as we have the capability to tap in at any level to spy on the activities of the system.

We structured the first level of our development environment using the hierarchical file system of UNIX. A read-only copy of the latest stable version of the system is in a source directory, and each of the project members owns a subdirectory under it. Each member can modify, test, and debug sections of code in his subdirectory without affecting the other members who may also be debugging. This feature was made possible by the UNIX *make* facility for creating, maintaining, and installing software. Someone working in a subdirectory who wants to put together a system using some changed source files simply asks *make* to build it. *Make* determines whether any source needs to be recompiled, and then loads the new code from the subdirectory and the rest from the source directory. Duplication is minimal as there is only one copy of the master source plus those pieces that people are working on in their subdirectories.

The Source Code Control System (SCCS) was our primary tool for dealing with version management issues. Whenever one wants to make a change to a piece of the system, one asks SCCS for a modifiable copy of the latest version. If no one else has a copy out, SCCS acquiesces and places the copy in the subdirectory. After successful testing of the modifications, one sends the modified copy back to SCCS and informs the system version manager of the change. The version manager asks SCCS to place a read-only copy of the new files into the source directory, and then gets *make* to build a new system. It is important that only well tested modifications make it to the source directory since all of the work in the subdirectories depends on the stability of that code. Fig. 6.1 depicts an execution monitor command menu, and Fig. 6.2 shows an execution monitor chain of context display.

```
type ?? for the list of commands
> > ??
> >

System multiple step ms, single step ss, continue cs, run rs
        display state ds, update freq us, breakpoint bs, trace ts
Image load li, inspect ii, save si
Graphics reset rg, print pg
Other monitor mc, statistics sc, context chain cc, receiver update ru
Window Help wh, Banner wb, Inspector wi, Smalltalk ws
        Context wc, Receiver wr, Method wm
Keys ↑C interrupt, ↑V quote, ↑X break, ↑Z suspend, ↑\core dump
        ↑ upArrow, ← leftArrow, ↑T ifTrue:, ↑F ifFalse:, ↑↑ control
        ESC select, DEL delete, ↑W deleteWord, ↑↑[0-9] fonts
** default radix is Decimal - prefix with 0 for Octal, 0x for Hex
** Shell sh * Help ?? * Exit qq
```

Figure 6.1

context	class	method	receiver	class
7c3a	16	72cc	238a	1a <Point>
7c06	16	552e	8aa	66a <InputSensor>
7c3e	16	232c	7908	3ef4 <StringHolderController>
7d32	16	4bae	7908	3ef4 <StringHolderController>
7cf6	16	650	7908	3ef4 <StringHolderController>
7c74	16	660	7908	3ef4 <StringHolderController>
7abe	16	632	7932	11f0 <StandardSystemController>
7cb2	16	648	7932	11f0 <StandardSystemController>
7d10	16	1ae8	7932	11f0 <StandardSystemController>
7c96	16	650	7932	11f0 <StandardSystemController>
7cae	16	660	7932	11f0 <StandardSystemController>
7d5c	18	5606	7d6e	16 <MethodContext>
79f8	18	784	798c	16 <MethodContext>

Figure 6.2   *active process: 7c40*   *priority = 4*

Central to the multi-level environment is the Smalltalk-80 virtual machine execution monitor (Fig. 6.1), a runtime facility offering the following services:

1. Transfer Smalltalk-80 images between object memory and the UNIX file system.

2. Variable step and run modes for the Smalltalk-80 virtual machine interpreter.

3. Manipulate Smalltalk-80 virtual machine-level breakpoints.

4. Display the current state of the Smalltalk-80 virtual machine.

5. Trace the chain of method and block contexts, as in Fig. 6.2.

6. Print the contents of the display bit map on a hardcopy device.

7. Enable Smalltalk-80 virtual machine functional tracing.

8. Invoke the object memory inspector.

In Fig. 6.3, a memory inspector subsystem command menu is presented. The last capability links the monitor to this inspector subsystem, a family of services concerned with object memory state:

1. Examine and change the current state of object memory.

2. Create new instances of classes in object memory.

3. Verify the current reference-count state of object memory.

4. Invoke garbage collection for object memory.

The Smalltalk-80 Implementation at Hewlett-Packard

type ?? for the list of commands
< < ??
< <
Load word lw, byte lb, float lf, string ls
Store word sw, byte sb, float sf, string ss
Length word wl, byte bl
Show header hs, object os, context cs, method ms
Reference Count display rc, verification vc, garbage collection gc
Instantiate Class withWords iw, withBytes ib, withPointers ip
Window Help wh, Banner wb, Inspector wi, Smalltalk ws
      Context wc, Receiver wr, Method wm
** default radix is Decimal - prefix with 0 for Octal, 0x for Hex
** answer 'y' or 'n' when asked 'more?'
Figure 6.3   ** Shell sh * Help ?? * Exit qq

To diagnose problems in dynamic memory management, we developed a facility to verify the reference counts of all objects in the system. It steps through the object table recording the number of pointers to each object and then checks this against the reference count field of each object. The routine produces a listing of objects with reference count dis-

HP Labs Smalltalk-84 System
> > ds
| RS| AC 7cca| 13501316 | Next b0/260 + | Last 76/166 P+1
> >

OTE7cca| 1VDfmPe[18	OTE7cba| 9VDfmPe[12	OTE135e| 2VDfmpo[54]
Se 7c92 < MethodConte	#00 7c7c < Text >	Hdr 0519= 0 5 s 12
PC 85	#01 7ca8 < TextStyle >	L00 0130 A 0010 C < Array
SP 7	#02 7cc0 < Point >	L01 0041 32D
Me 135e < CompiledMet	#03 0002 Nil	L02 0dd6 U ″ height: ″
RM 0002 Nil	#04 7ca4 < Rectangle >	L03 1360 U ″ in: ″
Re 7cba < Paragraph >	#05 7cda < Rectangle >	L04 1362 A 1366 C < Compo
T0 0061 48D	#06 0a52 < DisplayScr	L05 1302 U ″ lineAt:put: ″
T1 0087 67D	#07 0007 3D	L06 1376 U ″ composeLine
T2 000d 6D	#08 1560 < Form >	Index:inParagraph
T3 0093 73D	#09 0001 0D	L07 01fe U ″ max: ″
T4 7cdc < Composition	#0a 7cd8 < Array >	L08 1378 U ″ rightX ″
S1 006f 55D	#0b 000d 6D	L09 01d0 U ″ last ″
S2 0003 1D		L0a 12f4 U ″ updateCom
S3 7cf2 < TextLineInt		L0b 12f6 U ″ trimLines: ″
S4 000d 6D		#00 4021cd820a75820b756
S5 0061 48D		#10 75e287137c768142680
S6 7cba < Paragraph >		#20 6c1011b399a41c701214
S7 0002 Nil		#30 8714d813e76b0a12c0d
Figure 6.4		#40 6aa3de70da87701276

crepancies as well as those with permanent or overflow bits set. Usually all objects, except for a handful, have valid reference counts. The few exceptions are the objects cached by the system (e.g., the active context), and the Smalltalk object (SystemDictionary) which has an artificially increased reference count to prevent accidental deallocation.

Our system actually uses two displays: a graphics display for Smalltalk and a CRT terminal for the monitor and UNIX. Smalltalk, the monitor, and UNIX share the terminal keyboard. The presentation of information from the monitor facilities posed an interesting problem. It was impossible to squeeze everything into the 24 x 80 terminal format so we took a lesson from Smalltalk itself and implemented seven overlapping windows for the user interface. The user can select which windows to view and the system preserves the contents across selections. General command interaction uses a window consisting of the top four lines of the screen and the other windows do not overlap this region. Windows for diagnostic, inspector, and Smalltalk interaction fit into the other twenty lines. Fig. 6.4 shows the three vertically-overlapping 20 x 40 windows which display the active context, receiver, and compiled method components of the Smalltalk-80 virtual machine state. Most of the context and receiver information is in the leftmost 20 columns of their windows, so having those windows overlap was not a problem. The user can also close the receiver window to get full view of the context and the method.

Table 6.2 Notation for Displaying Objects

class	example	description
Small Integer	0205 258D	small integer value in decimal
Special Object	0006 True	name of object
Symbol	0132 U "Array"	(unique strings) U followed by string
String	0664 S "a string"	S followed by string
Association	0008 A 6f20 <Arc>	A followed by value field
Metaclass	73ea C <File>	C followed by class name
Other	72cc <Turtle>	class name within angle-brackets

The user can have the context, receiver, and method windows of the Smalltalk-80 virtual machine state display dynamically updated with execution. The frequency of update is selectable, and performance is acceptable even for small granularity updates. One can watch the stack values, temporaries, and instance variables change, and display enhancements indicate the current positions of the stack pointer and program counter. We follow a convention for single-line object descriptions in the window system. In all cases, we display the object pointer in hexadecimal format, and the additional object-specific information is described in Table 6.2. The motion-picture Smalltalk-80 virtual machine state display proved invaluable to the debugging effort. The performance of the system under full display is quite good.

Both the monitor and the inspector can escape to the UNIX shell to execute commands there. The monitor intercepts certain control characters and will halt execution, kill the system, or dump the core image to a file on request. As a special feature, the monitor traps all fatal errors and recursively invokes a new copy of itself to hunt for the cause. Then we can use the inspector to fix wayward values and continue execution.

Future Directions

As Smalltalk enters the real world there is much speculation over future directions for the system. Although the Smalltalk-80 distribution test process was thorough in eliminating problems in the system, many issues remain unresolved such as network interfacing and multiple inheritance, and there has been little time to implement the more ingenious optimizations. Hence there is much room for improvement in the design.

All of the test site implementations used high-level or assembly language to implement an interpreter for the Smalltalk-80 virtual machine. Unfortunately, this approach produced significantly degraded performance compared to native mode execution of the processor (a penalty of 40 to 200 times slower). The elimination of the Smalltalk-80 virtual machine as an intermediate stage could boost performance considerably, but this would necessitate the implementation of a Smalltalk-80-to-native-code compiler.

Early in our project we had investigated a native compiler strategy. Our bytecode execution frequency figures indicate that such an approach would be worthwhile. Over 70% of the Smalltalk-80 virtual machine bytecodes executed in normal usage (push, pop, store, jump, return) map to at most a few instructions in an ordinary computer. In addition, nearly 85% of all bytecodes executed (those above plus the special sends) translate to in-line sequences of instructions, including a procedure call escape for the exceptional cases. Only about 15% of Smalltalk execution requires the message lookup process where procedures perform the late binding. Because the Smalltalk-80 virtual machine compiler is written in the Smalltalk-80 language, the development of a native code version requires a stable Smalltalk-80 system to begin with.

In spite of the myriad optimizations proposed and implemented, a Smalltalk-80 system seems doomed to lower performance than more traditional programming systems. There are two areas where Smalltalk loses to other languages. One is the 15% of execution which requires message lookup. Message cache schemes lessen the penalty, but speed is still impaired by the symbol matching and indirection. The other area involves the automatic memory management provided by reference counting and/or garbage collection mechanisms. The memory manager is very expensive to operate and it is not clear that performance problems in this area can be solved. This may impact the ultimate success or failure of Smalltalk, as users of traditional programming systems may be reluctant to give up performance in exchange for Smalltalk.

Alternative implementation hosts also merit consideration. Although we have yet to implement the system on an HP 3000, we have derived performance estimates for the Smalltalk-80 virtual machine on the HP 3000 and the HP 1000 A Series minicomputer systems. With its stack-oriented architecture, an HP 3000 could be capable of 200,000 bytecodes per second. The HP 1000 A Series is a more attractive candidate because of its excellent price/performance ratio and compact packaging. Performance in excess of 100,000 bytecodes per second might be possible for an A Series processor with writable control store.

Implementations can benefit from special hardware for functions which do not perform well on general-purpose processors. Xerox solved this problem by adding special-purpose microcode for such functions to their general-purpose hardware. We have already commented on how the performance of our primitives suffered from lack of access to microcode or hardware support. This situation is most serious for graphics operations where microcode or instruction cache support for block moves would expedite matters by at least a factor of 10.

Since the Smalltalk-80 system is geared toward the personal computing community, the microprocessor is a natural area for investigation. However, most microprocessors do not have modifiable control stores and so special-purpose hardware may be the only efficient option to achieve acceptable performance. In fact, advances in VLSI design and fabrication have promoted the development of many such special-purpose chips for graphics control, memory management, and I/O support. A native code compilation system integrating these chips with one of the new 16- or 32-bit microprocessors could be an excellent Smalltalk-80 host.

There is also the issue of having an operating system alongside or underneath an implementation of the Smalltalk-80 system. The HP implementation runs on top of UNIX, which has significant advantages and disadvantages over the strategies of other implementors in the test program. UNIX has many features which assist the development of prototype software. For example, the debugging utilities are key components of our development environment. However, there are a few points where the integration of UNIX into Smalltalk could have helped us, such as in multiprocess control. As it stands we simulate this feature on UNIX, thus incurring additional overhead. The file system was another area where UNIX could have helped. By integrating the UNIX hierarchical file system into Smalltalk, we could have structured the system source into a hierarchical collection of files reflecting class relationships instead of the single large file currently used.

The Smalltalk-80 language itself is another direction for research. We find the language to be excellent for systems programming of applications with superior user interface characteristics. Contrary to popular belief, we do not feel that it is a programming language for the naive user community. Instead, it has proven itself to be a very good language for developing application kits to enable naive users to solve problems in limited domains, as in *ThingLab*[3]. The object orientation lends itself especially well to the programming of graphics problems. As other languages incorporate similar graphics capabilities, it will be interesting to note how their user interfaces compare with Smalltalk's.

There have been proposals to include types in Smalltalk, either through inference or declaration[4,5]. Each approach has its own merits, but more work needs to be done to determine the best way to integrate type structure into the system. In particular, we look forward to ways of using type information to optimize certain operations in the system.

Conclusions

The Hewlett-Packard team was curious about Smalltalk and we approached the task of implementing the Smalltalk-80 system with both reservations and enthusiasm. And indeed, some of our reservations were warranted: the Smalltalk-80 language did not prove to be a workingman's programming language and did not perform well enough on conventional hardware. The mystery surrounding Smalltalk for so many years had inspired grand expectations in us. In the end we were disappointed, but our curiosity was sated and we are perhaps better for it. The concepts embodied in Smalltalk have a heritage which goes back over 20 years, yet many have not achieved widespread acceptance by the research or marketing communities. There is little doubt now that the new economics of VLSI will make many of these concepts standard features of computing products.

It remains to be seen however, whether Smalltalk itself will succeed in the marketplace. All during the project we dreamed of a Smalltalk-80 product. These visions gradually became a nightmare as we discovered the pitfalls of an environment with the flexibility of Smalltalk. A Smalltalk-80 user can break the system by changing a single method. More important, one can make it incompatible with the distribution just as easily. From a product support standpoint, this would be chaos. Software distribution would be difficult to impossible.

Application software could assume very little about the runtime environment, since it might have been modified extensively by the user. In tracing down system problems, it would be tricky to determine whether the problem was in the distribution or in the changes made by the user. One solution would be to restrict what a user can change, but this defeats the whole purpose of Smalltalk. We can not see how an organization could hope to provide any form of comprehensive support for a Smalltalk product. The only way we can envision Smalltalk in the marketplace is as an unsupported package.

Acknowledgments

We would like to acknowledge the tenacious efforts of our fellow members of the HPL Smalltalk team in coping with the vagaries of a distribution test program. In particular, Alec Dara-Abrams for stalking the wild interpreter, Bob Shaw for graphics support beyond the call of duty on the Lexidata, and Bob Ballance for his work on the interpreter and primitives, especially in floating point and process control. Our project leader, Jim Stinger, provided technical arbitration and primitive design. Joe Falcone contributed in the object memory, development environment, and performance evaluation areas.

There are others who contributed to the project in advisory and managerial capacities. Ching-Fa Hwang, Dan Conway, and Sam Gebala helped review the chapters of the Smalltalk book and participated in the early discussions about target machines. We would also like to thank our department manager, Ted Laliotis, for his support throughout and beyond the life cycle of the project. None of this would have been possible without the work of Jim Duley and Paul Stoft, who were responsible for bringing the Smalltalk-80 system to Hewlett-Packard. Finally, we express our appreciation to David Casseres, Ann Falcone, Karri Kaiser, Glenn Krasner, Rick Meyers, and Steve Muchnick for their editorial assistance.

All of us involved with the Smalltalk-80 system at Hewlett-Packard appreciate the efforts of the Xerox Software Concepts Group. We gratefully acknowledge their support and tolerance during the test program.

References

1. Sansonnet, J. P., et. al., "Direct Execution of LISP on a List-Directed Architecture", Proceedings at the Symposium on Architectural Support for Programming Languages and Operating Systems, Palo Alto, CA, pp. 132–139, March 1982.

2. Ritchie, Dennis M., and Thompson, Ken, "The UNIX Time-Sharing System" *Comm. ACM* vol. 17, no. 2, pp. 365–375, July 1974.

3. Borning, Alan H., "The Programming Language Aspects of Thing Lab, A Constraint-Oriented Simulation Laboratory", *ACM Transactions of Programming Languages and Systems* vol. 3, no. 4, pp. 353–387, Oct. 1981.

4. Borning Alan H., and Ingalls, Daniel H. H., "A Type Declaration and Inference System for Smalltalk", Ninth Symposium on Principles of Programming Languages, pp. 133–141, Albuquerque, NM, 1982.

5. Suzuki, Nori, "Inferring Types in Smalltalk", Eighth Symposium on Principles of Programming Languages, Williamsburg, VA, pp. 187–199, 1981.

7

The Dorado Smalltalk-80 Implementation: Hardware Architecture's Impact on Software Architecture

L. Peter Deutsch
Software Concepts Group
Xerox Palo Alto Research Center
Palo Alto, California

Abstract

The implementation of the Smalltalk-80 virtual machine on the Dorado, an experimental high-performance microprogrammed personal computer, was strongly influenced by a few attributes of the Dorado hardware architecture: a large microprogram memory, a hardware instruction prefetch and decoding unit, an effective memory cache, and the use of base registers for memory addressing. Each of these features substantially reduced the complexity and/or improved the performance of the Smalltalk implementation.

Introduction

The Dorado is an experimental high-performance microprogrammed personal computer, the latest and most powerful descendent of the Xerox Alto. Because the Dorado is relatively easy to microprogram, and because it incorporates many architectural features for aiding implementors of higher-level languages, the Software Concepts Group chose the Dorado as the first target machine for implementing the Smalltalk-80 virtual machine. The first version of the implementation ran successfully in early 1981, after approximately six months' work by a single person.

Three excellent papers on the Dorado hardware architecture have appeared elsewhere[1], so we will only mention the machine's most important attributes. The Dorado is microprogrammed, with a 70 ns microinstruction time and a 36-bit microinstruction. The microprogram memory holds 4K microinstructions, all in RAM. The internal registers and data paths are 16 bits wide. The processor accesses main memory through a 4K-word cache, which can accept a reference every microinstruction and deliver data 1 or 2 microinstructions after a read request. The processor includes pipelined hardware for prefetching and decoding macroinstructions. Later we will describe other details of the Dorado hardware in connection with their impact on the Smalltalk-80 virtual machine implementation.

Emulator Architecture

The Dorado microinstruction memory (microstore) holds 4K instructions. In the standard Dorado microcode, approximately 1300 microinstructions implement I/O controllers and 700 microinstructions implement a simple macroinstruction set inherited from the Alto[2]. (The I/O control microcode is a consequence of the Dorado's I/O architecture, which emphasizes simple controller hardware and uses microcode multiprocessing to provide most of the control function.) The remaining 2000 microinstructions are available for implementing other macroinstruction sets and/or extending the Alto instruction set: normally they implement an instruction set specialized for Mesa[3]. The hardware instruction fetch unit (IFU, described in more detail below) allows switching between instruction sets in less than a microsecond, simply by reloading an IFU register.

In our Smalltalk-80 implementation, we had a number of choices:

1. Keep the Alto and/or the Mesa macroinstruction set, and implement the Smalltalk-80 virtual machine entirely in it/them.

2. Keep the Alto macroinstruction set; implement the Smalltalk-80 virtual machine mostly in microcode, and the remainder in Alto code.

3. Discard the Alto microcode; implement the Smalltalk-80 virtual machine mostly in microcode, and partly in Smalltalk extended with special primitives for manipulating memory or the I/O devices directly.

4. Discard the Alto microcode; implement the Smalltalk-80 virtual machine entirely in microcode.

We rejected approach 1 for performance reasons: although somewhat harder to write, microcode is approximately five times as fast as either Alto code or Mesa for straightforward instructions, and also offered the opportunity to fully exploit the available processor registers and the IFU.

It was likely that the microstore was not large enough for 4; 4 would also have deprived us of the ability to write debugging aids in Alto code or Mesa, and to use the standard debugger (as opposed to a microcode debugger) during Smalltalk development.

In finally choosing 2 over 3, we were motivated by several principal arguments:

- We wanted the parts of the Smalltalk-80 system written in Smalltalk to be completely portable, i.e. not contain code specific to any particular storage or I/O system, and were willing to tolerate a larger non-Smalltalk kernel to achieve this.

- Both the Dorado and the Dolphin, a less powerful machine for which we also wanted a Smalltalk implementation, already had Alto emulation microcode. Those parts of the Smalltalk system written in Alto code could be shared between the two implementations. We were also considering an implementation on the Alto, which has less powerful microcode and a smaller microstore. A system architecture which allowed us to move small functional units of code between microcode and Alto code implementations was likely to be more transportable between the three machines.

- Keeping the Alto emulator, which occupies less than 20% of the microstore, would relieve us of the 4K limit (by allowing us to write arbitrarily large fractions of the system in Alto code) without depriving us of a lot of microstore space.

It is interesting to note that Interlisp-D[4], where these desires were not as important, made the opposite choice. Interlisp-D originally adopted approach 2, later replacing it by 3. The Interlisp-D system now contains literally thousands of lines of machine-dependent source code written in Lisp: it has no clear division between a portable virtual machine and an implementation level, but the instruction set is much closer to the machine level and is much easier to implement efficiently.

Two features of the hardware architecture helped reduce the cost of approach 2 compared to 3, specifically by reducing the cost of passing control and data between the two implementation levels: quick switching between instruction sets in the IFU, and the fact that the Alto instruction set deliberately included a large number of undefined opcodes to which we could assign our own interpretation. We used these opcodes to optimize the transfer of information between the microcode and Alto code implementation levels. The appendix (p. 123) lists these opcodes in detail; we believe that any Smalltalk-80 implementation that uses a combination of microcode and an existing macroinstruction set will find this list a useful guide.

In retrospect, this decision to split the implementation between two levels worked out extremely well. The decision gave us a great deal of flexibility to move parts of the Smalltalk kernel between Bcpl (a system programming language which compiles into Alto code), Alto assembly language, and microcode as we investigated its performance characteristics. As it turned out, we only used Bcpl for initialization, since it could not generate our extended Alto instructions and since its subroutine calling sequence is less efficient than a hand-coded one by a factor of about 3. Typical Smalltalk-80 benchmarks show between 5% and 15% of the time being spent executing Alto code, and the remainder in Smalltalk microcode.

In the final implementation, the main part of the system is implemented entirely in microcode:

- Instruction set interpreter (with assistance from the IFU)
- Process switching
- Reference counting
- Object allocation and deallocation

In addition, the following primitive methods are implemented in microcode:

- Small integer arithmetic
- Subscripting and instance variable access: at:, at:put:, size, characterAt:, characterAt:put:, objectAt:, objectAt:put:, instVarAt:, instVarAt:put:
- Object creation (new, new:)
- Block context creation and execution: blockCopy:, value/value:, valueWithArguments:
- Process scheduling (signal, wait, resume, suspend)
- BitBlt (copyBits)

- Miscellaneous: asOop, ==, class, flushMessageCache, perform:, performWithArguments:

The following primitive methods for storage management were originally implemented in microcode, but were later translated into Alto code for reasons explained below: refct, become:, asObject, someInstance, nextInstance.

The following primitive methods are implemented in Alto code:

- 16-bit large integer arithmetic

- Floating point arithmetic

- All I/O primitives (disk, Ethernet, display, keyboard, mouse) except BitBlt

- The remaining storage management primitives: newMethod:header:, coreLeft

- Snapshot

The following optional primitive methods are not implemented on either the Dorado or the Dolphin: next, nextPut:, atEnd.

When the interpreter microcode encounters a Smalltalk method that includes a call on a primitive, it consults a table stored in main memory to determine whether the primitive is implemented in microcode (the table contains a microcode dispatch address) or Alto code (the table contains the address of an Alto code routine). In the latter case, the interpreter switches the IFU to Alto emulation, and the machine starts executing the Alto code that implements the primitive. The Alto code typically contains some special Smalltalk-specific instructions (described in the appendix on pg. 123) which allow it to interact with the Smalltalk world: LDSS instructions to access the receiver of the message and its arguments, SETDS and LDFD/STFD instructions to access the instance variables of the receiver, and finally a PRET instruction to return the result of the primitive and resume Smalltalk execution. All these trapped opcodes are of course implemented in microcode. PRET switches the IFU back to the Smalltalk instruction set and resumes execution with the next Smalltalk bytecode.

Instruction Sequencing

The Dorado's Instruction Fetch Unit (IFU)[5] prefetches and decodes instructions in a manner almost ideally matched to the Smalltalk instruction set. In fact the three language-oriented instruction sets designed at the Palo Alto Research Center (Lisp, Mesa, and Smalltalk) and the Dorado design influenced each other considerably. The IFU prefetches up to 6 bytes, accessing the memory through the same cache the processor uses, and only when the processor is not accessing it. The first 8-bit byte of an instruction indexes a 256-entry RAM. The entry in the RAM gives the address of the microcode that implements the instruction, says how many additional bytes the instruction uses (0, 1, or 2), and supplies a 4-bit parameter for any purpose the microcode wants. (For example, each group of Smalltalk "load" instructions uses the same microcode, but different parameter values corresponding to the offset of the desired variable within the context, instance, or literals.) The RAM also contains information which allows the IFU to execute certain unconditional jumps itself. The microcode that implements a given macroinstruction can read the parameter and the additional bytes from the IFU onto a convenient bus. The last microinstruction of each macroinstruction contains a field that informs the processor's control logic that the processor should ask the IFU for a new dispatch address for the next microinstruction; under this arrangement, there is normally no delay at all between macroinstructions. Thus the overhead of fetching, decoding, and dispatching on macroinstructions, and returning to a central loop after a macroinstruction is finished, is reduced essentially to zero. This overhead may take up as much as 20% of the time in an interpreter implemented without hardware assistance[6].

The entire job of instruction sequencing and decoding is handled by the IFU. The microprogram only intervenes to restart the IFU for jumps, message sends, and returns, and when switching between the Smalltalk and Alto instruction sets. The IFU RAM actually holds up to four instruction sets at once, and the overhead of switching is less than a microsecond if the first instruction to be executed is in the memory cache. Only 2.4% of execution time is spent waiting for the IFU to supply a dispatch address; we cannot determine what fraction of this time is due to cache misses and what fraction to competition with the processor for cache cycles. For a deeper discussion of IFU performance, see the Dorado papers.[7]

Memory Management

The Dorado provides hardware support for a paged virtual address space, but the Smalltalk-80 implementation makes no use of it— Smalltalk initializes the page tables to map virtual addresses one-for-one into real addresses. Recovering from a page fault at the microcode level is potentially complicated. A single Smalltalk instruction can make many memory references, so we would have had to adopt some combination of resuming execution of a Smalltalk instruction in mid-flight, arranging all instructions to be restartable, and/or letting the page fault handler complete the faulting reference. For this reason, and because past experience with a paged Smalltalk suggested that it would perform very badly if the working set exceeded real memory significantly, we did not go to the trouble of observing the microcoding restrictions which would make recovery from faults possible.

Recursive freeing of objects with zero reference count is implemented in microcode; the main loops of the compactor, but not the overall control, are also in microcode. This arrangement has worked out extremely well. In fact so little time is spent in recursive freeing (1.9%) that we might be able to move at least some cases of the rather complex recursive freeing algorithm into Alto code as well with relatively little performance penalty. This is partly a result of a minor interpreter change: when control returns from a context which has no other references to it, the interpreter essentially "unrolls" the top loop of the recursive freer, i.e., there is a special loop which iterates through the fields of the context (but only up to the current position of the stack pointer), decrementing the reference counts and calling the actual recursive freer if needed.

Memory Cache

The Dorado's memory cache is nearly as fast as the processor registers. A memory fetch in microinstruction N produces data in a register in microinstruction $N+1$ which can be used for computation in microinstruction $N+2$. Memory stores are even faster, taking a single microinstruction. The cache is pipelined, so a new fetch or store can be started in every microinstruction. As a result, we decided to implement even the very highest-bandwidth operations of the Smalltalk-80 implementation—pushing and popping quantities (particularly variables) on the stack—using memory references at the microcode level without significant time penalty. Thus for example, the microcode that implements the "load local variable" instruction reads the local variable using the current context as a base and the parameter supplied by the IFU as the offset, increments a stack pointer held in a register, and then writes the value onto the stack (in main memory) using the stack pointer as an offset from another base register.

In retrospect this decision was almost certainly correct. The memory references to the stack and the local variables in a context never cause cache misses. The bookkeeping required to manage a finite-size register stack (the Dorado has four 64-register stacks in the processor) would have been relatively complex, especially since Smalltalk does not always transfer control between contexts in LIFO order. However, this decision is critically dependent on the speed of the cache. If the cache had been only half as fast—taking 3 to 4 microinstructions to fulfill a request—it would probably have been better to store some of the current context in registers.

Despite its small size, the Dorado cache works effectively for Smalltalk. Our measurements show that cache misses account for only 11% of execution time. References to the stack and the current context never cause misses; most misses are caused by accesses to method dictionaries during message lookup, and to method headers when starting execution of a method.

Registers

The Dorado includes 256 16-bit working registers, organized as 16 groups of 16 registers each. One of the 16 groups is current at any time, selected by a processor register called RBase. Microinstructions supply a 4-bit register address within the current group, which is concatenated with RBase to provide the full register address. The Smalltalk microcode uses three groups:

- The "main" group, described in more detail just below

- A group used only by the compactor and recursive freer

- A group used almost exclusively by the process scheduler

Because changing the RBase register ties up a microinstruction field that is also involved in many other operations (such as memory references and constant generation), it is highly valuable to divide the registers into blocks according to major sections of the microcode control, to minimize the frequency of group switching. The convention we chose in the Smalltalk microcode was to define a single "main" group to be current throughout the entire microcode, except for local switching to access individual registers in other groups, and self-contained routines like the recursive freer which would restore the "main" group to currency when they were done.

Since the contents of the "main" group are a valuable indication to implementors as to what information should be held in machine registers, we list them here, in approximate order of decreasing utility:

SPR
: The stack pointer, relative to the base of the current context

9 temporary registers
: Also used for passing arguments and results to and from microcode subroutines

Nargs
: The number of arguments to the current method

Self	The Oop (object identifier) of the current receiver
SI	A flag indicating whether the last (or current) primitive is "fast" (entered directly in response to a special selector) or "slow" (entered through method lookup)
MyPC	The byte PC (relative within the method), saved whenever control might switch to another context or to Alto code
Context	The Oop of the current context
Method	The Oop of the current method

Note that direct pointers to the bodies of some of these objects (the receiver, context, and method) are also held in base registers, as described in the next section.

The limitation of 16 readable registers was much less of a nuisance than might be expected. The original Dorado prototype had 32 groups of 8 registers, which was a tremendous nuisance: the microcode shrank by about 15% from the prototype version simply through elimination of microinstructions whose main purpose was to switch register groups. Expansion to direct addressing of all 256 registers would probably eliminate only another 20 microinstructions: the figure is small because of our careful division of registers into meaningful groups. In other words, our experience indicates that for Smalltalk-80 implementation, there is a "knee" in the utility curve somewhere between 8 and 16 directly accessible registers.

The Dorado also includes 4 stacks of 64 registers which can only be accessed through a pointer register, the processor stack pointer (StkP). The microinstruction format supports pushing and popping quantities in the current stack as easily as addressing the current block of 16 addressable registers. Unfortunately, StkP is awkward to load and read, and recovering from over- or underflow is even more difficult. For these reasons, we chose not to use these stacks to model the Smalltalk stack, but only for temporary storage within the microcode. When a microcoded primitive fails, or other exceptional condition arises, the microcode resets StkP to a standard state before continuing with the recovery code. As indicated in the earlier section on the memory cache, we believe this choice is better than using the processor stack for caching parts of Smalltalk contexts.

Base Registers

The Dorado memory system provides 32 base registers which hold full 28-bit virtual addresses; the microinstructions that reference memory normally provide 16-bit displacements relative to a current base register, switched under microprogram control. Consequently, the Smalltalk microcode dynamically maintains the following addresses in base registers at all times:

TS
The current context for accessing local variables (home context when executing a block, current context otherwise)

SS
The context used for execution and stack — always the current context, even when executing in a block

RS
The receiver in the current context (self)

CS
The currently executing method (code)

In addition, it loads the following addresses at system initialization:

OTBase
The base of the object table (OT)

FreeLists
The base of the table of free list heads

MCacheBase
The base of the message lookup cache

SpecialBase
The SpecialSelectors array, used to handle sends of special selectors (must also be reloaded after memory compactions)

It is interesting to observe that the memory system is so fast, and the indirect or indexed addressing of registers so awkward, that the system actually runs (slightly) faster by putting the free list heads in memory than by putting them in addressable registers.

This choice of base registers is fairly obvious, except for the issue of whether or not to maintain a pointer to the receiver. Maintaining such a pointer requires reloading it at each activation or return; not maintaining such a pointer requires indirect access through the OT at each reference to an instance variable. (More complicated schemes are also possible, such as a flag to indicate whether the base register has been reloaded since the last change of context.) Measurements indicate that references to instance variables are slightly more common than context switches, so we come out slightly ahead by always loading the base register at a context switch.

While the base register model works well for memory references, loading a base register is awkward for two relatively minor reasons:

- Base registers are 28 bits wide, but the Dorado's data paths are only 16 bits. Thus loading a base register takes at least 3 microinstructions (one to select the register, and one to load each half).

- Because the Dorado implementation packs flag bits into the OT along with the data address, exactly as described in the Smalltalk virtual machine documentation, a masking operation is required. Also, again because of the 16-bit architecture, two memory references are required to fetch the OT entry.

As a result of these problems, the standard subroutine which loads a base register with the address of an object whose Oop is known (essentially the SETDS instruction described in the appendix below) takes 6 microinstructions; over 10% of execution time is spent in this subroutine (and various open-coded copies of it). By using 3 words per OT entry instead of 2, we could have eliminated the masking operation, saving 1 of the 6 microinstructions. However, besides adding 32K to the system's memory requirements, this design would have increased the cache working set size (and hence the wait time due to misses) significantly, so there might well have been no net speed improvement.

Microcode Multiprocessing

The Dorado micro-architecture includes multiple processes at the microcode level. The Smalltalk-80 emulator itself makes no use of this capability, which is primarily designed to allow a single processor to function effectively as a controller for multiple high-speed I/O devices. However, one of these processes can be awakened periodically, at intervals as short as a few microseconds, to collect a histogram of the address of the next microinstruction to be executed by the instruction set emulator. This facility proved invaluable in analyzing performance bottlenecks in the Smalltalk microcode; essentially all the measurements reported in this paper were obtained from the micro-address histogram. One particularly interesting number was the amount of time spent waiting for cache misses; we computed this by looking at the number of samples at addresses of microinstructions that had to wait for memory data to arrive, compared to the instructions immediately preceding and following these.

Appendix: Extended Alto Instructions

In the following descriptions of the extensions to the Alto instruction set, AC0-3 refer to four 16-bit registers which the Alto instruction set views as central registers, but which are addressable registers at the microcode level.

Many of these instructions are designed for use only from Altocode primitives, and consequently can cause "primitive failure" under certain circumstances. Primitive failure means that the execution of the primitive code is abandoned, and the Smalltalk method is executed instead.

The instructions are arranged below in groups, with the most heavily used groups listed first.

Access to Smalltalk Data

LDSS n — AC0 ← word n relative to SS+SPR-Nargs, the location of receiver and arguments on the stack in the current context. N = 0 is the receiver, n = 1 is the first argument, etc.

SETDS — AC0 = an Oop. Sets the DS base register to the real memory address of the object, taken from the OT. Causes primitive failure if AC0 is a small integer rather than an Oop.

LDFD n / LDF1 — AC0 ← word n relative to DS; for LDF1, n is taken from AC1 rather than from the instruction itself. The parameters .LENGTH, .CLASS, and .FLDS define the offsets of the length word, class word, and first field of an object, e.g. the assembly-language instruction to load the second field of an object would be LDFD .FLDS+1.

STFD n / STF1 — AC0 = a new Oop to be stored at word n relative to DS. This instruction does reference counting (increases the reference count of the object identified by AC0, decreases the reference count of the old contents): use STNFD (below) to store a non-Oop without reference counting.

LDNFD n / LDNF1 — AC0 ← word n relative to DS. Meant for use when the data being loaded are bits rather than Oops. Equivalent to LDFD in the current system, only provided for symmetry with STNFD.

STNFD n / STNF1 — AC0 = a new value to store into word n relative to DS. Does not do reference counting (see STFD above).

Conversion of Integers

IVAL — AC0 = a small integer; AC0 ← the value of the integer. Causes primitive failure if AC0 is not a small integer.

WRDVAL — AC0 = an Oop of a Smalltalk LargePositiveInteger, or a SmallInteger; AC0 ← the value of the number. Causes primitive failure if the Oop is not a LargeInteger, or if the value does not fit in one word.

MKINT — AC0 = an unsigned integer; AC0 ← the corresponding Smalltalk integer (small or large).

Primitive Control	**PRET**	A primitive has completed successfully. AC0 = the value to return from the primitive.
	PFAIL	Cause primitive failure.
Access to OT	**READOT**	Read the OT entry for a given Oop. AC0 = an Oop. AC0 ← address word from OT, AC1 ← flag word from OT.
	SETOT	Set the OT entry for a given Oop. AC0 = an Oop, AC1 = address word to store in OT, AC3 = flag word to store in OT.
Access to Microcoded Primitives	**SIGNAL**	AC0 = a Semaphore. Does a "signal" operation on the semaphore. Used only by I/O interrupts and the low space notification mechanism.
	CINST	AC0 = the Oop of a class, AC1 = the number of extra fields (for variable-length classes); AC0 ← the Oop of a newly created instance. DS is also set as for SETDS.
Compaction	**CLEANSTATE**	Store all of Smalltalk's state into memory in preparation for a compaction or a snapshot.
	ACOMPACT	Start a compaction. AC0 = the Oop of the display bitmap.
	CSEG	Prepare to compact the area of memory starting at AC0/1 and going up to an end marker which is the maximum legal Oop +3.
	CLOOP	Do the main compactor lOop. AC0/1 ← the end of the occupied area after compaction. AC2/3 ← the end of the occupied area just below the display bitmap, if the display bitmap was in the area being compacted.
	CRESUME	Resume Smalltalk execution after a compaction.
Miscellaneous	**RESUME**	Resume Smalltalk execution with the next bytecode. Used only during initialization, and for resuming after an interrupt. (All hardware interrupts cause control to go from the Smalltalk interpreter to Alto code.)
	SETCNT	Set the low-space trap parameter to AC0.
	READCNT	AC0 ← the number of Oops left before a low-space trap will occur -1.
Initialization and Post-mortem	**CONFIG**	AC0 ← the size of (real) memory in units of 32K, e.g. for a 512K Dorado, AC0 ← 16 decimal.
	SETOTBASE	Initializes the microcode base register that points to the OT. AC0 = low address of OT, AC1 = high address of OT.

DEADSTART Initializes the system. AC3 = a pointer to a block of memory laid out as follows:

0 base address of OT (low bits)

1 (high bits)

2 size of OT (# of OT entries)

3 the address of an 8K table for a microcode PC histogram, or 0 (low bits)

4 (high bits).

After initialization is done, Smalltalk execution begins, so control does not return to the instruction following the DEADSTART.

READOUT AC0 = a pointer to a readout area in memory, into which are stored the following values:

0 - Oop of current context (CONTEXT register)

1 - current stack pointer (SPR register)

2 - byte PC of current instruction (PCX register)

3 - unused but reserved for future use

4 - micro-PC from which crash occurred (LINK register)

5-19 - unused but reserved for future use.

References

1. Lampson, Butler W., "The Dorado: A High-Performance Personal Computer", Xerox PARC Technical Report CSL-81-1, Jan. 1981.

2. Thacker, C. P., et. al., "Alto: A Personal Computer", in *Computer Structures: Readings and Examples*, 2nd Edition, Eds. Sieworek, Bell, and Newell, McGraw-Hill, New York, 1981; (also Xerox PARC Report CSL-79-11 Aug. 1979).

3. Mitchell, James G., et. al., "Mesa Language Manual," Xerox PARC Report CSL-79-3, Apr. 1979.

4. Burton, Richard R., et. al., (The Interlisp-D Group), "Papers on Interlisp-D", Xerox PARC CIS-5, July 1981; (a revised version of Xerox PARC SSL-80-4).

5. See reference 1.

6. Markoff, John, "Smalltalk: A Language for the 80s", *InfoWorld*, cover story, Jan. 24, 1983.

7. See reference 1.

8

The Design and Implementation of VAX/Smalltalk-80*

Stoney Ballard
Three Rivers Computer Corporation
Pittsburgh, Pennsylvania

Stephen Shirron
Digital Equipment Corporation
Marlboro, Massachusetts

Introduction

VAX/Smalltalk-80 is an implementation of the Smalltalk-80 system written for the VAX family of computers running with the VMS operating system. This version differs from standard Smalltalk-80 implementations by using a basic word size of 32 bits and an incremental compacting garbage collector. This paper describes the rationale for these changes, their implementation, and various tricks that were developed to enhance the performance of this version of the Smalltalk-80 virtual machine. We also discuss some ideas for future work aimed at improving the performance of paged virtual object systems.

Some History

Our group at DEC (the Corporate Research Group) was involved in studying issues relating to personal workstations and graphics. We had been interested in the Smalltalk-72 and Smalltalk-76 systems for several years because they were the best examples of powerful personal workstation environments that we had seen. Consequently, we jumped at the chance to participate in the Smalltalk-80 review.

The VAX Smalltalk-80 implementation was our second, the first having been done for the PDP-11/23. The PDP-11 version was implemented as closely as possible to the virtual machine specification published in *Smalltalk-80: The Language and Its Implementation*. This version was notable primarily for its execution speed, which resembled molasses in December. By the time we were out of ideas to speed it up, the PDP-11 was executing about 5K bytecodes/second.

The PDP-11 version exhibited three major performance bottlenecks: the PDP-11 memory manager, the lack of writable microcode hardware, and the reference counter.

The memory management hardware on the PDP-11/23 was designed to map a 64Kbyte virtual space into physical space by using eight separate 8Kbyte segments. Our problem however, was not to map virtual space to physical, but rather to directly access the full 256Kbyte physical space of the PDP-11/23. This involved adjusting the map for every object access (as well as every object table access) to map it into the 64Kbyte directly addressable range. Since some Smalltalk-80 objects are larger than 8Kbytes, we had to adjust the map to point at the particular field we wanted. This was particularly painful since it took about 30 instructions to adjust the map. By setting up map segments for the objects commonly used by the interpreter (e.g. the context, method, self) at context switch and process switch, we eliminated most of this overhead. Nevertheless, the interpreter spent about half of its time with map box adjustment.

The PDP-11/23 had no writable microstore, so we wrote the bytecode interpreter and all the primitives in assembly language. If we had been able to write microcode, we could have achieved about a factor of two to four improvement in speed. The PDP-11 is not suitable for microcoding a Smalltalk-80 interpreter because the hardware is designed specifically for fetching and decoding its native instruction set.

The reference-counting scheme caused serious performance problems. Updating the reference counts of objects and tracing objects whose counts had gone to zero was the primary source of memory management overhead. Mapping problems aside, we felt that reference counting was inherently inefficient anyway because of the many places in the code that were required to update reference counts. Reference counting is probably the best scheme to use for small machines since it reclaims space immediately as it becomes garbage. All other garbage collection schemes leave a relatively large amount of garbage lying around between collections.

The space compactor was annoying since it caused the system to pause for several seconds whenever it ran. Our compactor was slow both because we compacted the whole memory at once, and because the memory map had to be constantly adjusted as it ran.

After playing with the PDP-11 version for a while we came to several conclusions about the Smalltalk-80 system:

1. A maximum of 32K objects is insufficient for a system that supposedly integrates the whole environment into one object space. We felt that 10 to 100 times that number of objects would be needed to properly support a rich environment. Even the base Smalltalk-80 system suffers from the small object name space as seen in the non-uniform handling of methods. These objects should be broken into a literal vector and a bytecode vector, but weren't for performance reasons and because that would have added about 6K objects to the base system. This non-uniformity requires a great deal of the code to handle methods specially.

2. The performance we achieved was clearly inadequate for real work. Compilation and browsing were far too slow to support rapid development work. Touch typing was virtually impossible since we could type faster than the input process could accept characters. We felt that a tenfold increase in speed would be needed before we would feel comfortable with the system.

3. Fifteen-bit SmallIntegers are too small. Although this is somewhat of a minor problem, it would clean up the array indexing code substantially if a SmallInteger was sufficient to index the largest possible array.

4. The reference-counting scheme should be discarded in favor of an incremental compacting garbage collector. Not only would this eliminate the problem of reclaiming circular garbage (which required us to implement a separate mark/sweep garbage collector), but would also reduce the work required when storing object pointers into other objects, especially contexts. Additionally, an incremental compacting garbage collector eliminates the pauses due to compacting space.

5. Some sort of virtual object storage is necessary to support large applications or sets of applications where millions of objects would be needed. Paging systems are commonly available and easy to use. We were interested in determining the performance of paging for a system like the Smalltalk-80 system, where the locality of reference between adjacent objects is much smaller than in traditional language environments.

These considerations led to our decision to implement a modified version of the Smalltalk-80 virtual machine on a VAX-11/780. The VAX was an obvious choice for us since most groups at DEC had one, and it would be much easier for people to use the Smalltalk-80 system if it ran on computers accessible to them. To this end we decided to implement a portable system that could be used on any VAX running VMS. We realized, of course, that we would be giving up a fair amount of performance by using a timesharing system. Our plan was to build a version for VMS, written in assembly code, and then convert it to run stand-alone with microcode assist. This latter phase has not yet been performed.

The following sections give details of the characteristics of our Smalltalk-80 implementation (which we call VAX/Smalltalk-80) and some suggestions for future work.

Word Size Changes

We reformatted the Smalltalk-80 image to use 31 bit object names and SmallIntegers, using the 32nd bit as a tag bit to distinguish between them. Object headers increased from 4 to 8 bytes. Non-Oop fields, such as those of BitMaps and Strings, were not changed. This reformatting increased the size of the base image by about 50%. After reformatting, the average object size in the base image was 40 bytes. Fig. 8.1 shows typical object formats.

A 4 byte size field allows objects up to 2^{24} bytes long, leaving a byte for various flags and an age field (described below). Our size field was a byte count of the object, eliminating the "odd" bit from the object table entry. Objects were stored on longword (4 byte) boundaries because longword fetches are faster on the VAX if naturally aligned. Fig. 8.2 shows the layout of the size field.

The object name space is vastly larger than the 32K objects supported by the standard Smalltalk-80 virtual machine. This not only allows keeping such things as the source code for the methods in the object space, but also allows us to use an incremental, compacting garbage collector. Unlike reference-counting schemes, an incremental compacting garbage collector does not reclaim either the names of objects or the space they take as soon as they become inaccessible. This requires that the name space be substantially larger than the maximum number of names otherwise needed. Although we could support two billion objects with a 31-bit name, we are limited to a much smaller number by the size of the virtual space allocated by VMS to the Smalltalk-80 process.

Although our version allocates 31 bits in an object reference for the name space, it is certainly feasible to allocate fewer (say 24) for the name reference and use the rest for tagging. Having tag bits in a reference can be useful when one object needs to appear in different guises depending on who references it. This would allow a "monitor" object to trap all messages from objects who refer to it as a monitor, but allow its "owner" to send messages to it directly, bypassing the monitoring. These tag bits could also be used to mark objects as being, for example, usable by the interpreter as CompiledMethods even if they are subclasses of CompiledMethod. Currently, the interpreter does not check

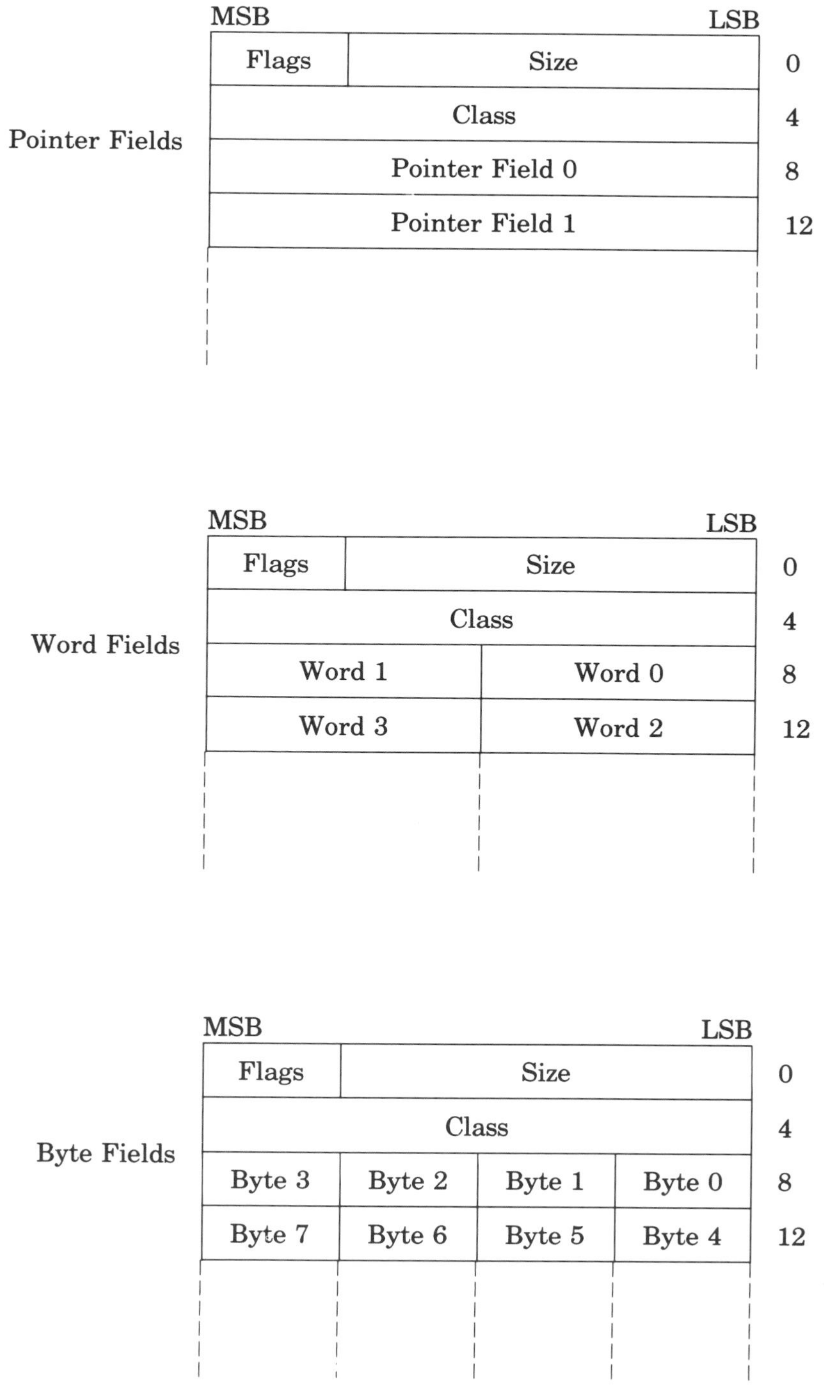

Pointer Fields

MSB			LSB	
Flags	Size			0
Class				4
Pointer Field 0				8
Pointer Field 1				12

Word Fields

MSB			LSB	
Flags	Size			0
Class				4
Word 1		Word 0		8
Word 3		Word 2		12

Byte Fields

MSB					LSB	
Flags	Size					0
Class						4
Byte 3	Byte 2	Byte 1	Byte 0			8
Byte 7	Byte 6	Byte 5	Byte 4			12

Figure 8.1

31	30	29	28	27	26	25	24	23	22	21	20	19	18	17	16
Age						X	P	Size (23:16)							

15	14	13	12	11	10	9	8	7	6	5	4	3	2	1	0
Size (15:0)															

Age – Age of the object in Flips
P – Set if object has pointer fields*
X – Unused
Size – Size in bytes of the object

Figure 8.2 *The P field is duplicated here so that the scanner need not refer to the OTE (Object Table Entry) to see if the object has pointer fields.

the class of objects such as CompiledMethods both for reasons of efficiency, and to allow using subclasses of these classes. Having tag bits that assert the compatibility of such objects with the ones expected would lead to greater safety in the interpreter.

In the standard virtual machine, only 15 bits are allocated for literal SmallIntegers. This is inadequate to index large arrays, so the indexing code must be able to use LargePositiveIntegers as indices. Since a 31-bit SmallInteger can index any array, our array primitives are simpler and faster.

Converting Smalltalk-80 to use 32-bit words was surprisingly painless. We found few places in the Smalltalk-80 code that depended on the word size. The worst one was that the decompiler found the first bytecode of a method by taking twice the number of literals and adding three (for the header and index origin). This prevented us from editing any of the methods to fix them, especially this one. We fixed this by creating a primitive that determined the initial PC of a method, and patching the initialPC method by hand to call this primitive. We recommend that these dependencies be removed from Smalltalk-80 systems by adding a primitive that returns information about the field size.

Garbage Collection

This is perhaps the most interesting aspect of our version, it is certainly where most of our effort went. The PDP-11 version (and prior experience with Lisp implementations) showed us that it is vitally important to have a reliable garbage collector early in the game. A buggy garbage collector has a tendency to randomly smash parts of objects in such a way that the damage does not come to light until much later. This makes the whole virtual machine rather difficult to debug, as you are not sure just which piece of code was responsible for the error. Since mark/sweep collectors can be simple enough to debug easily, we started out by using one.

After debugging the virtual machine with the simple mark/sweep collector, we turned our attention to the implementation of an incremental garbage collector. There were two candidates to choose from, the Baker[1] and the Lieberman-Hewitt[2]. Since the Lieberman-Hewitt garbage collector was an elaboration of the Baker, and significantly more complicated, we decided to implement the Baker first.

The Baker Garbage Collector

To gain a full understanding of this garbage collector, you should read Baker's work on the subject[3]. For those readers unfamiliar with this garbage collector, we present a brief description of it here.

The Baker garbage collector is an incremental, compacting garbage collector. By incremental, we mean that the process of collecting garbage is interleaved with the process of allocating space in such a way that the time required for collecting the garbage and compacting space is distributed fairly smoothly over time. The individual incremental executions of the collector have an upper bound on their time consumption proportional to the size of the largest object. This corresponds to the time it takes to move an object from one place to another. Under normal circumstances, no pauses in execution due to the garbage collector operating are perceptible.

The Baker garbage collector divides the virtual space into two equal-sized regions, or semispaces, called Fromspace and Tospace. Objects are copied from Fromspace to Tospace (hence the names) as they are found to be accessible. These copied objects are compacted sequentially at one end of Tospace. A scanning pointer starts at the base of this region, and moves field by field through the objects that were copied previously to Tospace, copying objects in Fromspace that are referenced by them. In this way, the objects in Tospace act like the stack commonly used by a mark/sweep collector. This scanning and copying continues until the scanning pointer runs out of objects. Newly created objects are placed at the far end of Tospace, so that they are not scanned. Fig. 8.3 shows the layout of Tospace.

In the original Baker scheme, whenever an object is copied, its old location (in Fromspace) is marked as a "forwarding pointer," and the new address is placed there. An access to a copied object is redirected to the new copy, and the reference is changed to point to the new location.

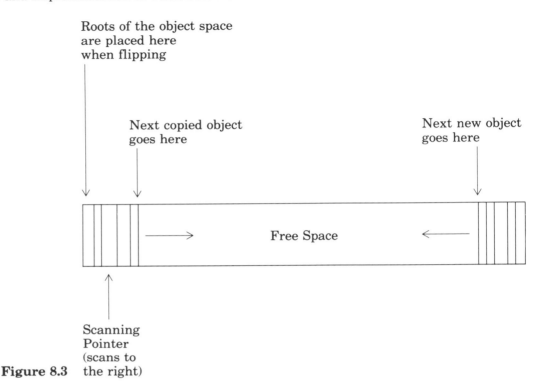

Figure 8.3   Scanning Pointer (scans to the right)

This is necessary for systems (such as Lisp) where objects are referenced by virtual address.

The whole process is started by an operation called a "flip", which switches the identity of Fromspace and Tospace, and immediately copies all the objects known to the interpreter (the "roots" of the world) to the bottom of the new Tospace. Flips may occur any time after the scanning pointer has reached the end.

We took the simplistic approach of flipping when there was insufficient space to satisfy an allocation request. This minimizes the copying activity at the expense of maximizing page faulting. Flipping when the scanning pointer runs out of objects to scan will minimize the number of pages needed for both semispaces by keeping the accessible objects as compacted as possible. It appears that the optimal time to flip should be dependent on the average lifetime of newly created objects, so that a flip will occur when the expected density of accessible objects falls below a reasonable value. The object of this tradeoff is to minimize the sum of the page faults due to accessing and creating objects and those due to copying objects.

Objects that must be copied as roots are those objects that may not be transitively accessible from any other object copied as a root. It is a good idea to copy all the objects that are "wired into" the virtual machine to insure that they never get deleted under any circumstances. The registers of the virtual machine are defined to always be in Tospace, so any objects referred to by them must also be copied at flip time. The objects that must be copied include the current context, all the objects it refers to that are cached by the interpreter (e.g. the method, receiver, self), any semaphores waiting for external events, the ProcessorScheduler object, the current DisplayBitMap (if it is not in a special location), and all the objects used by the interpreter such as nil and the selector doesNotUnderstand. If a list of these objects other than those relating to the current context is maintained, the list can be scanned incrementally to reduce the time required to perform the flip. It is not necessary to copy the object Smalltalk (the symbol table) at this time, although it is known to the interpreter, because the interpreter never uses it. If it is live, then it must be reachable from at least one of the objects which are actually used by the interpreter.

Whenever a reference to an object in Fromspace is stored into an object in Tospace, the Fromspace object must be copied to Tospace. This is necessary because the scanner may have already passed the Tospace object, or it is new. The interpreter registers are considered to always be in Tospace, since they are the first things scanned, so that object references stored in them must be checked and the objects copied if necessary. Although at first glance this seems to require more overhead than reference counting, it is actually much faster to test a flag than to increment a reference count and handle overflows. In practice, only a small number of objects need to be copied when their references are stored, and this copying would have been done by the scanner anyway.

The garbage collector is run (incrementally) every time an object is allocated. The amount of space to copy whenever a new object is created should be adjusted so that the scanning pointer finishes at the time a flip is desired (as per the above discussion). This will tend to distribute the copying activity as smoothly as possible. The semispaces must be large enough so that the probability of running out of room before the scanning pointer finishes is negligible. In practice, the largest semispaces possible should be allocated, as the middle pages of the semispaces will never be used, and will only contribute to page table overhead. Our implementation was not tuned in this fashion. Our system was set to copy four times as much space as we allocated so that we did not run out of room.

The net effect of this garbage collector is to copy all the objects which are live by virtue of being accessible (transitively) by the interpreter, from one space to another, leaving behind all the garbage. This old space can then be reused starting at the next flip.

With the Baker garbage collector objects are copied in a breadth-first order. This ordering has been shown to be substantially better than a random ordering for reducing page faults, though not as good as depth-first[4]. This ordering is largely invariant from one flip to the next, so that the copying will tend to proceed linearly through Fromspace, minimizing the page faulting due to the copying.

It is difficult to compare the performance of this garbage collector with reference counting schemes. There is no suitable analytical approach to this problem. We have not directly compared the two schemes in the same environment, but we can offer some observations based on our experience:

1. Reference counting uses less space (virtual or physical) than any other incremental scheme, as long as circular garbage is rarely created.

2. Smalltalk-80 systems would generate a fair amount of circular garbage if the programs did not explicitly unlink circular structures before deleting them. This manual intervention in what should be a completely automatic process of garbage collection is "unclean" because it prohibits easy sharing of circular data structures.

3. The Baker garbage collector is closer to a "real time" process because the time an activation takes is no more than the time to copy the largest object. A reference counter may take time that is proportional to the size of the largest network of objects.

4. Reference counting does not compact space incrementally. If objects are allocated from segments of limited size, the compaction time of a segment may be small enough to be unnoticeable. Segmentation may make it substantially more difficult to allocate large objects, such as bitmaps for high-resolution printers.

5. Reference counting is not sufficient by itself. An auxiliary mark/sweep garbage collector is needed to reclaim both circular garbage and objects whose reference counts have overflowed (if an overflow table is not used).

6. The Baker garbage collector traces accessible objects, while reference counters trace the inaccessible objects. Which is more efficient depends on the rate of garbage generation and of space flipping. The Lieberman-Hewitt garbage collector (see below) promises to radically reduce the amount of accessible storage that needs to be traced and copied, making it a clear winner in this category.

7. A detailed look at the implementation of both schemes shows that the virtual machine code has fewer places where the space checking for the Baker scheme must be performed, compared with the places where reference counts must be updated. In both schemes,

storing an object pointer usually requires that the stored pointer be checked, but reference counters require that the overwritten pointer be dereferenced, while the Baker does not.

For another comparison, it will be instructive to compare the processing necessary to perform a "store" with both reference counting and Baker. This is presented as a pseudo-Pascal code fragment in which the value of the ith field of object "objA" is stored into the jth field of the object "objB". The object table is expressed as an array of records containing the appropriate fields.

First, the reference-counting version.

store: objA intoField: j of: objB
```
    temp := objB[j];                    get the old value of objB[j]
    if not isSmallInteger(temp) then
      if ot[temp].refCount < > overflow then
        begin                           decrement refCount
          ot[temp].refCount := ot[temp].refCount - 1;
          if ot[temp].refCount = 0 then
            deallocate(temp);  if 0 then delete it
                                        recursive deallocation
        end;
    temp2 := objA[i];                   get the object pointer to store
    if not isSmallInteger(temp2) then
                                        SmallIntegers have no reference count
      if ot[temp2].refCount < > overflow then
                                        if refCount hasn't overflowed
        ot[temp2].refCount := ot[temp2].refCount + 1;
                                        increment refCount
    objB[j] := temp2;                   then store it
```

Next, the Baker version.

store: objA intoField: j of: objB
```
    temp := objA[i];                    get the object pointer to store
    if ot[objB].space = Tospace then
                                        if the dest is in Tospace
      if not isSmallInteger(temp) then
                                        and the source is not a SmallInteger
        if ot[temp].space = FromSpace then
                                        and the source is in Fromspace
          moveObject(temp)    move source from Fromspace to Tospace
    objB[j] := temp;                    then store it
```

Note that it is unnecessary to check if the destination object is in Tospace if it is the current context, since it would have either been created there or moved there when it became current.

Modifications to the Baker Garbage Collector

One difference between Smalltalk-80 object spaces and those of Lisp-like systems is that Smalltalk-80 objects are referenced by name, whereas in Lisp, objects are typically referenced by virtual address. This allows us to eliminate the forwarding pointers needed in Lisp systems using the Baker garbage collector, since in Smalltalk-80 systems the object table is the only place that the actual address of an object is stored. We also use a flag in the object table entries to note in which semispace an object is stored. This could be done by comparing the virtual address of the object with the base addresses of the spaces, but would be slower.

The use of object names rather than virtual addresses is both a blessing and a curse. The elimination of forwarding pointers simplifies the object accessing code, since no check need be made for a forwarding pointer, but adds an extra indirection for object accesses (the other being the virtual to physical mapping), and the difficult problem of reclaiming the names of objects which have become garbage.

The indirect addressing caused by using object names rather than virtual addresses is not nearly as expensive as having to handle forwarding pointers. The use of forwarding pointers requires that the accessing code test the virtual address pointer to see if it is in Fromspace, and if so, read the object header to determine if it is a forwarding pointer. If it is, the source of the reference must be changed to point to the new location. This is more expensive (without special hardware) than accessing objects indirectly through the object table. Most object references in Smalltalk-80 systems are to objects whose virtual address is cached by the interpreter (the context, method, and receiver) so that indirection through the object table is minimized. "Pure" objects need never be changed if they reference other objects by name, allowing them to be stored on read-only media like videodisks. An object table will take up about 10-20% of the space of the whole world of objects, but we don't feel that that is excessive given the benefits of naming.

Garbage objects are reclaimed by virtue of not being seen by the garbage collector, so there is no direct way to reclaim their names. One way to deal with this is to defer name reclamation until some convenient time, such as overnight. Although a 31-bit name space is big enough to do this, the object table would become quite large and sparse. This would be difficult to manage, so we looked for a way of incrementally reclaiming names.

At first, we implemented a mechanism whereby a flag was set in the object table entry for objects that were either newly created or copied to Tospace. At flip time, we scanned the object table, freed those names without the flag set, and cleared the flags in those that were set. This resulted in a pause of several seconds at each flip, due to page faulting in the object table. We could have just checked the pointers in the object table to find the ones that were still pointing at Fromspace, but we felt that the flag test was marginally faster.

Eventually, Steve Shirron developed a properly incremental method of reclaiming names that works in the following way.

Each object table entry has two flags, an "even" flag, and an "odd" flag. Each flip of the garbage collector alternates between being an "even" or an "odd" flip. As objects are created or copied to Tospace, the appropriate flag in the object table entry is set, without touching the other flag. A name reclaiming process is run incrementally every time a name is allocated. The name reclaimer scans the object table sequentially, starting over at each flip. For each object table entry, it checks to see if both flags are clear. If so, the object is dead and the name is reclaimed. If not, the flag corresponding to the previous cycle is cleared. In this way, names of objects that died in cycle N are reclaimed in cycle $N+1$.

The name reclaimer scans some number of entries each time it is activated. Since it is not fatal for the name reclaimer to not be done when a flip occurs (it merely finishes scanning the object table first), the number of entries to scan each time is not critical. The number of entries scanned per activation should dynamically depend on the amount of free space left, the average object allocation size, and the amount of object table left to scan, so that it will finish just before a flip occurs.

The Lieberman-Hewitt Garbage Collector

Lieberman and Hewitt observe that with the Baker garbage collector the cost of creating objects and garbage collection is not related to the objects' lifetimes[5]. Traditional environments commonly use stack storage for temporary objects, especially activation records, because stack management is very inexpensive. Stacks have the nice property that they are always compacted, so that allocating and deallocating objects of varying sizes does not cause fragmentation of storage. Language environments such as C and Pascal follow a strict control hierarchy, and the lifetimes of their temporary objects (local variables and activation records) are directly related to this hierarchy. In these environments it is either illegal or impossible to pass a reference to a stacked object to a previous level. These restrictions allow traditional languages to manage space very efficiently.

Most Lisp systems allow only hierarchical control flow so that they can allocate activation records on a stack. Temporary objects can be declared to the compiler as "local" to a function activation, which allows them to be deallocated when the function returns. Lisps which allow multiprocessing, such as Interlisp, use either multiple stacks or a structure known as a "spaghetti stack"[6]. Multiple stacks are difficult to manage because they may each grow to a potentially unbounded size. With spaghetti stacks, activation records are allocated from a heap and linked together. This facilitates the use of multiprocessing and environment closures. Even here, the cost of allocating activation records from a heap is not inordinately expensive because the virtual machine can deallocate them when they are deactivated.

Smalltalk-80 activation records (contexts) are objects just like any other object in the environment. Since a method may hand a reference to its context to any other object in the system, contexts may not be automatically deallocated when returning from a message send. Contexts are created at a very high rate, which makes the Smalltalk-80 system have pretty much the worst space management problems.

The Baker garbage collector is quite inefficient for Smalltalk-80 systems because the large number of contexts fill up free space rapidly, causing frequent flips. Since each flip causes all the accessible objects to be copied to the other semispace, the Baker garbage collector consumes too much time to be practical.

The Lieberman-Hewitt garbage collector eliminates this problem by dividing the world into a lot of little Baker spaces. These spaces are set up so that objects of about the same age are in the same space. Newer objects are more likely to die than older objects, so newer spaces are collected more often than older spaces. Garbage collecting a small space is quite a bit cheaper than garbage collecting the whole world at once. The individual spaces are collected separately, allowing the use of small Tospaces. Unfortunately, dealing with references that cross space boundaries is complex.

This "generation" scheme is ideal for Smalltalk-80 systems. The newest region will be filled with contexts rapidly, but when flipping the region, very few of the contexts will survive. This drastically reduces the amount of copying needed to maintain a compacted region. The scheme can be arranged so that a new generation is created whenever the newest region starts filling up with objects that have survived several flips.

The Static Object Region

We have not yet implemented the Lieberman-Hewitt garbage collector. There are several open questions about the details of this scheme that we want to answer before we try it. Instead, we implemented a scheme that is somewhat halfway between the Baker and the Lieberman-Hewitt. This scheme involved the use of a separate region called the static object region.

We noticed that of the approximately 700Kbytes of objects in the base Smalltalk-80 system, about 600Kbytes of them are relatively permanent, and need not be subject to the continual scrutiny of the Baker garbage collector. By dividing the objects into two groups, static and dynamic, we can remove most of the objects from the Baker regions and compact them together into the static object region. This region is not garbage collected dynamically because the objects in it are expected to have very long lifetimes.

The Static Object Region and the Baker region are equivalent to the oldest and the newest generation in the Lieberman-Hewitt garbage collector. By leaving out all the middle generations, we simplify the scheme at the expense of causing inefficiencies when running applications that generate lots of medium lifetime objects.

Static objects are differentiated from dynamic objects by their age. Each object has a 6 bit (arbitrarily chosen) age field. This field is used to keep track of how many flips the object had survived. An object older than 63 flips was placed in the Static Object Region the next time the region was regenerated. Fig. 8.4 shows the resulting layout of each object table entry.

Whenever a snapshot is requested (which already causes a long pause) we scan through all objects looking for "old" ones. A space is created that is just big enough to hold them, and then they are copied to it. The object table entries for these objects are marked to indicate to the Baker collector that they should be ignored. This space is dumped to the snapshot file separately from the "dynamic" objects, so that it is easy to recreate when rolling in a snapshot.

Dynamic objects referred to only by static objects must be saved by the Baker garbage collector. Instead of scanning all the static objects for references to dynamics, we use an "exit table." This table is a list of those static objects which may contain references to dynamic objects. The static objects referred to by this table are scanned by the Baker scanner and all dynamic object references found in them are handled appropriately. Each static object has a flag, which when set indicates that the static object has an entry in the exit table. Whenever an object reference is stored in another object, the flags are checked. If they indicate that the destination is a static object without an entry in the exit table, and that the source is a dynamic object, an entry for that static object is placed in the table. If later, that static object ceases to have references to dynamic objects, it is not removed from the exit table. This does not appear to be the source of any inefficiency. Surprisingly, the exit table had fewer than 50 entries after running for several

An Object Table Entry is a 32 bit word

31	30	29	28	27	26	25	24	23	22	21	20	19	18	17	16
ST	NE	W	X	M	SO	SE	P				Location (23:16)				

15	14	13	12	11	10	9	8	7	6	5	4	3	2	1	0
					Location (15:2)									X	F

F – Set if OTE is free
P – Set if object has pointer fields
SE – Even flag for OTE sweeper
SO – Odd flag for OTE sweeper
M – Mark–used by Mark/Sweep GC
W – Set if object has word fields
NE – Set if object is Static and is not in exit table
ST – Set if object is static
X – Unused

Figure 8.4 Location – Longword virtual address of object.

weeks, indicating that all but about 50 of the static objects only referred to other static objects.

The become: primitive causes problems because it switches the object pointers of two objects which may be in different spaces. A static object converted to a dynamic is the most difficult to manage. Rather than scan all the statics looking for those which refer to this new dynamic object (which would take a while), we add the new dynamic to a list called the "becomelist". This list is scanned by the garbage collector at flip time so that all the objects referred to by it are copied into Tospace. This insures that the new dynamic object is not deleted in case it is referred to only by static objects. It is fairly rare to convert a static object to a dynamic object, so we are not concerned by the possibility that it dies but is not seen as garbage. The exhaustive garbage collector that is run at snapshot time will get rid of it if it has died.

Converting a dynamic object to a static merely requires that the new static object be scanned for references to dynamic objects. If any are found, the new static is installed in the exit table. Only one object is scanned in this case, so no perceptible pause occurs.

Eventually, we have to collect the garbage that has accumulated in the static region. This is accomplished by an exhaustive mark/sweep garbage collector that is run at snapshot time. This same garbage collector also compacts the dynamic objects so that there is no wasted space in the snapshot image.

We found that the use of the static region resulted in a significant improvement in performance, more than doubling the apparent speed. Removing most of the objects from the Baker regions reduced page faulting substantially, because there were fewer objects to copy when a flip happened.

The implementation of this scheme was relatively simple compared to the full Lieberman-Hewitt. We acquired a lot of useful statistics from this that should allow us to do a good job of implementing the Lieberman-Hewitt garbage collector.

Virtual Object Space

In order to support a very large number of objects, some "virtual object" mechanism must be used. The Software Concepts Group has used variants of "object swapping" to achieve this with their OOZE and LOOM virtual object systems[7]. Since the VAX/VMS system supports a large paged virtual address space, we decided to use it directly to implement a virtual object scheme. This approach allowed us to defer issues relating to virtual memory performance until after we got the basic system running.

The virtual space is divided into several regions: two 1Mbyte "Baker" semispaces, 512Kbytes for the object table (ot), and approximately 600Kbytes for the static object region. The object table is set at 128K objects. This number was derived by doubling the size until we stopped running out of room. Although we do not know how much page faulting is due to accessing the object table, we suspect that it is substantial.

Ted Kaehler's paper (see Chapter 14) discusses the problems with straightforward paging systems (such as we used) and compares them with object swapping schemes. The gist of the argument against paging is that since there is a low locality of reference between adjacent objects in a page, and objects tend to be much smaller than pages, the majority of space in physical memory is taken up by useless objects that just happen to be on the same pages as useful objects. Object swapping schemes such as OOZE and LOOM compact the active objects into physical memory so that more active objects can fit at one time. This allows larger applications to run without faulting than with a paging system. Object swapping has two problems dealing with disks that like to transfer whole pages at once. First, a faulted-in object must be copied from the disk page buffer to the object region in core. This is probably not serious compared to the time it takes to access the object on disk in the first place. The second problem is that when faulting-out an old object (when it has been modified), the disk page(s) it belongs in must first be read so that the adjacent objects are not trashed. Although it is possible to write all the objects you need to fault out compacted together and appended to the end of the file, this will not only cause problems dealing with the fragmentation of the disk image, but makes for extra work in updating the directory of the objects on disk.

The VAX/Smalltalk-80 system is more properly thought of as a "mapped real memory" than a true virtual object memory because of the excessive paging we encounter when we have less than about 3Mbytes of real core for our use. A proper system should provide adequate performance whenever the set of active objects fits into the available real memory. There may be more than a 100 to 1 ratio between all objects and the active objects in a production Smalltalk-80 system. A virtual object system should be able to support such a system with ease.

Our goal is to design a hybrid of object swapping and paging that gives us a low faulting rate, yet runs on paged systems. This would allow us to use commonly available computers that have hardware to support paging, as well as allowing Smalltalk-80 systems to co-exist with other language environments on the same machine.

Our approach is based on the observation that you can create a compact set of active objects in a paged system merely by copying them from wherever they happen to be in virtual space into a region which is locked into core. Faulting out objects is accomplished by just copying them back. The disk activity of the paging system caused by this scheme is virtually identical to that of the object swappers. In addition, objects larger than a page need not be copied at all, allowing much larger objects than would be possible with an object swapper. A large linear virtual address space is helpful when implementing garbage collectors such as the Baker. With a paged system, when Fromspace is empty the pages underlying it can be deleted completely. Pages needed for Tospace can be quickly created by using those released from Fromspace. If a large amount of garbage is collected in each pass, then the amount of physical memory required is much less than what both semispaces would ordinarily require. If you need more space than is available physically, paging will happen automatically.

The Lieberman-Hewitt garbage collector would be a natural candidate for use here. Newer objects are accessed more frequently than older objects, so by keeping the newest regions in core and copying objects from older regions into a cache, we would obtain the benefits of both object swapping and incremental garbage collection.

The cache could be managed by combining the "clock" procedure[8] with a Baker-like semispace set. The clock procedure would repetitively scan a list of the cached objects. Those that had not been touched since the last scan would be copied back to their home (if they had been modified), those which had been touched would be copied to the other semispace. This would compact the cache incrementally. It is also possible to fault-out objects until a big enough hole is created to satisfy a faulted-in object, but this scheme may cause noticeable pauses whenever a flurry of objects are faulted out, as each will probably cause a page fault when written back. Fortunately, most of the objects would not have been modified and therefore need not be copied back. Some experimentation is called for here.

The object table should be implemented as a hash table in order to eliminate page faulting when accessing active objects. Objects in the cache, and those in the newer regions would have their names placed in the hash table.

Paging Performance

The straightforward approach we have taken, although easy to implement, spends most of its time waiting in a page fault state when there are other users on the system. VMS allocates most unused core for faulted out pages, so when the Smalltalk-80 system is running by itself (on Sunday mornings) the performance improves several fold as disk accesses are usually unnecessary for page faults. A lot of the paging overhead is due to the Baker garbage collector and the object name reclaimer scanning their spaces. Since the pages touched by the name reclaimer, and many of the pages touched by the Baker scanner are completely predictable, a mechanism whereby the pager could be requested to fault-in a page without suspending the program would have a substantial impact on the performance. Unfortunately, VMS does not have such a hook. We are looking into using a separate VMS process, mapped into the same space as the Smalltalk-80 process, to fault-in pages so that it would be suspended instead of the Smalltalk-80 process.

Anything that reduces the rate at which garbage is created will have a favorable impact on paging rates because of the reduced garbage collection activity. Smalltalk-80 systems seem to be much worse than modern compiled Lisp systems in the rate at which garbage is generated. This is attributable primarily to contexts, which must be allocated from the heap, and secondarily to the fact that Smalltalk-80 methods tend to require arguments packed into objects such as points and rectangles, which are almost immediately discarded. Editing text also creates a substantial amount of garbage as new strings are created for each modification. Some object-based systems allow variable-length objects to "grow" by allocating space for them that is larger than that actually needed. When an object such as a string needs more room, it can expand until it fills the contiguous chunk allocated for it by the memory system. If it needs more, it is automatically copied to a larger area. It may be worthwhile to use this technique in a Smalltalk-80 implementation.

Context Reclamation

We noticed that we were generating about a megabyte per second of objects that did not survive even one space flip. We found that these objects were almost entirely contexts. Some method of reducing this garbage without compromising the flexibility of the context linkages had to be found. We could not just reclaim contexts when they were returned from, since a reference to a context could be handed to another object.

We found that there are only two occasions when a reference to the active context was handed out: the PushActiveContext bytecode, and when the context was placed on a process or semaphore queue. We assumed that if either of these events happened, the current context and all its ancestors could be accessible by any other object, so must be reclaimed only by the garbage collector. Fortunately, these cases happen infrequently. If neither of these events occurred, the context could be reclaimed immediately upon returning. By maintaining a counter that is incremented every time a non-primitive send happens and zeroed when either of the special events happens, we reclaim contexts (small only) whenever we return and the counter is non-zero (decrementing the counter as we return).

These reclaimed contexts are linked together on a free list, and are used instead of heap space if there is anything on the list. When the garbage collector does a space flip, this list is cleared because the contexts are then in the wrong space and it would be silly to copy them to the new Tospace.

This little trick reclaims about 85-90% of the contexts. Occasionally, it is much worse (40-50%), apparently due to executing tight loops that perform a lot of blockCopys.

Dealing with a Timesharing System

The Smalltalk-80 system as distributed is not designed to either run background processes or co-exist on a timesharing system. This is due to the large number of places where the code loops waiting for a mouse button. The system can be converted to one which is entirely event driven by inserting wait messages to an "any event" semaphore into the loops. We found these loops by noticing whenever the idle process was not running, yet nothing else seemed to be happening. We would then type control-C to interrupt the Smalltalk-80 system and find out who was responsible. The debugger was then used to edit and recompile the offending methods. Converting all the interaction to an event-driven style allowed background Smalltalk-80 processes to run whenever the user was·not actively interacting with the Smalltalk-80 system.

It is generally considered uncivil to run programs that are not doing anything worthwhile on a timesharing system. To fix this, we replaced the Smalltalk-80 idle process with one that called two special primitives. The Smalltalk-80 code for this is as follows.

idleLoop
```
[true] whileTrue:
    [[Smalltalk collectGarbage] whileTrue.
    Smalltalk hibernate]
```

The collectGarbage primitive performed an incremental activation of the garbage collector, returning false if there was nothing left to do. The hibernate primitive suspended the Smalltalk-80 VMS process, letting other users run. The hibernate primitive returned whenever an external event happened. Since this loop runs at the lowest priority, it is preempted by any Smalltalk-80 process with something to do.

This made us more popular with the other users of the VAX, and also reduced the overhead of the garbage collector when interacting with the Smalltalk-80 system in a bursty manner (which is usually the case). The Smalltalk-80 process itself also benefited from this because the VMS scheduler assigns a lower priority to compute-bound processes. By hibernating often enough, the Smalltalk-80 process would preempt other users running compilers and the like, leading to a snappier response when browsing or editing.

The Message Cache

We implemented a message cache to speed up message lookup as recommended by the book. We found, however, that using a two-way set associative scheme was significantly better than the one-probe hash table described in the book. Our cache used a hash table where every key (constructed from the receiver's class and the selector Oop) had two possible locations in the cache, determined by the hash value and its complement. The location to store a message was determined by a ping-pong scheme in which a flag was toggled whenever a message was inserted into the cache. If the flag was set, the direct hash value was used, if cleared, the complement was used. This allowed two messages with the same hash value to co-exist in the cache. More elaborate caches using 4- and 8-way sets are feasible, but the payoff is less since all possible locations may have to be checked when looking up a message. In this cache we stored the full key for matching, the method's Oop, the fields of the method header and extension unpacked into bytes, and the address of the interpreter routine that handled that method. This latter information proved very helpful in speeding up the processing of message sends. Our hit rate was typically better than 90% with a 256 entry cache (two sets of 128 entries).

The Image Preprocessor

The differences in word formats between the Xerox and DEC hardware forced us to write a program (in C on the VAX) that read the standard Smalltalk-80 image, massaged it, and wrote out an image in our format. This was done originally for the PDP-11 version, and was extensively modified for the VAX version. This preprocessor did the following conversions:

1. Converted object headers to 32-bit word format.

2. Converted the size fields to be bytecounts.

3. Initialized the flags in the object header and object table entry.

4. Converted all pointer fields to 32-bit words by sign extending SmallIntegers and zero extending Oops.

5. Byte-reversed all the objects with byte fields (e.g. CompiledMethods) so that we could use the byte-addressing capability of the VAX directly.

6. Bit-reversed all the words in bitmaps (our lsb is on the left of a scanline).

7. Converted the IEEE format floating point numbers to DEC format.

8. Converted LargePositiveIntegers to SmallIntegers where possible.

9. Patched CompiledMethod initialPC to call a primitive.

10. Patched the PCs in all the contexts to reflect the increased storage taken by the literals.

11. Reformatted the object table because of the different flags and addresses.

12. Formatted the image header to have the information about the static region that we needed.

This preprocessor also gathered information about the number and sizes of the various types of objects.

Performance Measurements

It is difficult to come up with accurate performance figures for a system like this. Small changes in such things as the working set size have a major impact on the performance. Our performance monitoring software could not distinguish between time due to page faults and time due to other users preempting the Smalltalk-80 system (it left them both out). The page fault rate depended on the long-term history of the Smalltalk-80 session, and the time it took to handle faults varied according to the load on the VAX.

With that in mind, when using a working set of 512, 512 byte pages (the largest our system let us have), we observed that we were getting about 250 page faults/second during compiling or browsing. We seemed to get between 15K and 25K bytecodes/second (on Sunday mornings) when compiling or browsing.

We found that CPU time spent in the garbage collector code amounted to about 7% of the total when executing long tasks. Of course, the real time was substantially larger (except on Sunday mornings) due to page faulting in the garbage collector.

Conclusions

After using this version of Smalltalk-80 implementation for a while, we can make some useful observations:

1. 32 bit fields are the way to go.

2. Paging systems are very easy to use, but a lot of work needs to be done to achieve adequate performance.

3. Incremental garbage collection is generally superior to reference counting, both in ease of implementation and performance.

4. The Smalltalk-80 system is marginally usable on a timesharing system with 40 users.

References

1. Baker, Henry G., "Actor Systems for Real-Time Computation," MIT Laboratory for Computer Science, MIT/LCS/TR-197, 1978.

2. Lieberman, Henry, and Hewitt, Carl, "A Real Time Garbage Collector Based on the Lifetimes of Objects," MIT AI Memo no. 569, 1981.

3. See reference 1.

4. Stamos, James W., "A Large Object-Oriented Virtual Memory: Grouping Strategies, Measurements and Performance," Xerox PARC Technical Report SCG-82-2, May, 1982.

5. See reference 1.

6. Bobrow, Daniel G., and Wegbreit, Ben, "A Model and Stack Implementation of Multiple Environments," *Communications* of the *ACM*, vol. 10, pp. 591–602, 1973.

7. Kaehler, Ted, "Virtual Memory for an Object-Oriented Language," *Byte* vol. 6, no. 8, Aug. 1981.

PART THREE

Measurements and Analyses
of Implementations

9

The Smalltalk-80
Benchmarks

Kim McCall
Software Concepts Group
Xerox Palo Alto Research Center
Palo Alto, California

Introduction

At the first Smalltalk-80 "implementors meeting" on September 24-25, 1981, several of the groups pursuing implementations expressed a desire for some system facilities to help them measure the efficiency of their interpreters. Such facilities, which were unavoidably labeled "benchmarks," would provide an objective means of comparing implementations, gauging the value of intended performance enhancements, and tracking the progress of individual implementations over time.

This author was given the responsibility of adding such facilities to the system, and thus was born the class Benchmark found in the Smalltalk-80 virtual image.

In this paper I:

1. Describe the general framework of the timing and reporting facilities in class Benchmark;

2. Describe various individual tests (hereafter referred to as "benchmarks");

3. Explain how to write a new benchmark;

4. Suggest ways benchmarks can be used, i.e., how to gain useful information from them; and

5. Present the results of running the standard system benchmarks in several different implementations.

The Benchmark Framework

Class Benchmark contains a simple set of facilities for timing the execution of some block of code and reporting the result. The central message is

test: aBlock labeled: label repeated: nTimes.

aBlock must be a BlockContext that contains the code to be timed; and label should be a string describing this code, i.e., describing the system behavior that is being timed. Since timings are recorded in milliseconds, it often happens (e.g., when testing atomic system functions such as pushing a value onto the stack or popping it off) that a single execution of aBlock would yield a value so small that it would be dwarfed by the roundoff error. So the method allows us to specify the number of times the block should be executed (nTimes).

For example,

```
Benchmark new
    test: [20 factorial]
    labeled: 'testing 20 factorial'
    repeated: 100
```

would time 100 executions of the block

[20 factorial]

and report the result, using the label 'testing 20 factorial' for purposes of identification.

Reporting

Class Benchmark contains various facilities for reporting its results in a permanent, semi-permanent, or evanescent way.

A report consists of:

1) An *identification line*, giving the label, enclosed in square brackets.

2) A *total time line*, giving the number of times aBlock was executed and the total time (in seconds).

3) If the number of executions of aBlock is greater than one, a *single iteration line*, giving the time (in microseconds) taken to execute aBlock once.

For example, if it took 26133 milliseconds to run 100 repetitions of [20 factorial], the report would read

[testing 20 factorial]
    100 repetitions timed at 26.133 seconds
    261330.0 microseconds per repetition.

After each benchmark test, some feedback is printed in the SystemTranscript. The user can choose to print either the full report as described above or just the identification line. If she or he desires a more permanent record, the user may also elect to print a report on a file. For implementations that do not yet include a working file system, the report may be printed on a Stream.

The default reporting behavior will be to print the full report in the Transcript. To change the default, the user sends the message setOutputParameters to the instance of class Benchmark that is going to perform the test. In response to setOutputParameters, the instance of Benchmark will invite the user to select among the various reporting options.

In order to generate a file containing reports for a *series* of benchmarks, class Benchmark provides the message testList:. The setOutputParameters message is sent automatically in response to testList:. There are built-in facilities in class Benchmark for comparing two output files in order to chart progress over time or to compare two different implementations. These facilities are invoked by the message compareOldTimes:newTimes:outputTo:.

Timing

The actual timing is done by the method

    time: aBlock repeated: nTimes

This method times nTimes executions of aBlock and nTimes executions of an empty block (one that just returns nil), and then computes and returns the difference. This should report the actual time spent executing aBlock nTimes times, and subtract out the overhead of the counting and execution control structures. In the code for

    time: aBlock repeated: nTimes

some care was taken to insure that the control structures for counting up to nTimes would not dominate the execution of aBlock. For example, rather than using timesRepeat: for looping, we use an open coded loop. We also use a doubly-nested iteration loop when nTimes is large, to insure that all the counting is done using SmallInteger arithmetic.

The Standard System Benchmarks

The Smalltalk-80 virtual image includes two different kinds of benchmarks, those that measure specific parts of an interpreter and those that measure overall system performance. In order to be able to gauge the benefit of small changes to restricted parts of the interpreter, or to isolate specific areas in need of improvement, there is a set of benchmarks that test the efficiency of each of the most basic, simple operations of the interpreter. These test the basic bytecodes and the primitives. There is also a set of more global benchmarks that test the performance of the system at the higher-level activities invoked by a typical Smalltalk-80 programmer, such as compiling, decompiling, using browser facilities, and inserting, formatting, and displaying text. We call these the *micro-benchmarks* and the *macro-benchmarks* respectively.

The Micro-Benchmarks

Most of the micro-benchmarks consist of several repetitions of the particular bytecode or primitive to be tested. We need several repetitions of the very fast bytecodes in order to make the execution time of aBlock be so much greater than the execution time of the empty block that the rounded-off results will be meaningful. To keep the stack from overflowing, and to satisfy the demands of the compiler, the repetitions of the operation we intend to test are interspersed with pops or quick sends of the message = =. The micro-benchmarks all end with ↑nil. This makes aBlock's execution speed more directly comparable to the execution time of an "empty" block (which just returns nil). In the descriptions of the individual micro-benchmarks below, I generally give the percentage of bytes in the block (ignoring the ↑nil) that actually execute the behavior we are trying to test. I will present the standard system benchmarks in the order in which they occur in the method for setStandardTests in class Benchmark class. This list is intended to serve as a documentation reference, and the casual reader is invited to skip or skim it.

Please note that the inclusion in the benchmarks of the = = message or other byte codes that we really didn't want to test may greatly alter the execution speed of the block and compromise the meaningfulness of the results. For example, I thought that I had implemented the quick push of a constant (like 1) onto the stack about as efficiently as possible, and I was perplexed to learn that a machine-coded MC68000 implementation performed the testLoadQuickConstant benchmark faster than my own microcoded implementation. After looking at the code that actually implements the Smalltalk-80 virtual machine instruction 16r76 (118 decimal), I was even more perplexed, since my implementation looked considerably *more* efficient. Finally, I realized that most of the time reported by the benchmark was going into the execution of (and return from) the = = message which I had included just to satisfy the compiler. (This MC68000 implementation gave better results because it uses a delayed reference-counting scheme that greatly expedites pushes, pops, and simple primitive operations.)

testLoadInstVar

This benchmark measures how quickly an instance variable of the receiver can be pushed onto the stack. Because this variable is set to 1, there is little reference-counting overhead on the push (although there may be more on the other operations in the block). 50% of the bytes in the block are 16r0, a push of the receiver's first instance variable.

testLoadTempNRef

This benchmark measures how quickly a variable that is local to a method can be pushed onto the stack. Setting this variable to 1 avoids most reference-counting overhead on the push. 50% of the bytes in the block are 16r10, a push of the method's first local variable.

testLoadTempRef

This benchmark also measures how quickly a variable that is local to a method can be pushed onto the stack, but because the variable is set to some newly created point, the implementation's reference-counting mechanism (if any) will be fully exercised. Again, 50% of the bytes in the block are 16r10, a push of the receiver's first instance variable.

testLoadQuickConstant

This benchmark measures how quickly one of the "quick constants" (-1, 0, 1, 2, nil, true, false) can be pushed onto the stack. There is little reference-counting overhead on the push. 50% of the bytes in the block are 16r76, a push of the constant 1.

testLoadLiteralNRef

This benchmark measures how quickly an ordinary literal (a constant generated at compile time) can be pushed onto the stack. Because we have used the constant 3, there is little reference-counting overhead on the push. 50% of the bytes in the block are 16r21, a push of the method's second literal.

testLoadLiteralIndirect

This benchmark measures how quickly the contents of an indirectly accessed variable (such as a class variable or a global variable) can be pushed onto the stack. Because our variable refers to class Point, there is little reference-counting overhead on the push. 50% of the bytes in the block are 16r41, an indirect push of the method's second literal.

testPopStoreInstVar

This benchmark measures how quickly a value can be popped off the stack and stored in an instance variable of the receiver. Because this value is the SmallInteger 1, there is little reference-counting overhead on the push or the store. 50% of the bytes in the block are 16r60, a pop of the top of the stack into the receiver's first instance variable.

testPopStoreTemp

This benchmark measures how quickly a value can be popped off the stack and stored in a local variable of the method. Again, since this value is 1, there is little reference-counting overhead. 50% of the bytes in the block are 16r68, a pop of the top of the stack into the method's first local variable.

test3plus4

This benchmark measures the speed of SmallInteger addition. Because all values are SmallIntegers, there is little reference-counting overhead. 25% of the bytes in the block are 16rB0, a quick send of the message +.

test3lessThan4

This benchmark measures the speed of SmallInteger comparison. Because all values are SmallIntegers, there is little reference-counting overhead. 25% of the bytes in the block are 16rB2, a quick send of the message <.

test3times4

This benchmark measures the speed of SmallInteger multiplication. Because all values are SmallIntegers, there is little reference-counting overhead. 25% of the bytes in the block are 16rB8, a quick send of the message *.

test3div4

This benchmark measures the speed of SmallInteger division. Because all values are SmallIntegers, there is little reference-counting overhead. 25% of the bytes in the block are 16rBD, a quick send of the message //.

test16bitArith

This benchmark measures the speed of 16-bit integer arithmetic. Since some implementations use more than 15 bits to represent SmallIntegers (see Chapter 8), the reference-counting overhead will depend on the representation chosen for 16-bit integers. 25% of the bytes in the block are 16rB0, a quick send of the message +.

testLargeIntArith

This benchmark measures the speed of arithmetic on integers greater than 2^{16}. The reference-counting overhead will depend on the exact representation chosen for these integers. 25% of the bytes in the block are 16rB0, a quick send of the message +.

testActivationReturn

This very important benchmark uses a call on a doubly-recursive method to measure the speed of method activation and return. There is little reference-counting overhead associated with knowing when to end the recursion, but there may be a great deal in managing the Contexts that represent the activations. About 12.5% of the bytes executed during this benchmark are 16rE0, a send of the method's first literal (in this case, the Symbol recur:), and about 12.5% are returns, split evenly between 16r78, a quick return of the receiver, and 16r7C, a return of the value on the top of the stack.

testShortBranch

This benchmark times the short jump to the false branch of a conditional. Although there is not much reference-counting overhead, other operations may be *so* fast that reference counting takes a good proportion of the time. 16.7% (1/6) of the bytes in the block are 16r90, a short conditional branch.

testWhileLoop

This benchmark measures the speed of executing a simple "while loop." All loop-counting uses SmallInteger arithmetic. About 9% of the bytes in the block are 16rA3, long jump, and about 9% are 16r9D, a short conditional branch.

testArrayAt

This benchmark measures how quickly a value can be read from an Array. 25% of the bytes in the block are 16rC0, a quick send of the message at:.

testArrayAtPut

This benchmark measures how quickly a value can be stored into an Array. 20% of the bytes in the block are 16rC1, a quick send of the message at:put:.

testStringAt

This benchmark measures how quickly a value can be read from a String. 25% of the bytes in the block are 16rC0, a quick send of the message at:.

testStringAtPut

This benchmark measures how quickly a value can be stored into a String. 20% of the bytes in the block are 16rC1, a quick send of the message at:put:.

testSize

This benchmark measures how quickly a String can return its size. The String will be reference counted in reference-counting implementations. 33% of the bytes in the block are 16rC2, a quick send of the message size.

testPointCreation

This benchmark measures how quickly a Point can be created from two SmallIntegers. 25% of the bytes in the block are 16rBB, a quick send of the message @.

testStreamNext

This benchmark measures how quickly the next value can be read from a Stream. About 33% of the bytes in the block are 16rC3, a quick send of the message next.

testStreamNextPut

This benchmark measures how quickly the next value can be stored into a Stream. About 25% of the bytes in the block are 16rC4, a quick send of the message nextPut:.

testEQ

This benchmark measures how quickly two objects can be compared for identity. About 50% of the bytes in the block are 16rC6, a quick send of the message ==.

testClass

This benchmark measures how quickly an object can return its class. 33% of the bytes in the block are 16rC7, a quick send of the message class.

testBlockCopy

This benchmark measures how quickly a BlockContext can be created that has the current context as its "home context." 25% of

testValue

the bytes in the block are 16rC8, a quick send of the message blockCopy:.

This benchmark measures how quickly a simple BlockContext can be evaluated. 33% of the bytes in the block are 16rC9, a quick send of the message value.

testCreation

This benchmark measures how quickly a class can be instantiated. 33% of the bytes in the block are 16rCC, a quick send of the message new.

testPointX

This benchmark measures how quickly one coordinate can be extracted from a Point. 33% of the bytes in the block are 16rCE, a quick send of the message x.

testLoadThisContext

This benchmark measures how quickly the current context can be pushed onto the stack. 50% of the bytes in the block are 16r89, a quick push of the current context.

testBasicAt

This benchmark measures how quickly the value can be read from an unnamed (but indexed) field of a variable-length object. 25% of the bytes in the block are 16rE4, a send of the method's fifth literal, in this case the message basicAt:.

testBasicAtPut

This benchmark measures how quickly a value can be stored into an unnamed (but indexed) field of a variable-length object. 20% of the bytes in the block are 16rF5, a send of the method's sixth literal, in this case the message basicAt:put:.

testPerform

This benchmark measures the speed of the perform: primitive. 20% of the bytes in the block are 16rF1, a send of the method's second literal, in this case the message perform:with:.

testStringReplace

This benchmark measures the speed of the String replacement primitive.

testAsFloat

This benchmark measures the speed of the SmallInteger to Float conversion. 33% of the bytes in the block are 16rD1, a send of the method's second literal, in this case the message asFloat.

testFloatingPointAddition

This benchmark measures the speed of the floating point number arithmetic. 25% of the bytes in the block are 16rB0, a quick send of the message + which must be looked up in class Float.

testBitBLT

This benchmark measures the speed of the BitBlt primitive. 33% of the bytes in the block are 16rD2, a send of the method's third literal, in this case the message copyBits.

testTextScanning

This benchmark measures the speed of the primitive method that displays characters on the screen.

The Macro-Benchmarks

The macro-benchmarks provide examples of the main activities in which a Smalltalk programmer is typically engaged. Since the Smalltalk-80 virtual image does not contain many applications besides the programming environment as a whole, most of the macro-benchmarks test system support for programming activities.

testClassOrganizer	This benchmark measures the speed of conversion between the textual and the structural representations of a class organization. The example chosen is class Benchmark because its organization contains many categories.
testPrintDefinition	This benchmark measures how quickly a class definition, as it appears in the system browser, can be generated. The example chosen is an instance of class Compiler because it has a moderate number of instance variables.
testPrintHierarchy	This benchmark times the printing of a portion of the Smalltalk-80 class hierarchy. The example chosen is class InstructionStream because it has several subclasses.
testAllCallsOn	This benchmark measures how quickly all the methods in which a given selector is referenced can be found. The example chosen is the selector printStringRadix: because it has a moderate number of senders.
testAllImplementors	This benchmark measures how quickly all the implementors of a given selector can be found. The example chosen is the selector next because it has a moderate number of implementors.
testInspect	This benchmark measures how quickly a standard inspect window can be created. The example chosen is an instance of class Compiler because it has a moderate number of instance variables.
testCompiler	This benchmark measures the speed of the compiler on a slightly longer than normal method, one containing 87 tokens and compiling into 73 bytecodes.
testDecompiler	This benchmark measures the speed of the Decompiler by decompiling all the methods in class InputSensor.
testKeyboardLookAhead	This benchmark gauges keyboard response, simulating a typist who is able to type ahead.
testKeyboardSingle	This benchmark measures keyboard handling by simulating a typist who waits until each keystroke appears on the screen before typing the next one.
testTextDisplay	This benchmark measures how quickly a paragraph can display itself. The paragraph chosen contains 13 lines with no font or emphasis changes.

testTextFormatting	This benchmark measures the system facilities required to display a piece of source code in the system browser. First, the message pattern is discovered and highlighted (by making it bold). Next, the line breaks are determined which will allow it to be displayed between certain margins. Finally, the text is displayed.
testTextEditing	This benchmark measures text-editing speed by repeatedly inserting characters into a string and redisplaying the string.

Writing Your Own Benchmarks

Suppose you want to use the general benchmark facilities to test and record your system's performance of some tasks that are not already tested by class Benchmark. This is quite straightforward if you are testing some large system function, such as compilation, that does not require user interaction. As explained above, you send an instance of Benchmark the message

    test: aBlock labeled: label repeated: nTimes

where aBlock invokes the function whose speed you want to measure. But if you want to test a more atomic system facility, such as a primitive specific to your implementation or a simple system facility, primitive, or byte code for which I have not included a test (such as the performance of your low-level disk code), or if you want to test your system's behavior at a task that involves user input, I have a few words of advice.

First, advice for macro-benchmarks that require user input: It should be obvious that if the benchmark ever has to wait for input, the results will depend on the behavior of the user rather than that of the system. This is unacceptable. So unless you can be sure of feeding your benchmark all the input you need ahead of time (by "type ahead" for example), you will need to figure out a more creative way to discover the results you want. The implementors at University of California, Berkeley, (see Chapter 11), have developed a "script" facility in which the input events required to drive some application can be recorded and then played back later. This allows a script to drive an application or a benchmark, and thus avoids uneven waiting.

Next, advice for the designers of new micro-benchmarks: The main problem in defining a benchmark is being sure that the benchmark actually tests what you mean it to test. The main problem here is making sure that that operation is not swamped by other extraneous computation. For example, if you want to test the speed of your BitBlt primitive, you might think of a simple way of getting a BitBlt to occur, such as

Display reverse: (100@100 corner: 400@400)

which uses BitBlt to complement the bits in a rectangle on the screen. But this would probably be a mistake, because several (costly) message sends are required to turn this high-level description of a particular BitBlt into a completely specified call on the primitive. The Smalltalk-80 "spy" facilities contained in class MessageTally can help you discover whether your proposed benchmark times primitive or higher-level execution.

To solve this problem you need to find a much lower-level way of invoking the desired behavior. But sometimes you have to be very careful. For example, consider my original code for testing the speed of BlockContext creation. Smalltalk methods often call for unevaluated blocks of code to be passed as arguments. This happens, for example, in all code of the general form

1 to: 10 do: [:i | array at: i put: true].

When it sees something like this, the compiler realizes that it needs to create a BlockContext to serve as the second argument of the to:do: message. So it generates the following sequence of byte codes

pushThisContext   push0 (or 1 or 2, etc.)   sendMsg: blockCopy:

Now, I was interested in testing the speed of execution of this blockCopy: message. Since I wanted to follow my general rule of making sure that this operation was not swamped by other computation, I thought it would be smart to store the current context in a temporary variable and thus be able to get it onto the stack by a simple pushTemp instruction rather than a (at least in some implementation strategies) potentially more complicated pushThisContext instruction. The problem is that since the code that the benchmark repeatedly executes is itself passed as an unevaluated block, by the time this code is executed, my clever temporary variable no longer points at the current context, but rather at one further down the stack. This resulted in my benchmark testing an operation that would literally *never* be performed in any normal Smalltalk-80 system and that might go much slower (in certain very highly optimized implementations) than the behavior I had meant to test.

The micro-benchmark designer should also be careful to consider the effect of other "filler" bytes, as discussed above.

How to Use Your Results

What can you learn from the results of your tests? The micro-benchmarks can, of course, suggest parts of an implementation that need additional work. They will often help identify local gross inefficiencies. They can also serve to confirm that a simple local modification was, in fact, an improvement. But I think it is a mistake to place a great deal of emphasis on micro-benchmark performance. It seems that there are only a few micro-benchmarks whose performance correlates strongly with global (macro-benchmark) performance. Microcoded machines with stringent control store limits would be especially ill-advised to spend micro-instruction space speeding up the relatively insignificant micro-benchmarks.

The macro-benchmarks appear to be a good measure of overall system performance. Improvement in their performance correlates well with user-perceived system performance. I have found them very useful in gauging the effect of both small and large changes to my interpreter and in tracking my progress over time. For example, columns **A** and **B** of Table 9.1 compare the Dolphin interpreter before and after a change to the handling of the display that had a significant effect on performance. At other times however, testing the macro-benchmarks has served primarily to quell my enthusiastic anticipation of the value of some intended enhancement.

A Brief Analysis of Early Results

As this book attests, there are now several successful Smalltalk-80 implementations. The standard system benchmarks have been run in each of these implementations, and the reports are presented below. There are several interesting lessons to be gleaned from these results, which I will explore here.

It should be stressed that the figures we will be comparing were achieved on machines of vastly different speeds and hardware configurations. Some of our figures are very early results. Some come from implementations that were intended to teach the implementors about the structure of the interpreter and that placed very low priority on execution speed. Some implementations were written in high-level languages while others were written in microcode. None of these results is final, and none indicates the expected performance of any future products.

I include these figures because the fact that they were achieved on vastly different machines and in pursuit of different goals allows us to do interesting cross-correlations. We can learn which of the micro-benchmarks seem to be good predictors of the speed of the macro-benchmarks (which is what we really care about). And we can glimpse the results of various strategies such as reference counting versus garbage collecting.

I will present the results in two tables. Table 9.1 gives raw times for each of the benchmarks, and Table 9.2 gives times as a proportion of the average (geometric mean) time across all implementations. The time reported for each benchmark is the execution time for the entire benchmark (rather than for a single repetition), i.e., that given in the report's "total time line."

Table 9.1 The Benchmarks, Raw Times

A	B	C	D	E	F	G	H	I	J
Micro Tests									
testLoadInstVar									
4.47	3.72	0.28	5.85	27.6	3.85	23.41	10.62	5.89	10.02
testLoadTempNRef									
4.37	3.07	0.28	5.97	26.2	2.78	23.3	10.62	5.92	9.71
testLoadTempRef									
6.42	4.53	0.4	5.85	31.16	2.78	26.7	13.89	7.53	11.1
testLoadQuickConstant									
7.31	5.14	0.5	11.7	46.19	5.37	38.58	19.65	11.89	17.9
testLoadLiteralNRef									
4.46	3.11	0.28	6.03	25.51	2.88	19.22	10.62	6.02	10.9
testLoadLiteralIndirect									
7.33	5.06	0.49	6.6	29.0	3.92	24.49	15.41	8.13	11.9
testPopStoreInstVar									
3.12	2.81	0.18	6.75	27.68	5.62	20.63	7.98	10.49	6.95
testPopStoreTemp									
3.58	2.51	0.18	4.67	27.69	2.48	22.87	7.99	9.79	8.22
test3plus4									
3.48	2.42	0.16	7.43	24.56	3.1	25.97	8.7	10.52	8.04
test3lessThan4									
3.47	2.41	0.18	7.33	24.84	3.25	26.36	9.34	10.12	12.8
test3times4									
6.58	4.59	0.4	8.38	25.43	3.98	28.83	10.22	7.41	10.8
test3div4									
4.22	3.08	0.57	1.25	2.67	0.48	3.45	1.29	0.75	1.43
test16bitArith									
5.55	5.57	0.65	0.88	11.75	2.07	405.6	133.45	0.59	135.7
testLargeIntArith									
6.38	0.65	0.08	0.08	1.17	0.27	43.1	14.31	0.06	14.3
testActivationReturn									
11.07	7.39	1.01	16.2	55.38	8.68	73.41	26.38	16.84	21.5

	A	B	C	D	E	F	G	H	I	J
Table 9.1 (*Cont.*)										
testShortBranch										
	2.04	1.43	0.12	6.65	21.6	2.63	13.82	7.35	6.14	6.74
testWhileLoop										
	7.04	4.92	0.44	16.3	57.43	7.33	64.95	18.77	12.45	21.4
testArrayAt										
	2.48	1.7	0.19	4.03	30.71	1.65	13.74	5.73	2.51	5.85
testArrayAtPut										
	2.93	2.02	0.22	4.63	32.12	2.13	16.1	6.71	3.08	6.94
testStringAt										
	2.45	1.69	0.19	4.0	11.91	1.6	14.63	5.61	2.65	4.72
testStringAtPut										
	3.16	2.2	0.23	4.92	14.44	1.92	16.95	6.23	2.8	5.01
testSize										
	1.79	1.23	0.15	3.03	8.52	1.45	11.14	4.76	2.15	4.59
testPointCreation										
	1.66	1.17	0.37	1.67	5.52	1.4	6.29	4.3	1.28	3.37
testStreamNext										
	10.15	7.17	0.91	4.97	15.67	6.5	21.98	7.2	4.01	8.18
testStreamNextPut										
	12.32	8.77	1.05	5.88	28.71	7.58	26.26	9.33	5.18	9.84
testEQ										
	5.71	3.93	0.37	6.75	28.76	3.15	29.51	13.71	7.13	12.2
testClass										
	1.62	1.11	0.13	0.9	4.79	0.5	3.95	2.23	1.05	1.56
testBlockCopy										
	15.59	10.8	0.53	13.7	22.54	4.18	20.85	16.57	13.09	11.2
testValue										
	4.25	2.81	0.25	4.08	23.81	3.4	28.51	8.85	6.91	8.21
testCreation										
	4.03	2.78	0.35	6.65	32.58	3.82	16.37	11.04	4.13	7.33
testPointX										
	4.84	3.38	0.35	11.78	35.93	5.03	35.43	17.49	12.24	13.2
testLoadThisContext										
	6.04	4.19	0.4	5.9	29.76	3.05	33.72	14.21	5.36	10.6
testBasicAt										
	2.31	1.58	0.19	3.32	19.96	1.62	11.24	5.76	2.65	6.46
testBasicAtPut										
	2.79	1.91	0.22	3.85	31.89	2.15	13.91	6.44	2.76	6.63
testPerform										
	2.02	1.39	0.3	6.12	29.5	2.25	18.24	7.43	31.28	7.0

Table 9.1 (*Cont.*)

A	B	C	D	E	F	G	H	I	J
testStringReplace									
0.88	0.61	1.06	0.17	2.24	0.183	0.62	0.38	19.38	0.23
testAsFloat									
2.4	1.68	0.26	0.62	25.13	1.12	1.47	1.44	0.26	0.71
testFloatingPointAddition									
2.81	1.96	0.25	0.73	18.86	0.88	2.57	1.63	0.38	1.04
testBitBLT									
2.32	1.65	0.4	209.05	33.69	25.83	194.87	5.24	21.73	57.4
testTextScanning									
1.65	1.16	0.32	21.78	3.44	4.0	7.17	1.01	2.2	2.29

Macro Tests

A	B	C	D	E	F	G	H	I	J
testClassOrganizer									
12.3	8.51	1.25	16.03	80.79	8.58	65.02	24.53	16.82	27.4
testPrintDefinition									
8.49	5.58	0.84	10.43	47.37	6.0	48.21	15.61	11.66	15.9
testPrintHierarchy									
8.28	5.75	1.0	9.82	44.44	5.87	37.69	14.39	12.05	15.5
testAllCallsOn									
19.06	13.2	1.57	24.38	92.45	10.73	102.72	33.95	21.41	34.2
testAllImplementors									
6.13	4.3	0.61	7.95	34.33	4.22	36.11	12.33	8.55	12.7
testInspect									
15.55	10.6	1.83	19.08	69.23	10.65	91.81	30.09	19.32	26.6
testCompiler									
19.9	13.7	2.17	27.25	134.09	15.15	127.42	50.54	27.11	58.2
testDecompiler									
12.29	8.45	1.34	17.38	68.5	9.8	73.53	24.21	17.4	25.5
testKeyboardLookAhead									
3.37	2.34	0.49	23.08	13.07	3.7	25.13	5.28	4.85	8.99
testKeyboardSingle									
10.12	7.0	1.47	116.12	43.92	10.95	76.58	18.55	16.27	42.1
testTextDisplay									
9.28	6.5	1.2	41.43	32.8	12.92	47.44	11.95	13.88	23.8
testTextFormatting									
8.64	6.02	1.11	9.0	35.29	4.87	83.81	18.53	10.57	11.2
testTextEditing									
24.83	17.3	4.07	135.2	95.23	28.03	186.39	37.1	37.03	60.3

Table 9.2 The Benchmarks Normalized to the Average

	A	B	C	D	E	F	G	H	I	J
Micro Tests										
testLoadInstVar										
	0.772	0.642	0.0483	1.01	4.77	0.665	4.04	1.83	1.02	1.73
testLoadTempNRef										
	0.801	0.563	0.0514	1.09	4.8	0.51	4.27	1.95	1.09	1.78
testLoadTempRef										
	0.958	0.676	0.0597	0.873	4.65	0.415	3.98	2.07	1.12	1.66
testLoadQuickConstant										
	0.74	0.521	0.0506	1.19	4.68	0.544	3.91	1.99	1.2	1.81
testLoadLiteralNRef										
	0.819	0.571	0.0514	1.11	4.68	0.529	3.53	1.95	1.1	2.0
testLoadLiteralIndirect										
	0.989	0.683	0.0661	0.891	3.91	0.529	3.31	2.08	1.1	1.61
testPopStoreInstVar										
	0.581	0.523	0.0335	1.26	5.16	1.05	3.84	1.49	1.95	1.29
testPopStoreTemp										
	0.734	0.515	0.0369	0.957	5.68	0.508	4.69	1.64	2.01	1.69
test3plus4										
	0.669	0.465	0.0307	1.43	4.72	0.596	4.99	1.67	2.02	1.54
test3lessThan4										
	0.624	0.433	0.0324	1.32	4.46	0.584	4.74	1.68	1.82	2.3
test3times4										
	0.955	0.666	0.058	1.22	3.69	0.578	4.18	1.48	1.08	1.57
test3div4										
	2.82	2.06	0.381	0.835	1.78	0.321	2.3	0.862	0.501	0.955
test16bitArith										
	0.657	0.659	0.0769	0.104	1.39	0.245	48.0	15.8	0.0698	16.1
testLargeIntArith										
	5.5	0.56	0.0689	0.0689	1.01	0.233	37.1	12.3	0.0517	12.3
testActivationReturn										
	0.756	0.505	0.069	1.11	3.78	0.593	5.02	1.8	1.15	1.47
testShortBranch										
	0.543	0.381	0.032	1.77	5.75	0.701	3.68	1.96	1.64	1.8
testWhileLoop										
	0.623	0.435	0.0389	1.44	5.08	0.649	5.75	1.66	1.1	1.89
testArrayAt										
	0.736	0.504	0.0564	1.2	9.11	0.49	4.08	1.7	0.745	1.74
testArrayAtPut										
	0.74	0.51	0.0555	1.17	8.11	0.538	4.06	1.69	0.777	1.75
testStringAt										
	0.813	0.561	0.0631	1.33	3.95	0.531	4.86	1.86	0.88	1.57

Table 9.2 (*Cont.*)

A	B	C	D	E	F	G	H	I	J
testStringAtPut									
0.889	0.619	0.0647	1.38	4.06	0.54	4.77	1.75	0.787	1.41
testSize									
0.744	0.511	0.0624	1.26	3.54	0.603	4.63	1.98	0.894	1.91
testPointCreation									
0.825	0.582	0.184	0.83	2.74	0.696	3.13	2.14	0.636	1.68
testStreamNext									
1.52	1.08	0.136	0.745	2.35	0.975	3.3	1.08	0.601	1.23
testStreamNextPut									
1.46	1.04	0.125	0.697	3.41	0.899	3.11	1.11	0.614	1.17
testEQ									
0.854	0.588	0.0553	1.01	4.3	0.471	4.41	2.05	1.07	1.82
testClass									
1.33	0.91	0.107	0.738	3.93	0.41	3.24	1.83	0.861	1.28
testBlockCopy									
1.65	1.14	0.0559	1.45	2.38	0.441	2.2	1.75	1.38	1.18
testValue									
0.819	0.542	0.0482	0.786	4.59	0.655	5.5	1.71	1.33	1.58
testCreation									
0.759	0.524	0.0659	1.25	6.14	0.72	3.08	2.08	0.778	1.38
testPointX									
0.597	0.417	0.0432	1.45	4.43	0.621	4.37	2.16	1.51	1.63
testLoadThisContext									
0.921	0.639	0.061	0.899	4.54	0.465	5.14	2.17	0.817	1.62
testBasicAt									
0.745	0.509	0.0612	1.07	6.43	0.522	3.62	1.86	0.854	2.08
testBasicAtPut									
0.75	0.513	0.0591	1.03	8.57	0.578	3.74	1.73	0.742	1.78
testPerform									
0.402	0.277	0.0598	1.22	5.88	0.448	3.63	1.48	6.23	1.39
testStringReplace									
1.21	0.838	1.46	0.234	3.08	0.251	0.852	0.522	26.6	0.316
testAsFloat									
1.97	1.38	0.214	0.509	20.6	0.92	1.21	1.18	0.214	0.583
testFloatingPointAddition									
2.02	1.41	0.179	0.524	13.5	0.631	1.84	1.17	0.273	0.746
testBitBLT									
0.162	0.115	0.028	14.6	2.36	1.81	13.6	0.367	1.52	4.02
testTextScanning									
0.684	0.481	0.133	9.03	1.43	1.66	2.97	0.419	0.912	0.949

					Table 9.2 (*Cont.*)					
A	*B*	*C*	*D*	*E*	*F*	*G*	*H*	*I*	*J*

Macro Tests

testClassOrganizer

0.771	0.533	0.0783	1.0	5.06	0.538	4.08	1.54	1.05	1.72

testPrintDefinition

| 0.808 | 0.531 | 0.0799 | 0.992 | 4.51 | 0.571 | 4.59 | 1.49 | 1.11 | 1.51 |

testPrintHierarchy

| 0.811 | 0.563 | 0.0979 | 0.961 | 4.35 | 0.575 | 3.69 | 1.41 | 1.18 | 1.52 |

testAllCallsOn

| 0.874 | 0.605 | 0.072 | 1.12 | 4.24 | 0.492 | 4.71 | 1.56 | 0.981 | 1.57 |

testAllImplementors

| 0.78 | 0.547 | 0.0776 | 1.01 | 4.37 | 0.537 | 4.6 | 1.57 | 1.09 | 1.62 |

testInspect

| 0.82 | 0.559 | 0.0965 | 1.01 | 3.65 | 0.562 | 4.84 | 1.59 | 1.02 | 1.4 |

testCompiler

| 0.702 | 0.484 | 0.0766 | 0.962 | 4.73 | 0.535 | 4.5 | 1.78 | 0.957 | 2.05 |

testDecompiler

| 0.756 | 0.52 | 0.0825 | 1.07 | 4.22 | 0.603 | 4.53 | 1.49 | 1.07 | 1.57 |

testKeyboardLookAhead

| 0.614 | 0.426 | 0.0892 | 4.2 | 2.38 | 0.674 | 4.58 | 0.961 | 0.883 | 1.64 |

testKeyboardSingle

| 0.537 | 0.371 | 0.078 | 6.16 | 2.33 | 0.581 | 4.06 | 0.984 | 0.863 | 2.23 |

testTextDisplay

| 0.676 | 0.473 | 0.0874 | 3.02 | 2.39 | 0.941 | 3.46 | 0.87 | 1.01 | 1.73 |

testTextFormatting

| 0.822 | 0.573 | 0.106 | 0.856 | 3.36 | 0.463 | 7.98 | 1.76 | 1.01 | 1.07 |

testTextEditing

| 0.625 | 0.436 | 0.103 | 3.4 | 2.4 | 0.706 | 4.69 | 0.934 | 0.933 | 1.52 |

Here is a brief description of each implementation, with references to the related chapters in this book.

A. Xerox (see Chapter 7). Implementation written in microcode and machine code running on a 40Mhz Xerox Dolphin.

B. Xerox (see Chapter 7). Implementation written in microcode and machine code running on a 44.5Mhz Xerox Dolphin with special display alignment.

C. Xerox (see Chapter 7). Implementation written in microcode and machine code running on a Xerox Dorado.

D. U.C. Berkeley (see Chapter 11). Implementation written in C running on a DEC VAX-11/780, under 4.1BSD UNIX. Uses AED-512 over a RS-232 link for the display. Uses 32-bit Oops.

E. Tektronix (see Chapter 5). Implementation written in Pascal and assembly language running on an 8Mhz MC68000.

F. Tektronix (see Chapter 4). Implementation written in assembly language running on a 10Mhz MC68000.

G. Hewlett-Packard (see Chapter 6). Implementation written in high-level language (C) running on a DEC VAX-11/780 with 4 megabyte main memory running 4.1BSD UNIX. Portable among UNIX systems. "By the book" implementation; limited optimization. 16-bit and LargeInteger arithmetic performed with Smalltalk-80 code (no primitives); Float arithmetic using VAX format (not IEEE); some additional class and argument checking in primitives; standard reference-count management with 8-bit counts (contexts are reference counted); recursive marking garbage collector.

H. Apple (see Chapter 10). Implementation written in assembly language running on a 5Mhz MC68000. Synchronization of CPU memory accesses and display memory accesses reduces the effective processor speed to about 4.5Mhz.

I. Digital Equipment Corp. (see Chapter 8). Implementation written in assembly language, running on a DEC VAX-11/780 with 4 megabyte main memory, under VMS. SmallInteger and Float primitives implemented; LargeInteger primitives not implemented. All primitives do class and argument checking. Incremental compacting garbage collector.

J. Digital Equipment Corp. (see Chapter 8). Implementation written in Bliss-32, running on a DEC VAX-11/780 with 4 megabyte main memory, under VMS. "By the book" implementation using reference counting; moderately optimized. All arithmetic primitives implemented. All primitives do class and argument checking.

One can see from the above data that some micro-benchmarks matter very little to overall performance. Performance on the division and LargeInteger benchmarks for example, does not seem to be a very good predictor of overall performance. As might be expected, performance on the String replace benchmark correlates strongly with performance on the text editing macro-benchmark, but not for example, with compiler performance.

Another observation is that performance on the micro-benchmarks varies much more widely than performance on the macro-benchmarks. While this was to be expected, since the macro-benchmarks test performance over a much broader range of activities than do the micro-benchmarks (thus smoothing out peaks and valleys), I was surprised at the magnitude of this difference between the smoothness of the macro-benchmarks and the variations among the micro-benchmarks. (For the Dolphin implementation, the standard deviation for the micro-benchmark results is 0.86 while the standard deviation for the macro-benchmarks is only 0.087.) This leads me to the hypothesis that, for any reasonably efficient interpreter, virtually all macro-level performance is determined by a very few micro-level factors. This hypothesis is supported by the observation that while the Dorado performance on most of the micro-benchmarks is on the order of 15-20 times as fast as the Dolphin, performance on the macro-benchmarks is only approximately 10 times as fast. This appears to be due primarily to the relative speeds of activation and return in the two implementations. The activation/return benchmark correlates much more strongly with macro-level performance than do most other micro-benchmarks. So it appears that general system behavior is most strongly influenced by the speed of method activation and return. (This may be less true of machines with special stack hardware or other special hardware that would affect Smalltalk-80 bytecode performance in a non-uniform way.)

From an analytic point of view, this hypothesis, that (within reasonable bounds) overall system performance is most strongly determined by the speed of method activation and return, can be supported by two other general facts: method activation and return are by far the most expensive atomic operations the interpreter must perform; and a fairly high proportion of the byte codes encountered by a running interpreter cause activation or return. Of course, neither of these "facts" is universally true. The String replacement and BitBlt primitives can be much more expensive than an activation, so code that is very rich in these, such as text editing, can be expected to perform more like the relevant micro-benchmarks. Also, highly optimized code (such as that invoked by Smalltalk allCallsOn:) will "open code" important message calls rather than incurring the activation and return overhead and can therefore be expected to perform closer to the level predicted by the other benchmarks.

Exceptions to the general rule that macro-behavior is best predicted by the testActivationReturn benchmark are illustrated by the performance of implementation D on the testTextEditing and testKeyboardSingle macro-benchmarks. Most of D's normalized micro-benchmark scores fall in the range 0.8 to 1.6, but the scores for the display-intensive micro-benchmarks testBitBLT and testTextScanning are much worse. The display configuration that D uses is much slower than other implemenations and accounts for these low scores. While performance on most macro-benchmarks is very near 1.0, as predicted by the majority of the micro-benchmarks, the scores for testTextEditing and testKeyboardSingle are much worse (3.4 and 6.16) due to the fact that these are display-intensive macro-benchmarks. It is also worth noting that these particular macro-benchmarks seem to correlate strongly with user satisfaction. While D appears to be computationally acceptable in other respects, its users are generally not satisfied with its responsiveness.

Concluding Summary

Discoveries and warnings have been sprinkled throughout this paper; here is my chance to put them in one place.

Many of the micro-benchmarks contain operations that I had not meant to test, but that I included simply to satisfy the demands of the compiler or stack management discipline. These operations, although fairly fast, may be slower than the operations being tested and this may distort somewhat the meaningfulness of these benchmarks.

In writing your own benchmarks, you must be very careful to make sure that the operations you are trying to time are not swamped by other computation. For micro-benchmarks, it is good to look at the compiled code to see whether you have created the test you thought you had.

Most of the micro-benchmarks are not very good predictors of overall system performance. The speed of certain specialized applications may correlate well with some specific micro-benchmarks, such as BitBlt or String replacement, but it appears from our data that the efficiency of activation and return is the overriding determinant of system performance.

Finally, let me stress again that the data I presented in the analysis section represent early or interim results, designed for very different purposes, written in different level languages, and running on vastly different hardware. None of these are final, and none indicate the expected performance of any future systems. We thank the implementors for their courage in allowing us to publish such preliminary measurements.

10

An MC68000-Based Smalltalk-80 System

Richard Meyers
David Casseres
Apple Computer Inc.
Cupertino, California

Introduction

This paper describes some preliminary results of an MC68000-based implementation of the Smalltalk-80 system. The implementation was conducted as a research project by Apple Computer Inc. Our purpose in presenting this data is to provide to other implementors some of the information we wish we had known when we first set out to implement Smalltalk.

History

Apple Computer began its Smalltalk-80 research project in early October 1980. The project has been staffed by one engineer (Rick Meyers) and, for about half of the last 18 months, by a technical writer (David Casseres). Apple has consistently viewed Smalltalk as a research effort, and has afforded the project the freedom from schedules and from marketing considerations that allows research efforts to thrive.

Our Smalltalk-80 implementation has been running since April 1981 on a series of experimental Motorola MC68000-based computer systems. The Smalltalk-80 virtual machine described in this paper is a straightforward translation of the Xerox virtual machine specification to 68000 assembly language. The bytecode interpreter, object memory system, and primitive routines were written slowly and carefully by a single engineer. Other engineers contributed the BitBlt (screen display), text scanning (textual display), and floating-point arithmetic routines. To date, only about three weeks of effort have been devoted specifically to optimizing the virtual machine, and the only major optimization is the message lookup cache described later in the paper.

This paper reports on work in progress. The measurements reported were first made in June 1981 and were repeated in June and July 1982.

Memory Layout

The measurements were made on a Smalltalk-80 system configured to use about 793K bytes of memory. Estimates of the sizes of major system components are shown in Table 10.1. The virtual machine size includes BitBlt, text scanning, and the floating-point routines. The data does not include the program development system used to host Smalltalk, the file system and the device drivers, the system debugger, or the data areas used by program analysis tools.

Table 10.1 Memory Layout

Area	Bytes
virtual machine data	4K
virtual machine code	21K
display memory	32K
object table (24K objects)	96K
15K system-supplied objects (60K)	
9K user objects (36K)	
heap storage (10 heaps, 64K/heap)	640K
system supplied objects (407K)	
user objects (233K)	
Total	**793K**

Virtual Machine Structure and Size

At the time of this writing, our Smalltalk-80 virtual machine consists of 21,088 bytes of Motorola 68000 assembly-language code. The major system components have the following functions:

- Initialization and Utilities: Global initialization, memory image input, I/O operations, utilities

- Fetch Loop: Bytecode fetch and dispatch

- Bytecode and Primitive Tables: Addresses of bytecode and primitive routines

- Bytecode Interpreter: Bytecode interpretation, except the major activities such as send, return, and memory allocation

- Send/Return: Send and superclass send, primitive dispatch, context switch, argument transfer and return

- Multiprocessing: Process switch, semaphores, keyboard and time events

- Memory Management: Memory allocation, reference counting, heap compaction, and garbage collection

- Primitives: All primitives except for floating-point package, BitBlt and text scanning

- BitBlt: Class BitBlt, method copyBits

- Text Scanning: Class TextScanner, method scanCharactersFrom:to:-last:in:rightX:stopConditions:displaying:

- Analysis: Reference-count validation, statistics gathering and reporting

Table 10.2 shows a breakdown of the virtual machine into its major components. The file system and device drivers are excluded from these measurements. The table also indicates time spent in each component of the virtual machine.

Table 10.2 Virtual Machine Structure and Size

Function	Bytes	Size	% Time
initialization & utilities	2,274	10.8%	1.9%
fetch loop	18	0.1%	10.2%
bytecode & primitive tables	802	3.8%	--
bytecode interpreter	1,476	7.0%	16.0%
send & return	1,132	5.4%	39.2%
multiprocessing	1,338	6.3%	--
memory management	1,650	7.8%	22.6%
primitives (except those below)	5,128	24.3%	8.8%
floating-point	3,162	15.0%	0.0%
BitBlt	1,956	9.3%	0.5%
text scanning	1,258	6.0%	0.7%
analysis	894	4.2%	--

Virtual Machine Code Utilization

A sampling technique was used to measure the approximate percentage of the total time spent executing each instruction of the virtual machine. The virtual machine program counter was sampled every 10 milliseconds to construct a histogram of relative utilization for each possible program counter value. It should be noted that this technique fails to measure periodic activities which are based on interrupts, such as multiprocessing activity.

The Smalltalk-80 memory image supplied by Xerox Palo Alto Research Center contained a set of 35 benchmarks, included as methods in class Benchmark. The benchmarks test a number of individual bytecodes, common primitive operations, and several "macro" operations such as compilation and text formatting. The results of running Benchmark testStandardTests are reported in Chapter 9. The results reported in this section were gathered during execution of the Benchmark "macro" operations

> **Benchmark new testCompiler**
> **Benchmark new testDecompiler**
> **Benchmark new testInspect**
> **Benchmark new testTextEditing**
> **Benchmark new testTextFormatting**

Each of these tests was run five times in a period of just over 28 minutes; 170,922 samples were taken, one every 10 milliseconds. The time spent in each of the major system components is summarized in Table 10.2 above and in Fig. 10.1.

Several sections of the virtual machine deserve special attention. The bytecode fetch and dispatch, which usually requires five instructions, accounts for 10.2% of the total execution time. The relatively small (1132 bytes, 5.4% of total) send/return component of the system accounts for 39.2% of the execution time. Prior to implementation of a method lookup cache, this percentage was 52.5%.

The countDownOthers routine, which recursively decrements the reference counts for the fields of deallocated objects, requires 11.8% of the execution time. This fact, and the time spent in countDown, suggests that implementation strategies which avoid reference counting of contexts may yield substantial performance improvements.

Overall patterns of utilization indicate the value of *time* optimization for send/return and the memory management functions, and *space* optimization for most of the primitive operations, especially the floating-point routines. Fig. 10.1 shows the space and time used by each major system component.

Space Occupied by Code Time Spent in Code

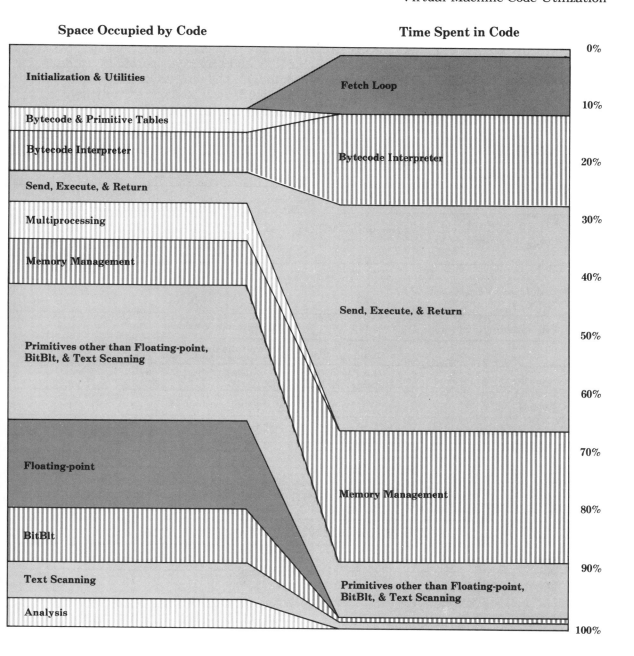

Figure 10.1

Bytecode and Primitive Frequencies

The Smalltalk-80 virtual machine implements 256 individual bytecodes (instructions) and approximately 100 primitive operations. In designing and optimizing an implementation, it is vital to know which bytecodes and primitives occur most frequently, and which are rarely used.

	0	1	2	3	4	5	6	7	8	9	A	B	C	D	E	F
0	Push Instance Variable (0 to F)															
1	Push Temporary Variable (0 to F)															
2	Push Literal Constant (0 to 1F)															
3																
4	Push Literal Variable (0 to 1F)															
5																
6	Pop Instance Variable (0 to 7)								Pop Temporary Variable (0 to 7)							
7	Push self	true	false	nil	−1	0	1	2	return from message self	true	false	nil	ret. msg.	TOS block		
8	Push	store	pop	send	send	send super	send super	pop stack	dup. TOS	push c'txt						
9	Jump (1 to 8)								Jump on False (1 to 8)							
A	Jump (iii−4)*256+jjjjjjjj								Jump on True ii*256+jjjjjjjj				Jump on False ii*256+jjjjjjjj			
B	+	−	<	>	<=	>=	=	~=	*	/	\\	@	bit Shift:	//	bit And:	bit Or:
C	Send Special Selector						==	class	block Copy:	value	value:	Send Special Selector				
D	Send Literal Selector (0 to F) with No Arguments															
E	Send Literal Selector (0 to F) with 1 Argument															
F	Send Literal Selector (0 to F) with 2 Arguments															

Notes:

To look up a hex bytecode, find the high-order digit on the left and low-order digit at the top.

☐ indicates a bytecode that is followed by one extension byte.

◩ indicates a bytecode that is followed by two extension bytes.

▦ indicates a bytecode that is not used.

Figure 10.2

Our implementation was instrumented to tally every bytecode and primitive executed. This instrumentation imposed a time overhead of about 22%, low enough to allow execution of reasonably large methods during analysis.

Bytecode and primitive frequencies are both directly dependent on the methods being executed while data is collected. Two separate measurements are reported here. In the first test we ran each of the Benchmark "macro" operations, listed above. Measurements continued through both the data collection and data reporting phases of the benchmarks. The second test consisted of browsing as rapidly as possible for about two minutes; it demonstrates the degree of variation involved.

Figure 10.2 is a bytecode summary matrix to aid in the interpretation of the bytecode frequency data.

Table 10.3 lists the percentage of total bytecodes executed in each major bytecode category, while executing the "macro" operations. A total of 3,750,200 bytecodes were executed while collecting this data.

Table 10.3 Bytecode Frequencies by Category in Benchmark Macro Tests

Hex Code	Operation	Percentage
00-0F	push instance variable	7.3%
10-1F	push temporary variable	19.1%
20-3F	push literal constant	2.3%
40-5F	push literal variable	1.1%
50-67	pop instance variable	1.9%
68-6F	pop temporary variable	3.9%
70-77	push self, true, false, nil, -1, 0, 1, 2	14.4%
78-7B	return from message self, true, false, nil	1.8%
7C-7D	return TOS from message/block	4.7%
80	extended push	1.3%
81	extended store	1.4%
82	extended pop	0.9%
83	extended send	0.6%
84	double extended send	0.0%
85	superclass send	0.2%
86	double extended superclass send	0.0%
87	pop stack	3.7%
88	duplicate TOS	0.1%
89	push context	0.3%
90-97	jump (1-8)	0.2%

Table 10.3 (*Cont.*)

Hex Code	Operation	Percentage
98-9F	jump on false (1-8)	4.8%
A0-A7	jump (iii-4)*256+jjjjjjjj	2.1%
A8-AB	jump on true ii*256+jjjjjjjj	0.0%
AC-AF	jump on false ii*256+jjjjjjjj	2.2%
B0-BF	send +, −, <, >, <=, >=, =, ~=, *, /, \\, @, bitShift:, //, bitAnd:, bitOr:	11.2%
C0-CF	send special selector, ==, class, blockCopy:, value, value:	7.1%
D0-DF	send literal selector with no arguments	3.4%
E0-EF	send literal selector with 1 argument	2.5%
F0-FF	send literal selector with 2 arguments	1.4%

In both of the tests, 18 of the 256 bytecodes accounted for over half of the bytecodes executed, as shown in Tables 10.4 and 10.5. Simple push operations (push self, push temporary variable, push 0, push 1) top both lists and account for over 30% of all bytecodes executed.

Table 10.4 Most Frequent Bytecodes in Benchmark Macro Tests

Hex Code	Operation	Percentage
70	push self	6.7%
10	push temporary variable 0	6.1%
11	push temporary variable 1	4.6%
12	push temporary variable 2	4.5%
76	push 1	4.4%
7C	return TOS from message	3.9%
87	pop stack top	3.7%
B0	send +	3.7%
01	push instance variable 1	2.4%
AC	jump on false (range 0 to 256)	2.2%
C0	send special selector 0	2.0%
B6	send =	1.9%
B1	send −	1.7%
A3	jump (range −256 to −1)	1.7%
B4	send <=	1.5%
75	push 0	1.4%
81	extended store	1.4%
78	return self	1.4%
	Total	**55.2%**

Table 10.5 Most Frequent Bytecodes in Browsing Test

Hex Code	Operation	Percentage
10	push temporary variable 0	6.9%
70	push self	5.4%
7C	return TOS from message	5.4%
11	push temporary variable 1	4.9%
12	push temporary variable 2	3.3%
B0	send +	3.3%
76	push 1	2.9%
00	push instance variable 0	2.4%
01	push instance variable 1	2.4%
87	pop stack top	2.3%
B1	send −	2.2%
D0	send literal selector 0 (no arguments)	2.1%
80	extended push	1.9%
C0	send special selector 0	1.8%
78	return self	1.6%
75	push 0	1.5%
AC	jump on false (range 0 to 256)	1.5%
82	extended pop and store	1.5%
Total		**53.3%**

Primitive executions were tallied during execution of the Benchmark "macro" operations. Primitive executions resulting from "send special selector" bytecodes and those resulting from normal send operations are included in the tally. Primitive failures are also included. The 20 most frequent primitives are listed in Table 10.6. The top five primitives account for over 50% of all primitive executions, and the top 20 account for almost 95%. As expected, all of the most common primitives are invoked directly from "send special selector" bytecodes.

Table 10.6 Most Frequent Primitives in Benchmark Macro Tests

Decimal #	Class	Method	Count	Percentage
1	SmallInteger	+	138,803	18.2%
7	SmallInteger	=	73,339	9.7%
60	Object	at:	72,429	9.5%
2	SmallInteger	−	65,399	8.5%
5	SmallInteger	<=	58,746	7.7%
110	Object	==	48,784	6.4%

Table 10.6 (*Cont.*)

Decimal #	Class	Method	Count	Percentage
61	Object	at:put:	38,657	5.0%
62	Object	size	36,075	4.7%
81	BlockContext	value/value:	35,092	4.6%
4	SmallInteger	>	34,170	4.4%
63	String	at:	27,256	3.3%
66	ReadStream	next	25,259	3.3%
6	SmallInteger	> =	13,010	1.7%
3	SmallInteger	<	11,724	1.5%
80	ContextPart	blockCopy:	9,894	1.3%
70	Behavior	new	8,695	1.1%
111	Object	class	8,402	1.1%
71	Behavior	new:	7,781	1.0%
11	SmallInteger	\\	6,039	0.7%
12	SmallInteger	//	5,594	0.7%
	Total			**94.4%**

Send Characteristics

Message sends play a key role conceptually in the Smalltalk-80 language, and have a major impact on the performance of Smalltalk-80 implementations. Three categories of bytecodes initiate send operations:

- Integer and common primitive bytecodes
- Special selector bytecodes
- Send and superclass-send bytecodes.

The final action taken as the result of a send can be any of the following:

- Primitive return of self
- Primitive return of an instance variable
- Successful execution of a primitive
- Activation of a CompiledMethod.

Sends involving primitives can either succeed or fail (usually because of improper argument classes). Our interpreter was modified to tally the various attributes of sends. The data in Table 10.7 was collected while executing the Benchmark "macro" operations.

Table 10.7 Analysis of Send Characteristics

Bytecode Initiating Send	Counts	Percent
Integer & common primitive bytecodes	515,099	51.9%
Special selector bytecodes	173,164	17.4%
Send and superclass-send bytecodes	305,065	30.7%
Final Action Taken		
Primitive return of self	1,673	0.2%
Primitive return of an instance variable	40,585	4.1%
Successful execution of a primitive	733,779	73.9%
Activation of a CompiledMethod	217,291	21.9%
Primitives		
Primitive successes	733,779	96.8%
Primitive failures	23,969	3.2%

Number of Arguments

In optimizing the activation code within the virtual machine, it may be helpful to know the distribution of the number of arguments passed by sends. The virtual machine was instrumented to construct the histogram shown in Fig. 10.3. Only sends resulting in activation of a CompiledMethod were considered. The data below is for the Benchmark "macro" operations. Zero-argument and one-argument sends occur with nearly equal frequency, and account for over 80% of all reported messages.

Arguments	Sends
0	96,130
1	79,858
2	23,823
3	10,518
4	4,455
5	308
6	1,462
7	72
8	270

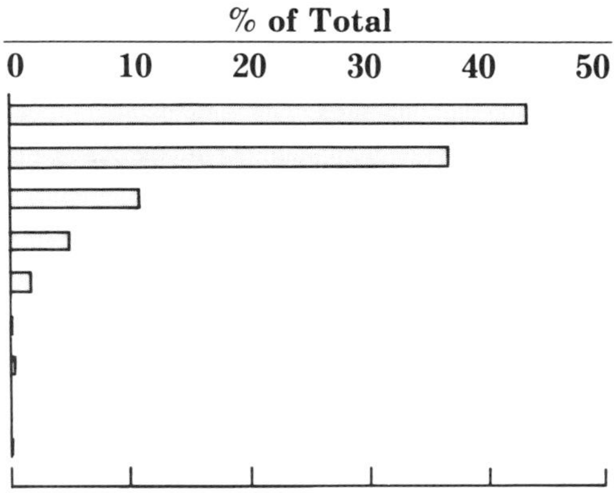

Figure 10.3

Message Lookup Chaining

The message lookup routines begin their search in the class of the receiver. If the message being sent is not in this class, the search continues up the superclass chain until an inherited message is found. Our interpreter was modified to gather statistics on the depth of search required. The method lookup cache was not in use when these statistics were collected. The data in Fig. 10.4 was gathered while executing the "macro" operations in class Benchmark.

About half of all sends are to methods defined in the class of the receiver, requiring 0 depth of search. Searches of depth 1, 2, 3, and 4 occur with roughly equal frequencies of about 7.5% to 15%. Relatively few messages require a search of depth 5 or more, but one search of depth 9 did occur.

Depth	Sends	% of Total
0	242,792	
1	56,771	
2	38,024	
3	75,968	
4	64,234	
5	12,455	
6	4,404	
7	7,892	
8	20	
9	1	

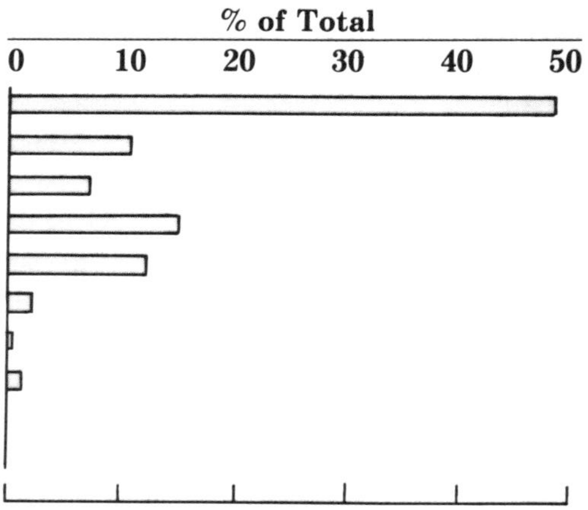

Figure 10.4

Performance Measurements

Performance measurements are included here to allow comparisons with other Smalltalk-80 implementations. These measurements were made on a single-user Motorola MC68000-based system with the system clock running at 5 MHz. (A 4-byte register-to-register add takes 1.6 microseconds. A 4-byte move from an absolute memory location to a register takes 3.2 microseconds. CPU memory accesses and display memory accesses are synchronized, slowing the CPU by 10-15%). The measurements are a snapshot of work in progress as of July 1982. The only major optimization in use was a 256-entry message lookup cache. The uninterpreted results of running Benchmark testStandardTests are reported in Chapter 9.

A traditional test of system performance is the number of bytecodes per second the system can execute. Bytecodes vary tremendously in complexity, from simple operations such as pushing a literal zero on the stack or branching to another bytecode to very complex primitive operations such as floating-point divide, string-to-string copy, or BitBlt operations. Therefore, bytecode-per-second measurements are extremely dependent on the methods being executed. We had no trouble collecting measurements ranging from 5000 to about 30,000 bytecodes per second.

Our analysis was done by modifying the virtual machine to count the actual number of bytecodes executed. This introduced an overhead of about 5%, which is compensated for in the final column of Table 10.8. Class Benchmark, method test:labeled:repeated: was also modified to allow collection of the bytecode counts. We have chosen to report data collected for each of the "macro" operations in class Benchmark. Measurements reported are the average of three trials. The message lookup cache was in use when these measurements were taken.

Table 10.8 Bytecodes/Second for Benchmark Macro Tests

Activity	Counts	ms Elapsed	Bytecodes/sec	+5%
compile dummy method	550,061	49,440	11,126	11,682
decompile Form & Class	2,391,154	203,440	11,753	12,341
create an Inspector	33,959	3,430	9,901	10,396
format a bunch of text	258,750	20,880	12,396	13,012
replace & redisplay test	350,985	38,580	9,098	9,552

Acknowledgments

The authors wish to thank the management of Apple Computer, and especially John Couch, Wayne Rosing, Nellie Connors, and Ron Johnston for providing the equipment, the environment and the freedom needed to implement the Smalltalk-80 system successfully on the MC68000. Thanks also go to Bill Atkinson and David Hough, who helped with the engineering effort.

11

Berkeley Smalltalk: Who Knows Where the Time Goes?

David M. Ungar
David A. Patterson
Computer Science Division
Department of Electrical Engineering
and Computer Sciences
University of California, Berkeley

Abstract

Sad deserted shore,
Your fickle friends are leaving.
Ah but then you know
It's time for them to go.
But I will still be here
I have no thought of leaving.
I do not count the time.
Who knows where the time goes?
Who knows where the time goes?
  *"Who Knows Where the Time Goes"**

We have implemented the Smalltalk-80 virtual machine in the C programming language for the Digital Equipment Corp. VAX-11/780 under Berkeley Unix. We call this system Berkeley Smalltalk (BS). An AED-512 terminal connected over a 9600-baud serial link serves as the display device. In four months one person wrote BS in about 9000 lines

---

*[Denny, Sandy, "Who Knows Where the Time Goes?" (BMI) Winckler Music, Judy Collins (BMI), Irving Music, used by permission]

of source code. Other Smalltalk-80 implementations on non-micropro-grammable computers have suffered from poor performance. We believe that a straightforward, literal implementation of the specification cannot achieve acceptable performance. This paper explains how the optimizations in BS have increased performance fourfold.

Introduction

The Smalltalk-80 book[1] includes a clear and intelligible definition of the Smalltalk-80 virtual machine. To learn about the performance consequences of following this definition, we have measured key components of:

1. An interpreter that follows the book exactly; and

2. Berkeley Smalltalk (BS), which meets the specification but does not mimic the definition in the book.

The results of this study are shown in Table 11.1 below. Berkeley Smalltalk is 4.8 times faster than a straight-forward implementation. The rest of this paper details the steps behind this result.

Table 11.1 Summary of All Optimizations
(all times are in microseconds per bytecode)

Activity	By-the-book	BS	By-the-book/BS
reference counting	50 (12%)	9.5 (11%)	5.3
dispatching bytecodes	124 (31%)	10 (12%)	12
BitBlt	0—100 (0—25%)	0—8.3 (0—10%)	12
allocation and freeing	19 (5%)	5.2 (6%)	3.7
OT indirection	29 (7%)	2.4 (3%)	12
method lookup	36 (9%)	3.8 (5%)	9.4
Subtotal	**358 (89%)**	**39 (47%)**	
other activities	44 (11%)	44 (53%)	
Total	**402μs (100%)**	**83μs (100%)**	**4.8**

Methodology

First, we identified the activities or operations that distinguish a Smalltalk-80 system from a conventional non-interpreted language. These include:

- Automatic free space reclamation (realized with reference counts),

- Bytecode decoding,

- Bitmap manipulation (BitBlt)[2],

- Allocating and freeing objects,

- Object table (OT) indirections, and

- Method lookup.

We measured the cost of each activity by writing test programs in C[3] that simply looped and performed the operations as defined by the book. The CPU execution times of these programs were compared with dummy programs that looped without performing the measured operation. Although we never implemented a complete interpreter by-the-book, we coded these key operations with as much ingenuity as those in BS. In this way, we hoped to measure only differences caused by underlying data structures rather than those attributable to clever "hacks" in the code.

Next, we derived a bytecode mix from a profile of a typical interactive session of seven million bytecodes[4]. This mix is shown in Table 11.2 below.

Table 11.2 A Typical Dynamic Bytecode Distribution

Instruction Type	Frequency	Explanation
push	43%	typically instance or temporary variable
full sends	11%	causes context switch
direct arith prims	8%	successful; another 2% fail
short circuit sends	5%	
direct special prims	3%	successful
primitives	3%	0.3% fail
return stack top	9%	assume 1 entry on stack
other returns	2%	assume 1 entry on stack
pop and store	5%	typically instance or temporary variable
pop	2%	
jump conditional	6%	from Baden's measurements[5]
jump unconditional	2%	from Baden's measurements[6]
store	1%	
unaccounted	1%	
Total	**100%**	

The Smalltalk-80 book and the BS source code gave us the types and numbers of key operations for each type of bytecode. Finally, we calculated a weighted average for the mean number of key operations per bytecode.

Multiplying the time per operation by the number of operations per bytecode gave us the time spent per bytecode on each operation (except BitBlt). To measure individual optimizations, we also computed the time spent by an implementation that performed all the optimizations *but* the one in question. Table 11.1 summarizes effects of optimizing these areas. We'll examine these areas individually in the following sections, discuss other optimizations, and draw some conclusions.

Reference Counting

Smalltalk-80 implementations, including BS, reclaim space by maintaining a reference count for every object. Two reference-count operations are required when the virtual machine stores an object pointer (Oop): one to account for the destruction of the word's former contents, and one to account for the creation of a new reference. Each reference-count operation must first verify that its operand represents a reference-counted object and not a small integer. Then it must increment or decrement the appropriate count and check for over- and underflow. When an object's reference count diminishes to zero, all of its references must be destroyed by recursively decrementing the counts of the referenced objects. Only then can the virtual machine reuse the space. Although each reference-count operation is not expensive, the cumulative time counting references threatens to throttle by-the-book implementations.

We designed the Oop and OT structures to speed up reference counting. We enlarged the book's reference-count variables from 8 to 32 bits to obviate overflow checking. The object table was split into separate arrays of reference counts, addresses, and flags to eliminate the multiplication needed to index an array whose elements are not a power of 2 long. The SmallInteger tag bit was moved to the high order bit of the Oop from the low order bit to avoid the right shift required to convert an Oop to an array index.

Oops by-the-book.

15 . . . 1	0
<OT Index>	0
<Integer>	1

Berkeley Oops

15	14 . . .	0
0	<OTIndex >	
1	<Integer >	

The Berkeley Oop format also reduced the overhead of reference counting by hastening the check to decide whether an object must be reference counted. Since the integers all have negative Oops, and the Oops not needing reference counting (invalid Oop, nil, true, false) have values 0 through 3; a single signed comparison can ferret out nonreference-counted Oops. A typical BS count operation became 25% faster—8.2µs to 6.3µs.

*Reference-
Counting
Operations Per
Bytecode*

BS incorporated many strategies from the Xerox Dorado[7] and Dolphin implementations[8] that reduce the number of reference-count operations. For example, when returning the top of stack, the result's Oop must be pushed onto the caller's stack. A straightforward implementation would *copy* the Oop into the new context and increment its reference count. Later, when freeing the callee's context, the implementation would decrement the result's reference count. Instead, *destructively moving* the Oop obviates these two reference-count operations. After storing the Oop in the caller's context, BS destroys the old reference from the callee's context by nilling it out. Since the net number of references does not change, the reference count stays the same. An implementation can also avoid a decrement operation when it can guarantee that the target field contains a nonreference-counted object (e.g. nil). If the implementation can count on the new contexts of a field to be nonreference counted, it can avoid the increment.

Perhaps the single most significant trick for optimizing reference counting is the stack management strategy we adopted from the Dorado implementation. A Smalltalk-80 interpreter must free a context on almost every return. Since the context may contain references to objects, a conventional implementation must sweep the entire context to free it. The stack occupies two-thirds of a context; most of the stack is never used. BS avoids sweeping the area above the top of the stack (TOS) by banishing references to objects from that area. Only nil, SmallIntegers, true, and false may reside there. Performing context freeing as part of the return operation whenever possible is another important optimization. In addition to saving the overhead of invoking the recursive freeing routine, many other fields in a context are sure to be nonreference counted and are thus ignored. With these changes, recursive freeing accounts for less than 2%[9] of the execution time. Moving the sender Oop and result Oop instead of copying them saved four more count operations in the return bytecode. Tables 11.3 and 11.4 enumerate the reference-count operations required for a full send and return.

Be warned: explicitly altering either the stack pointer or the fields above the top of stack (both pointless actions) can compromise the integrity of an implementation with this optimization. This hazard has not posed a problem for BS or the Dorado implementation.

Table 11.3 Reference-Count Operations for Full Sends

Operation	By-the-book	BS
decrement sender in new context	1	0
increment new sender	1	0
decrement old active context	1	0
increment new active context	1	1
decrement IP in old context	1	0
increment IP in old context	1	0
decrement SP in old context	1	0
increment SP in old context	1	0
increment context class	1	0
decrement method in new context	1	0
increment method in new context	1	1
decrement receiver in new context	1	0
increment receiver in new context	1	0
decrement argument in new context	1	0
increment argument in new context	1	0
Total for full send	**15**	**2**

Table 11.4 Reference-Count Operations for Returns

Operation	By-the-book	BS
decrement old active context	1	1
increment new active context	1	0
increment result	1	0
decrement result	1	0
increment old IP	1	0
increment old SP	1	0
Total to switch contexts	**6**	**1**
decrement old sender	1	0
decrement old IP	1	0
decrement old SP	1	0
decrement old unused field	1	0
decrement old receiver	1	1
decrement old method	1	1
decrement old stack contents	12	1
decrement context class	1	0
Total to free old context	**19**	**3**
Grand total for return	**25**	**4**

This stack management strategy also reduced the number of reference-count operations for pushes and pops. It saved a decrement for each push and saved two reference-count operations per pop and store. It did force pop operations to nil out the old Oop. Three reference-count operations were saved for each integer primitive since they can succeed only with nonreference-counted Oops. Table 11.5 lists the number of counts for each type of bytecode. The optimizations removed 70% of the reference counting.

Table 11.5 Reference-Count Operations by Bytecode

Instruction type	By-the-book	BS	By-the-book/BS
push	2	1	2.0
full sends	15	2	7.5
direct arith prims	4	0	(infinite)
special primitives	4	3	.67
short circuit sends	2	2	1.0
primitives	4	4	1.0
return stack top	25	4	6.3
other returns	26	5	5.2
pop and store	2	1	2
pop	0	1	0
jump conditional	0	0	
jump unconditional	0	0	
store	3	2	1.5
Mean counts per bytecode	**6.1**	**1.5**	**4.1**

Multiplying the time per count by the number of counts per bytecode gave us the total time spent for each bytecode on reference counting. Table 11.6 presents these data and reinforces the importance of the reference-count optimizations; if BS did not include them, it would run 1.5 times slower.

Table 11.6 Cost of Reference Counting

Measurement	By-the-book	BS	By-the-book/BS
mean counts per bytecode	6.1	1.5	4.1
mean time per count	8.2μs	6.3μs	1.3
mean count time per bytecode	50μs	9.5μs	5.3
mean time per bytecode	124μs	83μs	1.5
Fraction spent counting	**40%**	**11%**	**3.6**

Bytecode Decoding

The definition of bytecode decoding encompasses the computation performed identically for each bytecode. Both Dolphin and Dorado contain fast hardware to decode bytecodes, a luxury absent from a conventional computer like our VAX. In addition to the decoding itself, we included checking for process switches, fetching bytecodes, updating the virtual instruction pointer, and for BS, counting bytecodes. BS uses a 256-way branch table to decode single-byte bytecodes completely. We combined the check for process switching and input polling into a single counter that is decremented and tested for each bytecode executed. Although we did not measure this optimization by itself, we did duplicate the code for the directly executed primitives so they could be executed in-line. Open coding minimizes the number of subroutine calls; the most common bytecodes and primitives use none. We timed bytecode decoding for both BS and a by-the-book implementation. As Table 11.7 shows, fast dispatching is critical—BS would be 2.5 times slower without it.

Table 11.7 Bytecode Dispatching

Measurement	By-the-book	BS	By-the-book/BS
time to dispatch one bytecode	124µs	10µs	12
mean time per bytecode	207µs	83µs	2.5
% of time spent dispatching	**60%**	**12%**	**5**

BitBlt

BitBlt[10] is the workhorse of the Smalltalk-80 graphics system. It performs all bitmap manipulation and text composition. The large amount of computation for this operation makes it a prime target for optimization. BS uses an external display, and must pay communication costs for bitmaps as well as the computation costs.

Coping With an External Display

We found three techniques to cut communication costs to our external display: fill recognition, delayed output, and reordered output.

☐ *Fill Recognition*   The bulk of the computation on bitmaps fills a rectangular area with all ones or all zeroes[11]. These area fill operations involve 21 times more bits than other, more complex copying operations. BS determines which invocations of BitBlt merely fill areas and sends rectangle fill commands to the display for them. (BitBlt itself is optimized for this case with special-purpose routines.)

□ *Delayed Output*   Second, borrowing an idea from an HP version of Smalltalk[12], when displaying text, our output routine does not send individual character-sized blocks of pixels until the completion of an invocation of the text composition primitive, scanCharacters. At that point BS sends a complete word-sized block.

□ *Reordered Output*   Third, when sending a bitmap to the display device, the middle goes separately from the left and right edges. Since the middle is an integral number of bytes, no shifting is needed to align the pixels for the display device. Each row in the middle of the bitmap is sent as bytes, not bits.

Measuring the
BitBlt *Optimization*

The only display optimization that can be easily compared to the specification in the book is the special purpose code for area fill. We measured the time to fill a 1000 by 1000 bitmap with the slow, general code, and the time to fill the same bitmap with the fast code for zero and one fill. The data in[13] supplied the proportion of work done by BitBlt (number of bits) that could be done with the special-purpose fast code. A weighted average of the times then yields the mean time to fill a 1000 by 1000 bitmap. Profile data supplied the midpoint proportion of total time spent per bytecode on BitBlt. To derive the time spent in BitBlt per bytecode for BS, we multiplied the time per bytecode by this percentage. We obtained the BitBlt time per bytecode of the unoptimized version by multiplying this time by the ratio of the unoptimized time to fill a megabit to the BS time to fill a megabit. Table 11.8 shows the results of this calculation. We conclude that this optimization is important for sessions that involve graphics and text composition, it doubled the speed of the interpreter.

Table 11.8 BitBlt Area Fill Optimization

Measurement	*By-the-book*	*BS*	*By-the-book/BS*
time to fill 1000 x 1000 zeroes	2100ms	92ms	23
time to fill 1000 x 1000 ones	2100ms	97ms	22
time to fill 1000 x 1000 mixed bits	2100ms	2100ms	1
ratio of zero/one fill to mixed bits	21	21	1
avg. time per 1M bits	2100ms	180ms	12
% time copying	**0—57%**	**0—10%**	**1—5.7**
copybits time per bytecode	**0—100μs**	**0—8.3μs**	**1—12**
Mean time per bytecode	**75μs—175μs**	**83μs**	**1—2.1**

Allocation and Freeing

Unix includes a library package for allocating and freeing areas of memory[14], but it might be too general to be fast enough for a Smalltalk-80 system. The proliferation of dynamic objects in a Smalltalk-80 environment strains conventional memory allocators. In particular, every message send and return pair results in allocating and freeing a context object. Many Points are created and discarded in the graphics routines. The popularity of these two classes is shown in Table 11.9, the percentage of allocation frequency by size based on measurements[15].

Table 11.9 Sizes of Frequently Allocated Objects

Size	Allocation Frequency	Comments
18	84%	size of small context
2	9%	size of point object
28	1%	size of large context
other	6%	

BS exploits this pattern with an algorithm outlined in the specification[16]. We observed that when a small object such as a context is freed, the probability of an allocation request for an object of the same size in the near future is high. The obvious strategy then is to hold onto the space and OT entry for the freed object, and to recycle it for the expected allocation. Although the specification defines a small object as one with 20 or fewer fields, we extended it to 40 to cover large contexts as suggested by Peter Deutsch. For each size of small object (0-40), BS maintains a pool of free objects on a linked list. Thus BS can allocate a small object by removing one from the appropriate list, setting its class and reference count, and nilling out the object's fields. If a pool runs dry, the Unix storage allocator is invoked to obtain a chunk of memory 10 times the desired size. BS then divides the chunk into 10 free objects, and tosses them into the pool. If too many objects end up in the free pools, it is possible to run out of available OT slots. When this happens, OT entries must be released from the free objects. The memory space for large objects is obtained from the Unix allocator.

We measured the cost of an allocation with a test program that repeatedly allocated and freed 100 context-sized objects with a LIFO discipline. Both the Unix allocator and the BS allocator were measured. It will be useful for the analysis to trichotomize sends:

1. We call sends to methods that simply return self or an instance variable *short-circuit sends*. The method header names the field to be returned.

2. Other sends result in the invocation of runtime interpreter sub-routines. These are the *primitives*.

3. The longest sends activate a new context and transfer control to the target method. We call these *full sends*.

The frequency of full sends provided the context allocation frequency, and the total allocation frequency was obtained by dividing the number of contexts allocated per bytecode by the fraction of context allocations. The allocate, free, and nilling out time is just the product of the allocations per bytecode and the time per allocation. Table 11.10 shows this calculation. Our object allocation strategy bought only a modest improvement in overall performance. The Unix allocator is well-tuned, and the time allocating and freeing objects is amortized over the time spent using the objects.

Table 11.10 Cost to Allocate and Free Object			
Measurement	*Unix allocator*	*BS allocator*	*Unix/BS*
time to allocate and free	130µs	21µs	6.2
time to nil out object	19µs	19µs	1.0
Total	**149µs**	**40µs**	**3.7**
allocations per bytecode	.13	.13	1
alloc/free/nil time per bytecode	19µs	5.2µs	3.7
mean time per bytecode	97µs	83µs	1.2
Fraction of time spent allocating	**20%**	**6%**	**3.2**

There are more tasks involved in storage management than just allocating and freeing, but the large address space and physical memory of the VAX reduce the importance of most of them. BS usually needs about half a megabyte of physical memory, and fits comfortably on our 4 megabyte time-shared VAX. In particular, we have not observed any thrashing, and thus have ignored dynamic compaction. Garbage collection flashes by so quickly on a 32-bit computer with plentiful memory that it can be hidden in the time needed to save an image on disk.

Object Table Indirection

To read or write a field of an object, the Smalltalk-80 virtual machine must first determine the object's memory address from the Object Table. We optimized this object table indirection just as we optimized reference counting. Addresses, like counts, are stored in a separate array, and the same Oop format that facilitates indexing the reference array speeds accesses to the object address array. We used test programs to time the cost of an indirection. Indirection is so simple that the array access costs dominates; the data structures in the book would double the time for each object table indirection on a VAX.

Close scrutiny of the book and the BS source code yielded the number of indirections. BS avoids object table indirections by saving memory addresses of some objects in registers. In particular, it keeps the current receiver, active and home contexts, current method, top of stack, and next bytecode addresses in registers or local variables. Those primitives and bytecodes that do multiword transfers or read-modify-write operations also keep addresses in registers. Scattering addresses around in registers complicates compaction, but except for garbage collection, BS does not compact. Tables 11.11 and 11.12 enumerate the indirections performed for a full send and a return, respectively. The need to recursively free the old context increases the number of indirections for a by-the-book return.

Table 11.11 Object Table Indirections for Full Sends

Operation	By-the-book	BS
fetch send	1	0
copy receiver and argument	4	0
initialize new context	5	0
store old IP	1	0
store old SP	1	0
store new IP	1	0
store new SP	1	0
get address of new context	0	1
get address of new method	0	2
get address of new receiver	0	1
Total	**14**	**4**

Computing the indirections for the other operations was straightforward, except for the nonarithmetic primitives, where we cheated by assuming three indirections each. (These are only 6% of the bytecodes executed.) Table 11.13 gives the number of indirections required for each type of bytecode. A by-the-book implementation performs an indirection for every bytecode simply to fetch it; caching this address of the next bytecode is every implementor's favorite optimization. The optimizations are successful, they remove three-quarters of the indirections.

Table 11.12 Object Table Indirections for Returns

Operation	By-the-book	BS
fetch bytecode	1	0
pop result	1	0
push result	1	0
store old IP	1	0
store old SP	1	0
load new SP	1	0
load new IP	1	0
load new method register	1	0
load new receiver register	1	0
load active context	1	0
get address of new method	0	1
get address of new context	0	1
get address of new receiver	0	1
free context	2	2
recursive free of context	18	0
Total	**30**	**5**

Table 11.13 Object Table Indirections per Bytecode

Instruction Type	By-the-book	BS	By-the-book/BS
push	3	0	(infinite)
full sends	14	4	3.5
arith prim	4	0	(infinite)
special prim	4	1.5	2.6
primitives	5	3	1.7
short circuit sends	3	0	(infinite)
return stack top	28	5	5.6
other returns	30	5	6.0
pop and store	3	0	(infinite)
pop	2	0	(infinite)
jump conditional	2	0	(infinite)
jump unconditional	1	0	(infinite)
store	3	0	(infinite)
Mean indirections per bytecode	**7.0**	**1.2**	**5.8**

Finally, to obtain the time spent on object table indirection per bytecode, we multiplied by the number of indirections per bytecode. Table 11.14 shows these results. These optimizations reduce indirection from a major cost of the interpreter to merely 4% of the total cost. There have been proposals to use 32-bit Oops and eliminate the object table. Table 11.14 implies that eliminating the speed penalty of the indirection is a poor justification for abolishing the object table. There may of course, be other, more compelling reasons.

Table 11.14 Cost of Object Table Indirection

Measurement	By-the-book	BS	By-the-book/BS
mean indirections per bytecode	7.0	1.2	5.8
time per indirection	4.2µs	2.0µs	1.2
mean indirection time per bytecode	29µs	2.4µs	12
mean time per bytecode	110µs	83µs	1.3
Fraction spent indirecting	**26%**	**3%**	**9.0**

Method Lookup

Runtime type checking is a fundamental innovation of the Smalltalk-80 language. Every message send (procedure call) looks up the message's selector in the method dictionaries for the receiver's class (and superclasses). The Smalltalk-80 book recommends reducing the time spent for lookups with a cache. BS incorporates such a method lookup cache with 1024 entries. The cache slot is computed from the low-order 10 bits of the result of performing an *exclusive-or* (the book uses *and*) of the receiver's class and the selector. Conroy and Pelegri (see Chapter 13) have conducted a thorough study of Smalltalk-80 method cache behavior; Table 11.15 merely summarizes their findings for BS. The wisdom in the book is borne out, as BS would be 40% slower without the cache.

Table 11.15 Method Caching

Measurement	Without Cache	With Cache	Ratio
measured hit time		4.4µs	
measured miss time	187µs	284µs	
measured hit %	0%	94%	
mean lookup time	187µs	20µs	9.4
mean lookups per bytecode	.19	.19	1.0
mean lookup time per bytecode	36µs	3.8µs	9.4
mean time per bytecode	115µs	83µs	1.4
Fraction of time for lookup	**31%**	**5%**	**6.2**

Other Optimizations

Many other optimizations exist in BS. Standard programming tricks speed recursive freeing and garbage collection for certain popular classes. Subroutine calls and other overhead are trimmed in sends and returns. Floating point arithmetic is performed in hardware. Most of these optimizations are easily discovered and are unrelated to the distinguishing characteristics of the Smalltalk-80 system.

Other Interpreter Activities

As Table 11.1 shows, the activities we measured account for a total of $40\mu s$ per bytecode in BS. BS has been instrumented to measure the bytecodes executed per CPU-second; this is about 12000 for typical interactive sessions of browsing, editing, compiling, and so forth. Thus, BS spends 1/12000 second or $83\mu s$ per bytecode. That leaves $43\mu s$ unaccounted for. This represents the "useful work", in the sense that it contains no easy targets for optimization. It includes the execution of bytecodes and primitives.

Although we have optimized these activities in the obvious ways (e.g. open coding), these are the least interesting optimizations. We therefore made the conservative assumption that the unoptimized interpreter would be no slower.

Comparative Execution Times

How close is BS to an optimal Smalltalk-80 implementation? The fastest Smalltalk-80 implementation is Deutsch's Dorado interpreter. The Dorado is a powerful personal computer[17] with a microcycle time three times faster than the VAX-11/780. The Dolphin is a more modest machine; it is considered to be adequate but not comfortable. We decided to examine two test cases: our typical interactive session and Baden's Towers of Hanoi benchmark[18]. Peter Deutsch measured the performance of the Xerox implementations on the Hanoi benchmark. The numbers for the Xerox implementations for the typical interactive session reflect the best estimates of the Software Concepts Group. The execution rate for BS was measured as described above. Table 11.16

Table 11.16 Relative Performance (kilobytecodes per second)

Case	BS	Dolphin	Dorado
Interactive use	12	30	400
Towers of Hanoi	23	33	420

compares BS execution speed for the two test cases. Although BS performs well for a conventional machine, it suffers in comparison to the Xerox personal computers.

Conclusions

We have several minor reservations about the results in this paper. First, our methods yielded only rough approximations. We ignored the effects of the VAX hardware cache hit rate on the running times of our test programs. Bytecode frequencies can be expected to vary. Second, major optimizations often have synergistic effects on code complexity and execution time. Finally, we did not explore some important areas (e.g. context changing overhead). The intended value of this work lies in ranking the different optimizable areas and in quantifying the benefits of optimization. For instance, it clearly shows that reference counting remains a more promising target than allocation and freeing. These measurements and calculations do however, reinforce the need to optimize carefully and tune implementations of Smalltalk-80 virtual machines. When our optimizations in the measured areas were combined, they resulted in a fourfold improvement in performance.

Acknowledgments

We would like to thank the Software Concepts Group for creating the Smalltalk-80 system and bringing it out into the light of day. In particular, we owe our gratitude to Peter Deutsch who has offered both quintessential and patient technical guidance, and to Adele Goldberg who issued our entry visa onto the "Isle of Smalltalk". We thank the students here at Berkeley involved with the Smalltalk project: Scott Baden, Ricki Blau, Dan Conde, Tom Conroy, Dan Halbert, Ed Pelegri, Richard Probst, and Steve Sargent have contributed hard work, data, and insight to the task of understanding where the time goes. We owe a debt of thanks to Jim Stinger, Ted Laliottis, Bob Ballance, and the rest of the Smalltalk-80 group at HP Labs, who by permitting us to study their unfinished implementation, furnished us with a working model to study. Paul McCullough provided thoughtful and constructive comments to help smooth out the rough spots in this paper.

This effort was funded in part by Apple Computer and the State of California through the Microelectronics Innovation and Computer Research Opportunities program, and sponsored by Defense Advance Research Projects Agency, Department of Defense, Order No. 3803, monitored by Naval Electronic System Command under Contract No. N00039-81-K-0251.

References

1. Goldberg, Adele, and Robson, David, *Smalltalk-80: The Language and Its Implementation,* Addison-Wesley, Reading, Mass., 1983.

2. Ingalls, Daniel H. H., "The Smalltalk Graphics Kernel", *Byte* vol. 6, no. 8, pp. 168–194, Aug. 1981.

3. Ritchie, Dennis M., Johnson, Stephen C., Lesk, Michael E., and Kernigham, Brian W., "UNIX Time-Sharing System: The C Programming Language", *Bell System Technical Journal* vol. 57, no. 6, pp. 1991–2019, 1978.

4. Conroy, Tom, and Pelegri—Llopart, Eduardo, "CPU Time Profile of Long Interactive BS Session", Private Communication, May 1982.

5. Baden, Scott, "High Performance Storage Reclamation in an Object-Based Memory System", Master's Report, Computer Science Div., Dept. of E.E.C.S., Univ. of California, Berkeley, CA, June 9, 1982.

6. *Ibid.*

7. Lampson, Butler, "The Dorado: A High-Performance Personal Computer", Xerox PARC Technical Report CSL-81-1, Jan. 1981.

8. Deutsch, L. Peter, Berkeley Computer Systems Seminar, Fall 1981.

9. See reference 4.

10. See reference 2.

11. Cole, Clement T., Pelegri-Llopart, Eduardo, Ungar, David M., and Wayman, Russel J., "Limits to Speed: A Case Study of a Smalltalk Implementation Under VM/UNIX", Class Report CS-292R, Computer Science Div., Dept. of E.E.C.S., Univ. of California, Berkeley, CA, Fall 1981.

12. Stinger, Jim, et. al., Private Communications, 1981.

13. See reference 11.

14. Joy, William N., and Babaoglu, Ozalp, UNIX *Programmers Manual*, Computer Science Div., Dept. of E.E.C.S., Univ. of California, Berkeley, CA, Nov. 7, 1979.

15. See reference 5.

16. See reference 1.

17. See reference 7.

18. See reference 5.

12

The Analysis of the Smalltalk-80 System at Hewlett-Packard*

Joseph R. Falcone
Computer Research Center
Hewlett-Packard Laboratories
Palo Alto, California

Introduction

The implementation of Smalltalk at Hewlett-Packard Laboratories was the principal component of an investigation into personal computing environments. As we developed the implementation, we continually analyzed its performance to achieve a better understanding of the system. This program began in earnest in March of 1981 when we embarked on the first implementation. By November, the entire project was winding down and we placed more emphasis on performance analysis to complete it before the end. When the project closed in February of 1982, we had developed a vast body of performance data, collected by both programs and people. Since then only the performance analysis has continued (as an unofficial part-time activity). The HP Smalltalk project is described in more detail in Chapter 6.

Approach

The Smalltalk-80 system is difficult to measure, given the variability of user interaction which is fundamental to it. Repeating the identical test twice was nearly impossible so we designated a general collection of tasks as the *basic test,* touching all of the capabilities of the system at least once according to our view of personal computer usage patterns. During this test, the browser, compiler, decompiler, and window system are exercised in every conceivable way. With full performance monitoring, the test covers millions of bytecodes and takes over six hours. Our test should not be confused with the testStandardTests benchmarks. Early investigative work on our system used the testStandardTests benchmarks until we noticed that the results bore little relation to statistics gathered from normal usage. Hence we felt that it was not useful as a personal computing performance test.

In the following sections, we present measurements of the system compiled from many *basic test* experiments. The measurements cover a wide variety of system functions, from bytecode frequencies to memory access. These figures are probably accurate to within 10% for different mixes of Smalltalk-80 code. We conducted these tests on a pre-release version of the Smalltalk-80 system.

Bytecode Measurements

Table 12.1 Smalltalk-80 Virtual Machine Bytecode Frequency

SVM Bytecode	Static %	Dynamic %	Cumulative
push temporary variable 0	6.25%	6.48%	6.48%
push self (receiver)	6.28%	5.73%	12.21%
return stack top from message	3.22%	4.94%	17.15%
push temporary variable 1	3.39%	4.74%	21.89%
send +	1.19%	3.65%	25.54%
push temporary variable 2	2.12%	3.46%	29.00%
push constant 1	2.61%	3.26%	32.26%
send literal 0 with no args	1.66%	2.57%	34.83%
pop stack top	7.03%	2.42%	37.25%
send at:	0.77%	2.06%	39.31%
jump on false 0*256 + next	0.86%	1.93%	41.24%
push receiver variable 1	0.97%	1.72%	42.96%
push receiver variable 0	0.97%	1.70%	44.66%
send ==	0.90%	1.62%	46.28%
send −	0.83%	1.61%	47.89%
extended pop and store (all)	1.09%	1.51%	49.40%
push constant nil	1.33%	1.48%	50.88%
return self (receiver)	2.55%	1.43%	52.31%
send < =	0.18%	1.32%	53.63%

Table 12.1 (*Cont.*)

SVM Bytecode	Static %	Dynamic %	Cumulative
extended push (all)	0.68%	1.32%	54.95%
jump -1*256 + next	0.27%	1.29%	56.24%
pop and store temporary 1	0.87%	1.27%	57.51%
push constant 0	1.87%	1.26%	58.77%
push temporary variable 3	1.27%	1.18%	59.95%
extended store (all)	0.81%	1.17%	61.12%
pop and branch on false 2	0.76%	1.15%	62.27%
push temporary variable 6	0.42%	1.10%	63.37%
send literal 1 with no args	1.21%	1.05%	64.42%
push receiver variable 14	0.20%	1.05%	65.47%
pop and store temporary 2	0.71%	1.03%	66.50%
send >	0.32%	0.96%	67.46%
send =	0.91%	0.94%	68.40%
push temporary variable 4	0.82%	0.88%	69.28%
send literal 0 with 1 arg	1.63%	0.85%	70.13%
all others (213)	41.91%	29.87%	100.00%

Table 12.1 lists the static and dynamic frequencies of the Smalltalk-80 virtual machine instruction set. This distribution is remarkably uniform. Most dynamic instruction frequencies show at least one instruction at over 10%[1], but the highest in the Smalltalk-80 virtual machine is only 6.48% for pushing a temporary onto the stack, usually performed to work on an argument passed through the temporary variable area. However, as the following section will show, there is some regularity by category of bytecodes. The top 17 bytecodes consume more than 50% of execution and the top 34 are over 70% out of 247 designated bytecodes.

Pop stack top had the highest static frequency even though it was ninth in execution. The top three bytecodes in static frequency comprise one-fifth of all generated code. After that there is a steep drop and no bytecode rises above 3.39%. The less popular instructions tend to have higher static frequencies. Outside of the top 30, the bytecodes have a static/dynamic frequency ratio of 4 to 3.

There are 9 unused bytecodes in the Smalltalk-80 virtual machine instruction set, and the system never executed 18 other bytecodes in our tests. Twelve of these instructions were long jumps, and all were the longer varieties. The current Smalltalk compiler does not generate the *pop and jump on true* instructions. This is apparently to simplify the task of the decompiler. The other six untouched instructions were pushes and sends concerned with somewhat rare circumstances.

The Analysis of the Smalltalk-80 System at Hewlett-Packard

Table 12.2 Bytecode Frequency by Category

Bytecode Category	Static %	Dynamic %	Cumulative
stack push	44.01%	44.37%	44.37%
message send	29.00%	28.63%	73.00%
stack pop and store	13.32%	10.80%	83.80%
branch and jump	6.50%	8.59%	92.39%
return	7.17%	7.61%	100.00%

Table 12.2 groups the bytecodes into five categories for static and dynamic frequencies. The importance of message sends in Smalltalk is evident, but this can be misleading. The percentage of sends is so large because it includes both procedure calls *and* arithmetic and logical operations (note the absence of a *computational instruction* category). Also, because many of the sends are special or primitive operations which do not result in the execution of Smalltalk code, the percentage of return instructions is much lower.

Stack operations account for 55.17% of instructions executed, and 71.37% are instructions other than sends. The frequency of stack push and pop instructions points out the necessity of having an optimized independent path to the stack frame of the active context.

Send Bytecodes

Although the message send is perhaps the most important part of Smalltalk, it comprises only about one-quarter of execution time. More importantly, nearly half are *special* sends which do not require a dictionary lookup for their selector. These special sends perform functions which are typically in the instruction set of a processor, such as arithmetic and logical operations for small integers.

Approximately every third instruction is a message send and sends requiring dictionary lookups occur every 6.67 bytecodes. Of the sends needing dictionary searches, 36.64% invoked primitives, and the rest resulted in the execution of a Smalltalk method which, along with process switches, accounted for a context switch every 6.50 bytecodes.

Of the special sends, 78.92% are arithmetic and logical operations. The remaining special sends fell further into the minority by a change in the third test image release which required 11 of the 16 cases to look up the selector in a special messages array rather than invoking a primitive directly. As a result, some of these special sends actually result in the execution of Smalltalk code if the selector in the array does not bind to a primitive for the receiver in question. Of course this allows one to dynamically modify system behavior or to change this set of primitives if future requirements should dictate. These other special sends include high level operations such as instantiation, indexing, length and class query, block evaluation, and point coordinates.

Table 12.3 Frequency of Message Sends by Flavor

Flavor of Send	Percentage	Cumulative Percentage
primitive	66.86%	66.86%
method	21.42%	88.28%
pseudo-primitive	11.72%	100.00%

There are three flavors of message sends:

Primitive	Those which invoke C or machine code routines.
Method	Those which activate Smalltalk code.
Pseudo-primitive	Those which return directly after performing an operation encoded in the header of the compiled method.

The method sends are the best known of those in Table 12.3. At about one-fifth of all sends executed, this indicates the amount of optimization possible through the proper choice of the set of primitives. The pseudo-primitives, which offer an inexpensive way to access instance fields, execute half as frequently as traditional method sends. In all, 78.58% of sends do not *immediately* result in the execution of Smalltalk code. This does not take into account those primitives which fail and then activate Smalltalk backup code (discussed later).

Table 12.4 Frequency of Primitive Method Invocations by Type

Type of Primitive	Percentage	Cumulative Percentage
arithmetic	56.30%	56.30%
selector	28.66%	84.96%
common	15.04%	100.00%

Primitive invocations also break down into three categories:

Arithmetic	Arithmetic and logical operations invoked with no lookup.
Common	Operations invoked without lookup in the special messages array.
Selector	Those sends where selector lookup associated a primitive with the method.

As one might expect, the arithmetic primitive invocations dominate the statistics in Table 12.4. Overall, 71.34% of primitive invocations are *direct* from bytecode dispatch and require no special handling.

Table 12.5 Failures of Primitive Methods by Type

Type of Primitive	Percentage	Cumulative Percentage
arithmetic	81.36%	81.36%
selector	15.93%	97.29%
common	2.71%	100.00%

Several interesting figures arise from Table 12.5 which shows primitive failures by type. Only 4.49% of primitive operations fail, and most of these are the result of small integer arithmetic range violations. In fact, arithmetic primitives are 2.6 times more likely to fail than selector primitives and 8 times more likely than common primitives. The true figure for arithmetic failures is probably even higher because we did not implement certain primitives in the selector category (e.g., large integer arithmetic) and an invocation of one of them leads directly to a primitive failure. Still the failure rate for arithmetic primitives is only 6.49%, a testament to the utility of signed 15-bit arithmetic.

Table 12.6 Frequency of Message Sends by Flavor
(adjusted for primitive failures)

Flavor of Send	Percentage	Cumulative Percentage
successful primitive	63.86%	63.86%
method and primitive backup	24.42%	88.28%
pseudo-primitive	11.72%	100.00%

Comparing Table 12.6 with Table 12.3, we see that primitive failures account for only a three percent increase in the number of Smalltalk methods activated. This is a very small price to pay for significantly better performance than equivalent Smalltalk routines.

Table 12.7 Send Bytecode Frequency by Category

Send Category	Static %	Dynamic %	Cumulative
special arithmetic	19.00%	37.65%	37.65%
selector send	53.81%	32.71%	70.36%
common send	19.74%	27.21%	97.57%
extended selector	7.45%	2.43%	100.00%

The SVM send instructions fall into the four categories listed in Table 12.7.

1. *Special Arithmetic.* Arithmetic and logical operations invoked with no selector lookup. Their dynamic frequency is twice the static, indicating the popularity of these operations. Together with the common send instructions, these dominate dynamic frequency at over 64%.

2. *Common Send.* Special operations which either execute directly (five cases) or indirectly through the lookup of a selector in the special messages array. Although these bytecodes have a higher static frequency than special arithmetic sends, they execute 10% less of the time.

3. *Selector Send.* An instruction specifying where the selector is found in the literal frame of the compiled method. These sends can access the first 16 literal selectors in the compiled method, and they take 0, 1, or 2 arguments. The static frequency concurs with our flavor analysis as selector send bytecodes constitute more than 50% of all sends in methods, but less than one-third of execution.

4. *Extended Selector.* These are 2- and 3-byte extended versions of the regular selector sends for greater literal access range and/or larger numbers of arguments. They come in two flavors: one is an ordinary message send to receiver; the other starts message lookup in the superclass of the receiver. The 2-byte version can access the first 16 selectors with 0 to 7 arguments. The 3-byte version allocates a byte to the selector index and the argument count, with a range of 0 to 255 for each. These are rarely executed so their static frequency is triple the execution rate.

Table 12.8 Send Bytecode Frequency

Send Bytecode	Static %	Dynamic %	Cumulative
+	4.10%	12.74%	12.74%
selector 0, no args	5.84%	9.01%	21.75%
at:	2.67%	7.18%	28.93%
==	3.11%	5.66%	34.59%
−	2.87%	5.64%	40.23%
<=	0.64%	4.61%	44.84%
selector 1, no args	4.16%	3.66%	48.50%
>	1.09%	3.38%	51.88%
=	3.13%	3.28%	55.16%
selector 0, 1 arg	5.61%	2.97%	58.13%
x	0.56%	2.73%	60.86%
y	0.45%	2.71%	63.57%
selector 0, 2 args	1.93%	2.42%	65.99%

Table 12.8 *(Cont.)*

Send Bytecode	Static %	Dynamic %	Cumulative
selector 1, 1 arg	3.10%	2.17%	68.16%
@	2.11%	2.07%	70.23%
all others (66)	58.63%	29.77%	100.00%

Table 12.8 is a closer look at the send bytecodes. Addition (+) is the most popular message sent, executing at triple its static frequency. However, a selector send follows closely revealing the importance of the more flexible versions in spite of all the special cases. The next two entries in the table are primitive sends for array access (at:) and object equivalence (==). The three other primitive sends in the table all deal with points—creation and access. The graphical nature of the Smalltalk-80 user interface increases the use of the coordinate point so that messages for point handling account for over 7.5% of all messages sent. Overall, the selector sends have much higher static frequencies than the rest.

Table 12.9 Special Arithmetic Send Bytecode Frequency

Bytecode	Static %	Dynamic %	Cumulative
+	21.56%	33.85%	33.85%
−	15.11%	14.96%	48.81%
<=	3.35%	12.26%	61.07%
>	5.74%	8.96%	70.03%
=	16.47%	8.71%	78.74%
@	11.12%	5.50%	84.24%
<	4.92%	4.53%	88.77%
bitAnd:	2.01%	2.62%	91.39%
bitShift:	1.96%	2.42%	93.81%
>=	1.94%	1.79%	95.60%
\\	1.53%	1.57%	97.17%
//	3.35%	1.06%	98.23%
*	6.24%	0.86%	99.09%
~=	2.68%	0.63%	99.72%
bitOr:	0.29%	0.26%	99.98%
/	1.75%	0.02%	100.00%

The statistics for special arithmetic sends in Table 12.9 are comparable to those for the computational instructions of conventional languages and architectures[2]. Additions occur over one-third of the time, and together with subtractions, comprise nearly half of arithmetic send execution. The sixth entry is a bit unusual—an instruction for creating a point from the receiver as the X value and the argument as the Y value. Multiplication and division account for only about 3.5% of special arithmetic sends. The static and dynamic frequencies show interesting differences. The execution frequency of $<=$ is four times the static, while the opposite is true for @ and $=$ where the static frequencies are twice the dynamic. The multiplication bytecode is fifth in static frequency with a rate eight times its execution percentage.

Table 12.10 Common Send Bytecode Frequency			
Bytecode	*Static %*	*Dynamic %*	*Cumulative*
at:	13.51%	26.41%	26.41%
==*	15.77%	20.81%	47.22%
x	2.85%	10.02%	57.24%
y	2.26%	9.95%	67.19%
value:*	2.09%	6.86%	74.05%
size	9.71%	4.91%	78.96%
blockCopy:*	19.29%	4.75%	83.71%
new	10.59%	4.57%	88.28%
at:put:	7.18%	3.38%	91.66%
class*	2.90%	3.05%	94.71%
nextPut:	4.95%	1.87%	96.58%
value*	2.67%	1.48%	98.06%
new:	4.40%	1.47%	99.53%
next	1.77%	0.47%	100.00%
atEnd	0.00%	0.00%	100.00%

Table 12.10 lists the frequencies for common send bytecodes. The selectors marked by an asterisk in the table are those messages which do not require any dictionary lookup before invoking a primitive. Those without the asterisk get their selectors from a special messages array and then proceed via the normal send process. Array access (at:) and object equivalence ($==$) constitute nearly one half of common send execution. Although array element loads (at:) are eight times more frequent than array element stores (at:put:), the opposite is true for streams. Writes on streams (nextPut:) are four times more frequent than reads (next). Nearly all of the common send instructions show significant differences between static and dynamic frequencies, ranging as high as a 4 to 1 ratio in both directions.

Table 12.11 Primitive Method Invocation Frequency
(excluding arithmetic primitives)

Class & Primitive	Percentage	Cumulative Percentage
<Object> at:	25.89%	25.89%
<Object> ==	19.91%	45.80%
<BlockContext> value	8.10%	53.90%
<Object> size	7.78%	61.68%
<String> at:	5.76%	67.44%
<Object> at:put:	5.75%	73.19%
<BlockContext> blockCopy:	4.38%	77.57%
<Behavior> new	4.25%	81.82%
<Object> class	2.81%	84.63%
<BitBlt> copyBits	2.47%	87.10%
all others (31)	12.90%	100.00%

The 10 primitive methods in Table 12.11 total nearly 90% of all invocations. Array, string, and stream access account for nearly 40% of these. With a few exceptions, the leading non-arithmetic primitives perform very simple functions. The most notable exception is copyBits, a very complex primitive made even more so because of our external graphics display system. Two of the primitives manage block execution and account for over 12% by themselves.

Table 12.12 Superclass Chain Traversals by Length

Length of Traversal	Percentage	Cumulative Percentage
0 (receiver)	56.20%	56.20%
1 (superclass)	17.36%	73.56%
2	6.72%	80.28%
3	6.18%	86.46%
4	5.33%	91.79%
5	4.32%	96.11%
7	2.11%	98.22%
6	1.67%	99.89%
8, 9 & 10	0.11%	100.00%

Table 12.12 gives the number of links traversed to look up messages in the dictionaries of superclasses. The zero category corresponds to messages understood by the class of their receiver and therefore no links are traversed. The average traversal distance is 1.18, but the majority of messages never go to the superclass. Nearly 14% search four or more dictionaries, thus skewing the figures in that direction.

Table 12.13 Message Dictionary Probes by Number

Number of Probes	Percentage	Cumulative Percentage
1 (direct hit)	61.16%	61.16%
2	11.97%	73.13%
4	4.71%	77.84%
3	4.08%	81.92%
5	2.54%	84.46%
9	1.45%	85.91%
8	1.41%	87.32%
12	1.34%	88.66%
23	1.28%	89.94%
6	1.19%	91.13%
all others (31)	8.87%	100.00%

The statistics in Table 12.13 for message lookup are for method cache misses. Our method cache hit rate is 93% for a 509 element cache. There is an average of 3.89 probes into each message dictionary after a cache miss. Combined with the superclass chain traversals, each send missing the cache requires an average of 8.48 probes of message dictionaries, searching the message dictionaries of the class and superclass of the receiver in the typical case. The appearance of figures over 10 in the table is the result of very long hash collision chains. If a message dictionary is nearly full this will happen, but it is more likely that the very simple hash function used by Smalltalk is causing many collisions.

Push and Pop Bytecodes

Table 12.14 Push Bytecode Frequency by Category

Push Category	Static %	Dynamic %	Cumulative
temporary variable	35.45%	44.45%	44.45%
special	33.95%	29.57%	74.02%
receiver variable	11.30%	17.19%	91.21%
extended (all)	1.54%	2.97%	94.18%
literal variable	8.97%	2.96%	97.14%
literal constant	8.79%	2.86%	100.00%

Push instructions can access four different memory areas in the Smalltalk-80 execution environment:

1. *Temporary Variable.* The area just above the stack in a method context is the temporary frame where the Smalltalk-80 language passes arguments and allocates local and temporary variables.

2. *Receiver Variable.* The instance variables of the receiver of the message.

3. *Literal Variable.* A variable accessed through a pointer to an association in the literal frame of a compiled method.

4. *Literal Constant.* A constant value in the literal frame of a compiled method.

Table 12.14 lists the frequencies of these plus the special push instructions for frequently used constants and environment values, such as self (the receiver of the current message). The extended category includes all four flavors of push instructions. The static frequencies for literal access are triple the execution rate, which is less than 6%. Literal constant access is particularly low because of the push constant instructions for 2, 1, 0, −1, false, true, and nil. These seven bytecodes alone constitute 15.71% of all pushes.

The access ranges of push instructions vary. The standard temporary and receiver variable push instructions can access the first 16 entries, while the literal frame pushes have a range of 32. The extended push instructions can access up to 64 entries. When this range is not enough, other tactics are necessary. For example, to access instance variable number 73 of the receiver, we can do the following:

1. Push self [the Oop of the receiver]

2. Push literal constant n [73]

3. Send at:

This takes two pushes and a primitive invocation, so one can appreciate the value of the extended push instructions.

Table 12.15 Push Bytecode Frequency

Push Bytecode	Static %	Dynamic %	Cumulative
temporary variable 0	14.19%	14.61%	14.61%
self (receiver)	14.26%	12.92%	27.53%
temporary variable 1	7.70%	10.70%	38.23%
temporary variable 2	4.81%	7.79%	46.02%
constant 1	5.92%	7.34%	53.36%
receiver variable 1	2.20%	3.88%	57.24%
receiver variable 0	2.19%	3.82%	61.06%
constant nil	3.03%	3.33%	64.39%
extended (all)	1.54%	2.96%	67.35%
constant 0	4.24%	2.84%	70.19%

Table 12.15 (*Cont.*)

Push Bytecode	Static %	Dynamic %	Cumulative
temporary variable 3	2.89%	2.67%	72.86%
temporary variable 6	0.95%	2.48%	75.34%
receiver variable 14	0.46%	2.35%	77.69%
temporary variable 4	1.87%	1.99%	79.68%
receiver variable 2	1.75%	1.65%	81.33%
temporary variable 7	0.59%	1.62%	82.95%
temporary variable 5	1.40%	1.49%	84.44%
literal variable 2	2.10%	1.30%	85.74%
all others (85)	27.91%	14.26%	100.00%

Pushes involving the receiver and the first three temporary slots account for nearly half of execution in Table 12.15. These top four entries correspond roughly to usage of the first four parameters or local variables in an ordinary language subroutine. After the special push of constant 1, there is a steep drop in execution percentage. There is little disagreement between static and dynamic frequencies for these instructions.

Table 12.16 Special Push Bytecode Frequency

Special Push Bytecode	Static %	Dynamic %	Cumulative
self (receiver)	42.00%	43.70%	43.70%
constant 1	17.45%	24.82%	68.52%
constant nil	8.92%	11.26%	79.78%
constant 0	12.50%	9.61%	89.39%
constant 2	4.02%	3.98%	93.37%
active context	7.59%	3.13%	96.50%
constant false	3.11%	1.91%	98.41%
constant true	1.97%	1.45%	99.86%
constant −1	0.53%	0.09%	99.95%
stack top	1.91%	0.05%	100.00%

The special pushes offer a shortcut for popular push operations. When it determines a value to be constant, the compiler can use the special push instructions to avoid additional memory accesses and to conserve space in the literal frame where it usually puts constants. However, in some cases the special pushes are the only mechanism for reaching certain environment values, such as the receiver of the current message and the active context. In Table 12.16, push self accounts for over 40% of special push execution, and the top four comprise nearly 90%. Both push -1 and duplicate stack top have a combined static frequency of nearly 2.5% (0.83% overall), but execute only once every 2400 pushes (or 5400 bytecodes).

Table 12.17 Pop and Store Bytecode Frequency by Category

Pop & Store Category	Static %	Dynamic %	Cumulative
pop and store temporary variable	25.16%	36.51%	36.51%
pop stack top	52.77%	22.36%	58.87%
pop and store receiver variable	7.84%	16.30%	75.17%
extended pop and store (all)	8.15%	13.96%	89.13%
extended store (all)	6.08%	10.87%	100.00%

The pop and store instructions in Table 12.17 roughly parallel the push operations, with a few differences. The SVM prohibits storing directly into the literal frame of compiled methods, but one can modify literal variables through their association in the literal frame via the extended pop and store instructions. In addition, the range of the regular pop and store instructions for temporary and receiver variables is 8 entries instead of 16. Because of these factors, the extended versions of the instructions total nearly 25% of all pop and stores executed. The pop stack top bytecode is also almost one-quarter, leaving regular temporary and receiver variable access at a little over half. The story is different for static frequencies where pop stack top leads at over 50%, more than double its dynamic rate. The other categories show dynamic frequencies from 40% to 100% higher than their static figures.

The difference in execution between loads and stores on this system is interesting. The figures for temporary and receiver variable operations are very similar. However, the extended pop and store instructions execute over eight times more frequently than extended pushes (24.83% vs. 2.97%). This is because the only way to modify literal variables is through the extended pop and store instructions, whereas there is a separate regular bytecode for pushing literal variables. In addition, as noted, the range of pop and store instructions is more limited, hence forcing the use of extended instructions more frequently. Finally, popping the stack top is almost 500 times more frequent than duplicating it (22.36% vs. 0.05%).

Table 12.18 Pop and Store Bytecode Frequency

Pop & Store Bytecode	Static %	Dynamic %	Cumulative
pop stack top	52.77%	22.36%	22.36%
extended pop and store (all)	8.15%	13.96%	36.32%
temporary variable 1	6.53%	11.76%	48.08%
extended store (all)	6.08%	10.87%	58.95%
temporary variable 2	5.36%	9.53%	68.48%
receiver variable 1	1.57%	4.36%	72.84%
receiver variable 0	1.61%	3.99%	76.83%
receiver variable 4	0.87%	3.44%	80.27%
temporary variable 6	1.50%	3.26%	83.53%
temporary variable 4	2.22%	3.11%	86.64%
temporary variable 3	3.23%	2.89%	89.53%
temporary variable 7	0.82%	2.82%	92.35%
all others (7)	9.29%	7.65%	100.00%

Table 12.18 provides a more detailed look at the pop and store bytecodes. Temporary variable 0 is not among the top 12, and in general, the frequency of variable access is not in numeric sequence. In fact, pop and store operations on temporary variable 1 are six times more frequent than those on variable 0 (11.76% vs. 1.82%). This indicates that methods manipulate temporary variables more than arguments, since temporary slot 0 is usually occupied by the first message parameter.

Return, Branch, and Jump Bytecodes

The system spends nearly one-sixth of execution on these transfer of control instructions. The return bytecodes are the most sophisticated of them, having to reset the sender as the active context upon leaving a method. The special case sends have diminished the importance of returns by relegating their use to the relatively small percentage of method sends. We divide the other control transfer bytecodes into *branches* for the single-byte short versions and *jumps* for the multiple-byte long ones. These are not very significant either because the tiny size of Smalltalk methods leaves precious little space for much transfer of control.

Table 12.19 Return Bytecode Frequency

Return Bytecode	Static %	Dynamic %	Cumulative
stack top from Method	44.90%	64.83%	64.83%
self	35.54%	18.82%	83.65%
stack top from Block	14.08%	8.10%	91.75%

Table 12.19 (*Cont.*)

Return Bytecode	Static %	Dynamic %	Cumulative
false	2.30%	5.59%	97.34%
true	1.78%	2.63%	99.97%
nil	1.40%	0.03%	100.00%

Nearly three-quarters of all methods and blocks return top of stack as shown in Table 12.19. Most of the rest return self, while a very tiny portion return nil. Although the default return for Smalltalk-80 code is self, such returns account for less than 20%. The static frequencies of return self and stack top from block are nearly double their execution. At the other end, only one of every 3300 methods returns nil, raising doubts as to the value of this variant, which is executed once every 43,802 bytecodes on average.

Table 12.20 Branch and Jump Bytecode Frequency by Category

Branch & Jump Category	Static %	Dynamic %	Cumulative
pop and branch on false	40.71%	49.50%	49.50%
pop and jump on false	13.21%	22.56%	72.06%
jump	27.46%	21.42%	93.48%
branch	18.62%	6.52%	100.00%
pop and jump on true	0.00%	0.00%	100.00%

Because Smalltalk-80 methods tend to be very short, one expects to find low execution frequencies for long jumps, and the data in Table 12.20 concurs. However, the most frequent unconditional transfers are the long jumps, outnumbering short branches by more than three to one. Overall, the conditional and unconditional short branches account for 57.02% of transfers. The conditional branches and jumps execute over two and a half times more frequently than the unconditional ones. As noted before, the current compiler does not use the pop and jump on true instruction.

Table 12.21 Branch and Jump Bytecode Frequency

Branch & Jump Bytecode	Static %	Dynamic %	Cumulative
jump 0*256 + next	13.21%	22.56%	22.56%
jump -1*256 + next	4.21%	15.01%	37.57%
pop and branch on false 2	11.63%	13.38%	50.95%

Table 12.21 (*Cont.*)

Branch & Jump Bytecode	Static %	Dynamic %	Cumulative
pop and branch on false 4	7.76%	8.53%	59.48%
pop and branch on false 3	6.65%	7.33%	66.81%
pop and branch on false 6	2.78%	6.59%	73.40%
jump 0*256 + next	23.20%	6.39%	79.79%
pop and branch on false 1	3.16%	5.10%	84.89%
pop and branch on false 5	4.60%	4.77%	89.66%
branch 1	8.15%	3.44%	93.10%
pop and branch on false 8	1.74%	2.81%	95.91%
all others (9)	12.91%	4.09%	100.00%

The first two entries in Table 12.21 comprise nearly 90% of all long jumps executed. The rest of the table is dominated by the short conditional branch instruction. There is little consistency to the static and dynamic measurements. For the two unconditional long jumps in the table, the backward jump executes at more than three times its static frequency while the forward jump has a greater static frequency by nearly four to one. The branches and jumps in the *others* category have a low execution frequency but appear statically more than three times as often.

Memory System Measurements

The performance of the object memory system is vital to a Smalltalk-80 implementation. We recognized this early, and we were able to improve memory system performance substantially through regular analyses of profile data. The following tables are the culmination of this effort.

Object/Class Distribution

Table 12.22 Classes in the System by Number of Instances

Class of Objects	Percentage	Cumulative Percentage
CompiledMethod	25.83%	25.83%
Symbol	21.84%	47.67%
Array	15.45%	63.12%
String	9.11%	72.23%
Association	3.81%	76.04%
Point	2.91%	78.95%
ClassOrganizer	2.80%	81.75%
MethodDictionary	2.80%	84.55%

Table 12.22 *(Cont.)*

Class of Objects	*Percentage*	*Cumulative Percentage*
Character	1.66%	86.21%
LargePositiveInteger	1.44%	87.65%
RemoteString	1.40%	89.05%
Metaclass	1.40%	90.45%
Float	1.33%	91.78%
TextLineInterval	1.09%	92.87%
all others (296)	7.13%	100.00%

Table 12.22 ranks the classes in the system according to the number of extant instances of each. Compiled methods and symbols (selectors) comprise nearly half of the objects in the system, and over 75% of the objects are instances of the top five classes. With over 200 classes in the system, this indicates that many have very few instances. In fact, 56.48% of classes (excluding metaclasses) have no instances at all and exist mainly for the behavior inherited by their subclasses; 26.38% have exactly one instance (a system controller, object, or dictionary). In all, 76.38% of all classes have fewer than 10 instances. This is a result of a particular style of Smalltalk programming making extensive use of an existing set of basic classes and certain paradigms.

Table 12.23 Classes in the System by Memory Usage

Class of Objects	*Percentage*	*Cumulative Percentage*
CompiledMethod	34.69%	34.69%
Array	13.19%	47.88%
Symbol	11.72%	59.60%
DisplayBitmap	9.76%	69.36%
String	9.74%	79.10%
Bitmap	8.62%	87.72%
MethodDictionary	4.18%	91.90%
ClassOrganizer	0.88%	92.78%
Metaclass	0.77%	93.55%
Dictionary	0.62%	94.17%
Association	0.60%	94.77%
all others (296)	5.23%	100.00%

Table 12.23 lists the classes by the amount of memory used by their instances. Compiled methods and symbols occupy nearly half the object space. The percentage for DisplayBitmap depends on the size of the display screen currently in use. In our case, a 640 x 480 pixel bit map was

active. The leading classes result from code (CompiledMethod, Array, Symbol, MethodDictionary and Metaclass) at 64.55% and graphics (DisplayBitmap and Bitmap) at 18.38% for a total of 82.93%.

Object Memory Access

Table 12.24 Object Memory Accesses by Type

Type of Access	Percentage	Cumulative Percentage
load pointer	72.45%	72.45%
store pointer	14.84%	87.29%
load word	7.59%	94.88%
store word	4.82%	99.70%
load byte	0.23%	99.93%
store byte	0.07%	100.00%

The *load pointer* and *store pointer* routines fetch and store object pointers in memory. The word and byte routines deal only with non-pointer 16- and 8-bit quantities. Because our interpreter caches the instruction and stack pointers, the memory access figures in Table 12.24 include neither stack push/pop operations nor bytecode instruction fetch. However, those aspects of execution have well-defined behavior and are very easy to monitor. The bias introduced by such factors can be significant. For example, if we include bytecode fetches with the other memory accesses, the share of *load byte* operations increases from 0.23% to 16.90%. This bias tends to cloud the real issues (bytecode fetch, like death and taxes, is inevitable).

These figures show *load pointer* dominating the memory accesses. This is not surprising in an object-oriented memory system. Pointer object accesses accounted for over 87% of all memory traffic. The memory system must endure nearly five accesses per bytecode, a figure which is due partly to the experimental nature of the system. A better implementation of the interpreter could reduce the number of accesses, but that was not our goal.

Load and store operations occur 40 times more frequently for words than for bytes. At 12.41% word accesses seem relatively high since they are not used by the system for any common operations. Instead, the infrequent but massive bit map operations are responsible for this rate of access.

Table 12.25 Load Pointer Operations by Class

Class of Object	Percentage	Cumulative Percentage
MethodContext	27.55%	27.55%
MethodDictionary	25.06%	52.61%
CompiledMethod	15.70%	68.31%
Array	7.00%	75.31%

Table 12.25 (*Cont.*)

Class of Object	Percentage	Cumulative Percentage
Class Array	4.95%	80.26%
BlockContext	3.11%	83.37%
Class String	1.29%	84.66%
Class LargePositiveInteger	1.25%	85.91%
all others (258)	14.09%	100.00%

The breakdown of *load pointer* operations by classes in Table 12.25 points out the memory intensive nature of some operations. The method and block context loads are for receiver and argument passing as well as operations occurring while they are neither the active nor the home context (since access to those are through a cache). The hash probes to the selector portion of message dictionaries comprise part of the method dictionary figure. The compiled method loads are from the literal frame for constants, pointers, and selectors. The array accesses correspond to the method pointer portion of the message dictionary—in other words, the method Oop fetch after a successful cache hit or search.

Table 12.26 Store Pointer Operations by Class

Class of Object	Percentage	Cumulative Percentage
MethodContext	81.96%	81.96%
BlockContext	8.43%	90.39%
Point	1.95%	92.34%
CompositionScanner	1.85%	94.19%
DisplayScanner	1.23%	95.42%
all others (102)	4.58%	100.00%

Context initialization, including receiver and argument passing, dominates *store pointer* operations in Table 12.26. Again this does not include operations on home or active contexts. Graphics and text manipulation consumes the remainder of the stores.

Table 12.27 Load Word Operations by Class

Class of Object	Percentage	Cumulative Percentage
DisplayBitmap	69.30%	69.30%
Bitmap	30.22%	99.52%
Float	0.40%	99.92%
Array	0.08%	100.00%

Bit map access constitutes over 99% of word object loads and stores. These bit maps come in two flavors: the bit map associated with the display and subsidiary bit maps used as graphics workspaces to prepare material for BitBlt to the display bit map. In Table 12.27 the relatively high percentage for Bitmap loads results from the transfer of their contents to the display bit map. Accordingly, Table 12.28 shows that *store word* operations are almost completely devoted to the display bit map, the eventual recipient of all words loaded. This indicates that the majority of graphics operations do not warrant the use of subsidiary bit maps, but rather operate directly on the display bit map.

Table 12.28 Store Word Operations by Class

Class of Object	Percentage	Cumulative Percentage
DisplayBitmap	97.41%	97.41%
Bitmap	2.06%	99.47%
Float	0.31%	99.78%
Array	0.11%	99.89%
LargePositiveInteger	0.11%	100.00%

String processing accounts for nearly 75% of all byte loads in Table 12.29. This is a result of the actions of the compiler, decompiler, and text editor. For byte stores, string processing declines by one-third as operations on large integer objects double their share to lead Table 12.30. Compiled methods are rarely the subject of byte accesses, and in general, byte accesses account for a tiny fraction of all types, mainly because the bytecode instruction fetches have direct access to the current compiled method.

Table 12.29 Load Byte Operations by Class

Class of Object	Percentage	Cumulative Percentage
String	67.96%	67.96%
LargePositiveInteger	25.46%	93.42%
Symbol	6.50%	99.92%
CompiledMethod	0.08%	100.00%

Table 12.30 Store Byte Operations by Class

Class of Object	Percentage	Cumulative Percentage
LargePositiveInteger	52.26%	52.26%
String	46.69%	98.95%
CompiledMethod	0.66%	99.61%
Symbol	0.39%	99.92%

Allocation and Instantiation

Table 12.31 Object Instantiation Types by Number

Type of Instantiation	Percentage	Cumulative Percentage
pointer object	98.34%	98.34%
byte object	1.20%	99.54%
word object	0.46%	100.00%

Pointer objects dominate the instantiation statistics in Table 12.31. Byte objects show a relatively higher rate of instantiation than word objects, probably because of the fine granularity of string processing. Such extremely lopsided statistics lead one to seriously question the need for type distinctions between pointer and non-pointer objects.

Table 12.32 Object Instantiation Types by Amount

Type of Instantiation	Percentage	Cumulative Percentage
pointer object	99.11%	99.11%
word object	0.49%	99.60%
byte object	0.40%	100.00%

Table 12.32 shows the percentage of memory allocated to the three object types. Pointer objects lead this category by an overwhelming margin with an even greater share than in Table 12.31. The next places are reversed, with word objects taking second. Though the system instantiates byte objects more frequently than word objects, the average word object is more than three times larger. A breakdown by classes and sizes will further clarify this situation.

Table 12.33 Object Instantiations by Size in Words

Size of Instantiation	Percentage	Cumulative Percentage
18 words	83.86%	83.86%
2 words	11.47%	95.33%
38 words	1.90%	97.23%
1 word	0.88%	98.11%
all others (98)	1.89%	100.00%

Instantiations are listed by object field size in Table 12.33. The three most popular sizes exceed 97% of all instantiations, suggesting a correlation with the preceding type figures. These sizes are those chiefly used for small contexts, points, and large contexts, respectively.

Table 12.34 Average Instantiation Size by Type

Type of Instantiation	Average Size in Words
pointer object	16.50 words
word object	14.53 words
byte object	6.67 words
all objects	16.38 words

From Table 12.34, the average allocation size is less than 17 words. The memory system actually stores byte objects in words, sometimes wasting an odd byte, as a relic from Xerox word-addressed memory architectures. However, there are so few byte objects in the system that this waste is not significant. The system averages about one instantiation for every dozen bytecodes executed. This makes for an allocation rate of 1.4 words per bytecode.

Table 12.35 Pointer Object Instantiations by Class

Class of Object	Percentage	Cumulative Percentage
MethodContext	83.02%	83.02%
Point	8.32%	91.34%
BlockContext	4.18%	95.52%
Rectangle	2.25%	97.77%
all others (79)	2.23%	100.00%

Method and block contexts comprise over 87% of pointer object instantiations (Table 12.35). In Smalltalk, the system creates and activates a method context for every non-primitive send, thus leading to their prominent position in these statistics. Over 10% of instantiations are for points and rectangles. Applications use points for screen management, since they are the fundamental reference for graphics operations.

Table 12.36 Pointer Object Instantiations by Size

Size of Object	Percentage	Cumulative Percentage
18 words	85.28%	85.28%
2 words	10.99%	96.27%
38 words	1.93%	98.20%
all others (37)	1.80%	100.00%

In Table 12.36 note that point size objects (2 words) are more prevalent than the large context size (38 words). The typically short methods of Smalltalk rarely require the deep stack provided by a large context.

The preceding tables actually underestimate the dominance of contexts in memory allocation. Context instantiations consume nearly 97 out of every 100 words allocated by the system. This is because the average context size (18.44 words) exceeds the mean size for all other objects by 14.52 words, thus boosting the context share from 87% to 97%. For pointer objects alone, if we exclude contexts the average object size drops to 3.28 words.

Even though bit maps are the most frequently accessed word objects, the system creates very few of them (only 3.69% of word object instantiations). Floating point objects are the most frequently instantiated word objects and their size (2) is the most popular, both at 96.31%. Most bit maps were at least 100 words, but so few were created that there was little impact on the average size of word objects. As evidence, the average size of word objects instantiated, excluding those of size 2, was 341.72 words.

Table 12.37 Byte Object Instantiations by Class

Class of Object	Percentage	Cumulative Percentage
LargePositiveInteger	87.12%	87.12%
String	12.59%	99.71%
CompiledMethod	0.17%	99.88%
Symbol	0.12%	100.00%

Large integers lead byte object instantiations by a substantial margin (Table 12.37), and together with strings, they encompass nearly all of them. Smalltalk does create many large integers because certain system functions use numbers greater than those small integer objects can contain. A number of solutions are possible: redesign those system functions to stay within the small integer range, implement the arbitrary precision arithmetic primitives in firmware or hardware, or increase the range of small integers through an implementation with 32-bit object pointers.

Table 12.38 Byte Object Instantiations by Size in Bytes

Size of Object	Percentage	Cumulative Percentage
2 bytes	37.91%	37.91%
1 byte	22.94%	60.85%
4 bytes	16.39%	77.24%
0 bytes	8.59%	85.83%
3 bytes	2.46%	88.29%
16 bytes	1.88%	90.17%
200 bytes	1.10%	91.27%
9 bytes	0.91%	92.18%
all others (94)	7.82%	100.00%

As one might expect, the byte object instantiations exhibited a more uniform distribution of sizes than the other types (Table 12.38). This reflects the fact that text varies greatly even within an application, and could vary with choice of identifiers, different user interfaces, or foreign language systems.

Memory
Reclamation

Table 12.39 Reference Count Size by Amount of Memory Reclaimed

Size of Count Field	Percent of Memory Reclaimed
2 bits	65.21%
3 bits	83.34%
4 bits	92.42%
5 bits	95.67%
6 bits	97.31%
7 bits	99.87%

The number of bits necessary for reference counts can be important, especially for those considering hardware implementations of count caches and managers (see Chapter 19). Table 12.39 shows that 4 bits can reclaim over 90% of memory, while 6 bits can manage over 97%. Because of the availability of fast byte access and arithmetic on our host machines, our system uses an 8 bit reference count field in a 16-bit header with additional separate permanent object and count overflow or exemption flag bits. Using our reference-count verifier, we have found only a few non-permanent object counts over 255, while some of the permanent kernel objects have hundreds of references.

Table 12.40 Pointer Chasing for Count Down Operations by Depth

Count Down Extent	Percentage of Count Downs	Cumulative Percentage
exempt	75.42%	75.42%
decremented, > zero	20.55%	95.97%
sons exempt	0.06%	96.03%
son decremented, > zero	3.52%	99.55%
grandsons exempt	0.20%	99.75%
grandson decremented, > zero	0.18%	99.93%
deeper levels (12)	0.07%	100.00%

The most expensive side of the dynamic memory management scheme involves reference count decrement and the possible pointer chasing and object deallocation. There are nearly two reference count decrements for every bytecode executed. Table 12.40 shows to what depth the associated pointer chasing went during experiments with the system. Objects with active reference counts accounted for 24.58% of count down invocations and the other 75.42% were on small integers or objects exempt from count management (either permanent or count overflow). Only 4.03% of count down invocations resulted in a decrement to zero and a subsequent deallocation for a rate of one every 13.61 bytecodes. Nearly all of these deallocations caused some pointer chasing to decrement the counts of objects referenced from the fields of the now dead object; the average depth of such pointer chases was 1.13 levels.

Table 12.41 Objects Disposed through Garbage Collection by Class

Class of Object	Percentage of Disposed	Cumulative Percentage
MethodContext	49.61%	49.61%
Process	18.74%	68.35%
BlockContext	13.49%	81.84%

Table 12.41 (*Cont.*)

Class of Object	Percentage of Disposed	Cumulative Percentage
String	3.83%	85.67%
Array	2.41%	88.08%
Association	2.06%	90.14%
all others (28)	9.86%	100.00%

Table 12.41 lists the trouble makers: the objects which compose inaccessible cycles. The high ranking of contexts has to do with the problem of passing a block context as an argument to a message and then having it passed down the line a few levels of sends. When it is all over, there is usually a three or four context cycle (almost invariably with at least one block context).

System Specifications

The size of our implementation varies with the modules included in the compilation. Table 12.42 lists the major system modules and their specifications. The primitive methods use over four times as much code as the bytecode interpreter itself. Although the memory and interpreter modules contain only about one-quarter of the code, they contain almost all of the macros and over half of the procedures in the system. We designed many of these procedures and macros as part of an implementation palette which we drew upon to build the system. As a result of this approach, some of them actually are never used. The extent of our development environment is apparent from its sheer size. The local routine module contains implementation-dependent code for the graphics device among other things.

Table 12.42 Module Specifications in the Hewlett-Packard Smalltalk-84 System

Module	# of Macros	# of Procedures	# of Statements
primitive methods	5	109	4600
development environment	18	34	2300
object memory	103	54	2000
local routines	0	50	1300
bytecode interpreter	88	22	1000
Totals	**214**	**269**	**11,200**

The code size of our system ranges from 50 kilobytes in an optimized version using procedures to 100 kilobytes for the multi-level debug version using in-line macros. The static data area ranges from 300 to 500 kilobytes, and the dynamic allocation from 400 to 500 kilobytes. Total memory usage falls between 750 kilobytes and 1 megabyte. The system installed at HP Labs has 80 kilobytes of code, 350 kilobytes of static data, and 400 kilobytes of dynamic data.

Throughout the implementation process, the execution profile of the system changed continually. At the beginning of July, the system was spending most of its time in the management of object memory. The top 14 procedures consumed 90% of execution time, and object memory management accounted for over half of that. As the implementation progressed, we steadily improved the performance of the most expensive routines. For example, we were able to reduce the overhead of object memory allocation and freeing to less than 6%. In our latest version, the top 14 procedures consume less than two-thirds of the time and one must add up the first 31 routines to reach 90%. One-quarter of the time is spent in bytecode fetch, event recognition, and the execution of all bytecodes except sends. The major object memory operations of allocation, garbage collection, and reference count management consume another 25%. The message send process takes 25% of the time, including message binding and context initialization. Finally, primitive functions use the final quarter of execution time.

Table 12.43 VAX Instructions Executed for Each Bytecode Category

Bytecode Category	Minimum	Maximum	Average
stack push	11	33	16
stack pop and store	2	47	28
return	43	81	46
branch and jump	3	13	11
message send	33	> 1000	120

Recently we investigated the VAX assembly code generated from our C modules. The main interpreter loop is 12 instructions long. Table 12.43 lists the additional instructions executed for each instruction category. The cost of maintaining contexts as separate objects plus the message lookup process contributed heavily to the relatively high figures for sends and returns. The 15-bit signed arithmetic required for small integer objects was also very expensive to implement on the VAX.

The performance of the system also changed substantially over the course of several months. By the first week in July 1981, our system was executing around 500 bytecodes per CPU second with slow object memory, and over 1000 bytecodes per CPU second with fast memory. A week later we were at 750/1500 bytecodes per CPU second (fast/slow memory versions). By early September, the interpreter was executing better than 2000 bytecodes per CPU second (fast memory version). Two weeks later it had increased to 2800 bytecodes per CPU second. The fifth version of HP Smalltalk boosted this to 4000 bytecodes per second. The final version of HP Smalltalk-84 performs at 5000 bytecodes per second on the average, with a peak rate around 25,000.

Table 12.44 Hewlett-Packard Smalltalk-84 testStandardTests Benchmark Results

Test	Description	Iterations	Seconds	Speed
LoadInstVar	load instance variable	20,000	3.183	12,570
LoadLiteralIndirect	load literal indirect	20,000	3.500	11,430
LoadLiteralNRef	load literal constant	20,000	3.350	11,940
LoadQuickConstant	load	100,000	15.950	12,540
LoadTempNRef	load 1 as a temp	20,000	3.384	11,820
LoadTempRef	load 0@0	20,000	3.851	10,390
PopStoreInstVar	store 1 in an inst. var.	200,000	24.083	16,610
PopStoreTemp	store 1 in a temp	200,000	23.600	16,950
16bitArith	add 20000 plus 20000	10,000	442.783	3730
3div4	divide 3 by 4	100,000	36.320	11,010
3plus4	add 3 plus 4	100,000	27.752	14,410
3times4	multiply 3 times 4	100,000	30.884	12,950
LargeIntArith	add 80000 plus 80000	1000	47.034	4000
ActivationReturn	activations and returns	16,383	42.084	4090
ShortBranch	short branch on false	100,000	14.850	26,940
WhileLoop	simple while loop	10,000	7.800	11,540
ArrayAt	send at: to an array	20,000	15.000	5330
ArrayAtPut	send at:put: to an array	20,000	17.884	5590
Size	send size to a string	20,000	11.367	5280
StringAt	send at: to a string	20,000	17.284	4630
StringAtPut	send at:put: to a string	20,000	18.983	5270
StringReplace	replace part of a string	5000	67.385	4630
BlockCopy	send blockCopy: 0	20,000	22.000	3640
Class	send class to a point	20,000	4.334	13,840
Creation	send new to Point	20,000	16.608	3610
LoadThisContext	load a context	20,000	4.620	8660
PointX	send x to a point	20,000	7.867	7630
StreamNext	send next to a stream	20,000	23.934	2510

Table 12.44 (*Cont.*)

Test	Description	Iterations	Seconds	Speed
StreamNextPut	send nextPut: to a stream	20,000	28.534	2800
Value	send value to a block	20,000	31.433	1910
Compiler	compile dummy method	5	140.932	3890
Decompiler	decompile Form and Class	1	645.200	3710
Inspect	create an inspector	1	10.500	3540
TextFormatting	format a bunch of text	5	63.633	4030
TextEditing	text replacement	20	215.667	3120

Table 12.44 gives the results of running the testStandardTests set of benchmarks on the HP Smalltalk-84 system. Note that this is an earlier version of the benchmarks than the one in the current Smalltalk-80 image. The table includes the time in seconds reported by Smalltalk for running each entire test, and the speed of execution in bytecodes per second. We ran the tests on a single-user VAX-11/780 with 4 megabytes main memory under 4.1BSD UNIX. The system was in a normal configuration with display, keyboard, and mouse active. Clearly, the primitive method situation is the most serious. The benchmarks for primitive methods averaged about 5000 bytecodes per second, seriously limiting opportunities for greater speed.

Conclusion

Our curiosity about the Smalltalk-80 system had lead us down a primrose path. When the termination of the project washed away the path, we traded in our programming language robes for the lab coats of the pathologist. The result of our post mortem was simple: there was little hope for performance high enough to lure users away from traditional programming systems. Although we did not have the luxury of iterating and refining our implementation, the experience of those who did is very discouraging. No one in the test program was able to achieve performance considerably above 25 KIPS. Even with microcode assist, it is difficult to imagine an implementation performing at better than 50% of native mode operation. In our experience, though users like the functionality of a Smalltalk system, they are unwilling to accept a significant loss in performance.

**Acknowledg-
ments**

The analysis of the Smalltalk-80 system at Hewlett-Packard Laboratories was basically a post-mortem. Nearly all of the work described in this report happened after the project terminated. I appreciate the patience and understanding of my management during the period when I spent my spare time generating and analyzing the body of statistics.

References

1. Clark, D. W., and Levy, H. M., "Measurement and Analysis of Instruction Use in the VAX-11/780", Proceedings of the Ninth Annual Symposium on Computer Architecture, pp. 9-17, Austin, TX, 1982.

2. *Ibid.*

13

An Assessment of Method-Lookup Caches for Smalltalk-80 Implementations

Thomas J. Conroy
Eduardo Pelegri-Llopart
Computer Science Division
Department of Electrical Engineering and
Computer Sciences
University of California, Berkeley

Abstract

A unique feature of the Smalltalk-80 language is the dynamic binding of methods to a message based on the class of its receiver. This binding requires a lookup of the selector in the message dictionaries of the superclass chain for the receiver. A way to avoid this time-consuming process is to cache the most frequently used information. In this paper, we present an assessment of the cost effectiveness of this mechanism. A theoretical analysis characterizes the behavior of the cache in terms of variables dependent on both the particular implementation and on the Smalltalk code being executed. One result is that the benefits of the cache heavily depend on the relation of the speed of the implementation to the speed of the cache accesses, and also on the instruction mix being executed. For software implementations of virtual machines, a method-cache can greatly enhance performance. We then present the implementation of the software method-cache in BS, the Smalltalk-80 implementation at UC Berkeley (see Chapter 11). Measurements from this implementation show that the cache increased execution speed by 37%.

Introduction

A unique feature of the Smalltalk-80 language is the dynamic binding of methods based on the class of the receiver. Conceptually, given a receiver and a message selector, the actions to perform are[1,2]:

1. Determine the class of the receiver,

2. Search for the message selector in the message dictionaries of the receiver's superclass chain, and

3. Retrieve the method associated with the message selector in the dictionary where the search succeeded.

A direct implementation of this *lookup* process is time-consuming since a large number of bytecodes involve method-lookup. A solution to this problem is to *cache*[3] the result of the whole lookup process. A cache can provide a fast by-pass of the lengthy search.

A method cache stores combinations of receivers and message selectors, allowing look-ups to be retrieved quickly when the combinations needed for the look-up are in the cache. For those combinations not found in the cache, a full look-up has to be done. An additional overhead present in caching is the cost of trying to keep the more frequently required combinations on the cache. Clearly, the feasibility of this technique depends on how often the bypass succeeds and the relative cost of each alternative.

The effect of the technique on the performance of an implementation is related to the cost of look-ups, the cost of the remaining components and the relative occurrence of each part. In this short paper we present an assessment of this cache mechanism using a simple theoretical analysis and measurements from a software implementation of the Smalltalk-80 virtual machine, (see Chapter 11).

Analysis

This analysis compares the behavior of a straightforward implementation of a Smalltalk-80 virtual machine to an implementation with a method-cache. Subscripted capital letters represent virtual machine implementation-dependent quantities, while greek letters represent Smalltalk-80 code-dependent quantities. Specifically,

- A with a subscript represents the time for completing a method look-up,

- S represents the number of bytecodes/second (speed), and

- F represents the fraction of total time spent in doing method-lookups.

We stress the distinction between Smalltalk-80 code-dependent and implementation-dependent quantities because the former are constants independent of the implementation. For example, implementations may differ drastically in the number of bytecodes executed per second, but for the same Smalltalk-80 code, the number of method-lookups per bytecode would be identical. The following table lists the variables used and their definitions.

Table 13.1 Parameters and Definitions

Implementation Dependent Values

A_{miss}	method lookup time for a cache miss*
A_{nc}	method lookup time without a cache
A_{hit}	method lookup time for a cache hit

Implementation and Smalltalk Code Dependent Values

A_{xK}	average method lookup time for an xK entry method cache
S_{nc}	number of bytecodes/sec without a cache
S_{xK}	number of bytecodes/sec with an xK entry method cache
$S_{optimal}$	the number of bytecodes/sec possible assuming zero access time for method lookup
F_{nc}	fraction of total time spent in lookup without a cache
F_{xK}	fraction of total time spent in lookup with an entry xK cache
φ	hit ratio (also depends on cache characteristics)

Smalltalk Code Dependent Values

β	number of lookups/bytecode

*Strictly speaking, A_{miss} and A_{nc} also depend on the length of the superclass chain, and hence on the Smalltalk code being executed.

An implementation will be characterized by: A_{miss} and A_{hit}, S_{nc} and A_{nc}, and φ and β. These values, together with the equations shown below, are used to obtain the remaining values of interest.

The fraction of time spent doing method lookups is related to the number of lookups per bytecode, the lookup access time, and the number of bytecodes per second by the relationship $F = S\beta A$. Applying this relationship to a cache and a non-cache implementation gives

$$F_{nc} = \beta A_{nc}S_{nc} \quad \text{and} \quad F_{xK} = \beta A_{xK}S_{xK}.$$

The average cache access is given by the usual relation

$$A_{xK} = \varphi A_{hit} + (1-\varphi)A_{miss}.$$

The speed (bytecodes per second) depends partly on how much time is spent in method lookup. $S_{optimal}$ assumes the time to be zero.

If $T_{optimal}$ and T_{nc} are the times required to execute N bytecodes at speeds $S_{optimal}$ and S_{nc}, then we have

$$S_{optimal} = \frac{N}{T_{optimal}} = \frac{S_{nc}\,T_{nc}}{T_{nc}\text{-}total\ lookup\ time}$$

where *total lookp time* $= N\beta A_{nc}$.

Replacing *total lookup time* by its value, and simplifying, we obtain

$$S_{optimal} = \frac{S_{nc}}{1 - S_{nc}\,\beta A_{nc}} = \frac{S_{nc}}{1\text{-}F_{nc}}.$$

Similarly, the speed of the cache implementation, S_{xK} is derived. The difference is that the cache's average method lookup access time is used instead of the non-cache access time.

If T_{nc} and T_{xK} are the times required to execute N bytecodes at speeds S_{nc} and S_{xK} we have

$$S_{xK} = \frac{N}{T_{xk}} = \frac{S_{nc}\,T_{nc}}{T_{nc} - total\ time\ gained\ by\ caching}$$

where *total time gained by caching* $= N\beta(A_{xk} - A_{nc})$.

obtaining,

$$S_{xK} = \frac{S_{nc}}{1 - S_{nc}\,\beta(A_{nc} - A_{xK})} = \frac{S_{nc}}{1 - F_{nc} + S_{nc}\,\beta\,A_{xk}}$$

Using the equations above, the ratio $S_{xK}/S_{optimal}$ is computed. This ratio expresses how close the implementation comes to the theoretical lower limit of zero access time for method lookups, and may be expressed as

$$\frac{S_{xK}}{S_{optimal}} = \frac{1 - S_{nc}\,\beta A_{nc}}{1 - S_{nc}\,\beta(A_{nc} - A_{xK})} = \frac{1}{1 + S_{optimal}\,\beta A_{xK}}.$$

Furthermore, the ratio S_{xK}/S_{nc} gives the factor increase in execution speed of a cache implementation compared to a non-cache implementation. This ratio can be written as

$$\frac{S_{xK}}{S_{nc}} = \frac{1}{1 - S_{nc}\,\beta(A_{nc} - A_{xK})}.$$

If we consider a given cache organization, and a fixed program behavior, the speed increase has the form $1/(1\text{-}KS_{nc})$, where $K = \beta(A_{nc}\text{-}A_{xK})$.

One use of this formula is to determine the speed increase that a non-cache-implementation will get by using a caching scheme. In the next section we present a particular Smalltalk-80 implementation, and on p. 245 we present some measurements on its behavior. Implementors can use these measurements as guidelines to obtain for their particular case, approximations to the expected gains.

The Implementation in Berkeley Smalltalk

Currently, Smalltalk-80 virtual machines are being implemented on general purpose computers. Smalltalk-80 implementors should consider adding a software cache for method-lookup. As an example of the considerations involved, we now present, in some detail, the implementation used in BS. BS executes on the VAX-11 family of computers, under the UNIX operating system. The programming language used is C. The algorithms were coded with extreme care (sometimes checking the code produced by the C compiler), and macros were used whenever possible.

Cache Structure

The implemented cache is of the direct-mapped variety. The underlying data structure consists of four arrays, each with 1K entries. The first three arrays have entries 2 bytes long (one VAX-11 word); the last one 1 byte long. The first two arrays (CacheSel and CacheClass) contain the Oops of the combinations for selector and class that are cached. The remaining two (CacheMethod and CachePrimitive) contain the actual information: the method Oop, and an indication of whether it is a primitive or not.

The organization as separate arrays allows the use of the VAX-11 *index* mode to access all desired information. Thanks to a careful management of the available registers on the hardware, most of the time the fastest modes can be employed. Thus, to access CacheSel[i], if i is in register r0, we can simply use

    movw CacheSel[r0],

Note that an implementation as a field in an array of records would produce much longer code, including shifts (or divides) to access the appropriate entry in the array, plus additional code to access the field.

Recently BS has been extended to include a playback facility. With this facility, a script of all the bytecodes executed in a session can be obtained, and later replayed to reproduce the session. In this way we have been able to study the effect of different cache sizes on the hit ratio. For a particular interactive session of about 2M bytecodes, using as a hash function a simple EX-OR the hit ratios found were:

Table 13.2 Hit Ratio and Cache Size

entries	64	128	256	512	1024	2048	4096
hit ratio	65.3%	77.0%	86.1%	90.4%	93.1%	95.0%	95.4%

This makes a cache of size 1K or 2K the more adequate for most situations.

□ *The lookup algorithm*   The lookup algorithm is simple. An entry on the cache is selected using some function of the class and selector Oops. Then a comparison is done to check the validity of the information associated to the entry. On a hit, the required information is already obtained. On a miss we have to go through the complete lookup search; when the correct binding is found, the entries in the cache are updated with the appropriate information.

Clearly, the selection of the hashing function is important. Three simple functions are:

1. hash(class,selector) ← (class EXOR selector) AND cacheSize

2. hash(class,selector) ← (class AND selector) AND cacheSize

3. hash(class,selector) ← (class ADD selector) AND cacheSize

As the difference in speed between an EXOR and an ADD is small, on the order of .07 us (approximate value for the 2 register versions of these instructions on a VAX-11/780), 1 and 3 have similar qualities. Although AND requires two instructions on the VAX-11, it also has a similar speed. The total access time in the case of a hit, A_{hit} is reasonably small because of the explicit handling of registers done in C.

The playback facility of BS has allowed us to compare the different functions. The results for the same sample as mentioned above are as follows:

Table 13.3 Hit Ratio and Hash Function

Function	Hit Ratio	A_{hit}	A1K
1.	93.1%	4.4	23.6
2.	61.6%	4.5	111.82
3.	94.8%	4.5	19.08

It is clear that 2 is a loser and its use is discouraged. The function originally used in BS was 1; its performance is acceptable. The best choice is

3, the hashing function currently being used in BS (and also in the Dolphin and Dorado implementations[4]).

Measurements in BS

We now present some measurements of the BS implementation. They show a 32-37% increase in the execution speed of the implementation.

When these measurements were made, the hashing function used was the one referred to as 1 above; otherwise the implementation is the one presented there. Two different Smalltalk-80 programs were executed to obtain representative samples. One program was an interactive session of editing, browsing, and short arithmetic computations comprising 6.8 million bytecodes. The other was the Tower of Hanoi problem, a computation intensive problem, comprising 1.5 million bytecodes.

On a VAX-11/780, the constants for cache accesses for BS are

$$A_{hit} \quad 4.4 \ \mu sec$$
$$A_{nc} \quad 187 \ \mu sec$$
$$A_{miss} \quad 284 \ \mu sec$$

The data from the two programs and the computed results are summarized in the table below.

Table 13.4 Berkeley Smalltalk Results

Parameter	Interactive	Tower of Hanoi
φ (hit ratio)	0.943	0.996
β lookup/bytecode	0.186	0.078
$A_{1K} \ \mu sec$	20.4	5.52
S_{nc} bytecodes/sec	8,750	17,350
$S_{optimal}$ bytecodes/sec	12,570	23,230
S_{1K} bytecodes/sec	12,000	23,000
F_{nc}	0.304	0.253
F_{1K}	0.046	0.010
$S_{1K}/S_{optimal}$	0.955	0.990
S_{1K}/S_{nc}	1.372	1.326

The numeric values for the parameters and values were obtained using various mechanisms. A_{hit} was obtained from the VAX-11 code that accesses the cache. The exact time used by the sequence of instructions is difficult to measure because of the effect of the VAX-11/780 cache; timing the instruction loop gives an overly optimistic value since all the code ends up in the cache. A_{nc} and A_{miss} were obtained by profiling the execution of the updating routines[5]. The difference between the A_{nc} value and the A_{miss} is the time required to update the cache. The cache is updated every time there is a cache miss. The profile tool also gave the number of lookups and the number of bytecodes executed, used to determine β, and the number of misses, used to determine φ. Finally, S_{1K} was obtained from the user time it took to execute the programs. The remaining values were obtained from the equations.

There are several important points to make. The software cache achieves an average method access time of 20.4 microseconds for the interactive session. The Tower of Hanoi problem is atypical and tends to give a best case result since the small amount of code generates few cache misses. Nevertheless note that both hit ratios are high, 94% and 99%. The cache of 1K entries increases execution speed by 37.2 percent (interactive), and 32.6 percent (Hanoi). Execution speed is slower than $S_{optimal}$ by only 4.5 percent (interactive) and 1.0 percent (Hanoi). (Note that, since the two execution profiles are different, we cannot compare the two executions directly.)

Conclusions

Fast method access is important in achieving better Smalltalk-80 performance. We have presented the main parameters and relations involved in the method lookup process. From these it has been shown that the benefits of adding a method cache depend on the relation of the overall speed of the implementation to the speed of the cache accesses, as well as on the more traditional considerations of hit ratio and miss/hit access speeds.

On an optimized VAX-11/780 implementation, the addition of a software-supported method cache produced a nine-fold reduction of the time required by the lookup process. This by itself, increased the overall speed of the Berkeley Smalltalk-80 implementation by 37%.

Acknowledgments

We heartily thank all the people on the Smalltalk island, both at Berkeley and at Xerox Palo Alto Research Center. We especially thank the two Daves, Dave Ungar for making BS a reality, and Dave Patterson for encouraging us to write this paper. Without them this work would have never existed. We also want to thank all the reviewers, their comments largely increased the readability of this paper.

References

1. Goldberg, Adele, and Robson, David, *Smalltalk-80: The Language and Its Implementation*, Addison-Wesley, Reading, Mass., 1983.

2. Krasner, Glenn, "The Smalltalk-80 Virtual Machine", *Byte* vol. 6, no. 8, pp. 300–320, Aug. 1981.

3. Lipway, J. S. "The Structural Aspects of the System/360 Model 85 II: The Cache", *IBM Systems Journal* vol. 7, no. 1, pp. 15–21, 1968.

4. Deutsch, L. Peter, Private Communication, 1982.

5. Graham, Susan L., Kessler, Peter B., and McKursick, Marshall K., "Gprof: A Profiler Using Call Graphs", in Proceedings of the Sigplan Conference on Compiler Construction, June 1982.

PART FOUR

Proposals for the Future of the Smalltalk-80 System

14

LOOM—Large Object-Oriented Memory for Smalltalk-80 Systems

Ted Kaehler
Glenn Krasner
Software Concepts Group
Xerox Palo Alto Research Center
Palo Alto, California

Introduction

The Smalltalk-80 virtual machine is specified as a memory-resident system containing up to 2^{15} objects. When full, it typically occupies about 2M bytes of memory. Unfortunately, many machines do not have this capacity in main memory, and many applications require, or will require, more than this capacity. To solve this space problem, one typically uses a virtual memory system in which the resident, "real" memory is used as a cache for the larger mass storage, "virtual" memory. LOOM, Large Object-Oriented Memory, is a virtual memory system designed and implemented for the Smalltalk-80 system. The most important feature of the LOOM design is that it provides virtual addresses that are much wider than either the word size or the memory address size of the computer on which it runs.

LOOM is a single-user virtual memory system that swaps objects and operates without assistance from the programmer. Virtual memory systems may be characterized by the amount of attention that the programmer must pay to the transfers between virtual and real memories, by the extent to which the memory is shared among users, and by the granularity of transfer between memory levels. Overlay mechanisms are an example of systems that require much programmer attention, while all common paging systems require none[1]. Databases may be viewed as the extreme in allowing sharing; the virtual memory for Interlisp-D[2] is one example of a single-user virtual memory. Most overlay systems transfer program segments, while paging systems transfer disk pages, and a few systems such as the OOZE virtual memory for Smalltalk-76[3] transfer objects.

The LOOM Design

We view virtual memory design as a process of trying to determine what happens most often, making it go fast, and hoping that it will continue to be what happens most often. Our experience with previous Smalltalk systems gave us three major assumptions on which we based the LOOM design: programmers and users have a large appetite for memory, object-swapping is an efficient and effective scheme, and the Smalltalk-80 design for handling resident objects is worth keeping. From these assumptions and the desire to provide a large number of objects on a machine with a narrow word width, we created the major design decisions.

- LOOM assumes that the object is the unit of locality of reference. It swaps individual objects between primary and secondary memory, and allows into main memory only those objects actually needed by the interpreter. Unlike paging systems, LOOM packs objects in main memory at maximum density.

- LOOM is designed for machines with 16-bit words. Fields of objects in main memory are 16 bits wide.

- The address space of the secondary memory is large. LOOM allows as many as 2^{31} objects.

- The interpreter accesses objects in main memory exactly as it does in a resident Smalltalk-80 interpreter. When the necessary objects are already in main memory, the interpreter runs as fast as it did in the resident system.

In order to allow the large number of possible objects, and yet treat the resident objects in the same way they are treated in a non-LOOM Smalltalk-80 implementation, we decided to create two different name spaces. The same object is identified by names from different spaces when it resides in different parts of the system, as shown in Fig. 14.1. The identifier of an object is called an *Oop*, which stands for "object pointer." An object in secondary storage has a 32-bit Oop (a long Oop), and each of its fields containing a pointer to another object holds that

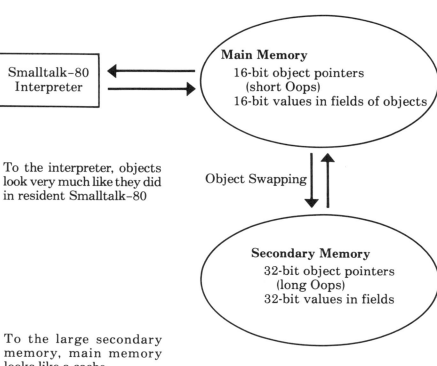

To the interpreter, objects look very much like they did in resident Smalltalk-80

To the large secondary memory, main memory looks like a cache.

Figure 14.1

pointer as a 32-bit Oop. An object cached in main memory has a 16-bit Oop (a short Oop) and 16-bit fields. As in the resident Smalltalk-80 implementation, main memory has a resident object table (*ROT* or sometimes called an OT), which contains the actual main memory address of each resident object. An object's short Oop is an index into the ROT, so that the object's address can be determined from its Oop with a single addition and memory reference. When an object is brought into main memory from disk, it is assigned a short Oop, and those of its fields that refer to other objects in main memory are assigned the appropriate short Oop. Fields pointing to objects that are not resident are handled specially, the details of which make up the crux of LOOM.

Thus, when all objects in the working set are in main memory, LOOM behaves just like a resident Smalltalk-80 implementation—all objects have short Oops that index the ROT, providing their actual core address. When an object in core must access one of its fields that refers to an object that is not in core, something special must happen. LOOM brings that object into core, assigns it a short Oop, and resumes normal Smalltalk execution. The main memory resident space of 2^{15} objects acts as a cache for up to 2^{31} objects on the disk.

The LOOM Details

The important issues in the LOOM design implementation are:

- The representation of resident objects,
- The representation of objects in secondary memory,
- The translation between representations, and
- The identification of times when the translations must occur.

The Representation of Resident Objects

Resident objects are represented in a manner similar to their representation in a resident Smalltalk-80 system. Each object has as its name in main memory, a short (16-bit) Oop. The Oop indexes the ROT in order to provide the starting address of the object's body, as shown in Fig. 14.2. The ROT entry also has reference-count bits, and a few other bits, described later. The body of each object contains a word for the length of the body, a pointer to the object's class, and the object's fields. Each field is either a pointer to another object or a collection of "bits", in the same manner as resident Smalltalk-80 fields. We will only deal with pointer fields here. Each field (as well as the class pointer) that refers

Format of Objects in Main Memory

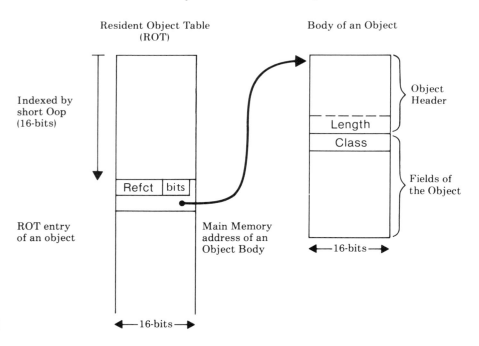

Figure 14.2

to another resident object contains the short Oop of that object. Fields that refer to non-resident objects (objects on secondary storage) contain a short Oop of one of two types, a *leaf* or a *lambda*.

In addition to these fields, resident objects in a LOOM system have three extra words. Two of these words contain the long (32-bit) Oop of that object. The third word, known as the delta word, contains a delta reference count and some other bits. The short Oop of an object is not only an index into the ROT for that object's address, but is also the result of a hash function applied to that object's long Oop. See Fig. 14.3, p. 256. The algorithm for translating an object's short Oop to its long Oop is:

1. Index the ROT with the short Oop to get the body address
2. Load the long Oop from the first two words of the body

The algorithm for translating an object's long Oop to its short Oop is:

1. Convert the long Oop into a short Oop by applying the hash function
2. Index the ROT with this short Oop to get a body address
3. Look at the first two words of the body
4. If they match the long Oop, then the short Oop is correct
5. If not, create a new short Oop from the current one with a reprobe function (e.g., add 1), and go to step 2

The Representation of Objects in Secondary Memory

Secondary memory is addressed as a linear space of 32-bit words. Objects start with a header word that contains 16 bits of length and some status bits. Each pointer field in the object is 32 bits wide. Non-pointer fields (such as the bytes in Strings) are packed, with 4 bytes in each 32-bit word. Resident Smalltalk-80 SmallIntegers are rather short to be occupying a full word on the disk. However, since they represent legitimate object pointers, their 15 significant bits are stored along with a flag value in a 32-bit pointer field on the disk. The long Oops in pointer fields are 31-bit disk pointers, addressing as many objects as will fit into 2^{31} disk words (32-bit words). Fields of objects on secondary storage always refer to objects in secondary storage and do not change when the object to which they point is currently cached in main memory. As shown in Fig. 14.4, no information about primary memory is ever stored in secondary memory. Information such as an object's short Oop, its location in primary memory, or whether it is currently cached in primary memory are never recorded in secondary memory.

Finding an Object's Long Oop from Its Short Oop

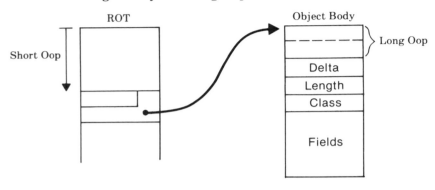

Finding an Object's Short Oop from Its Long Oop

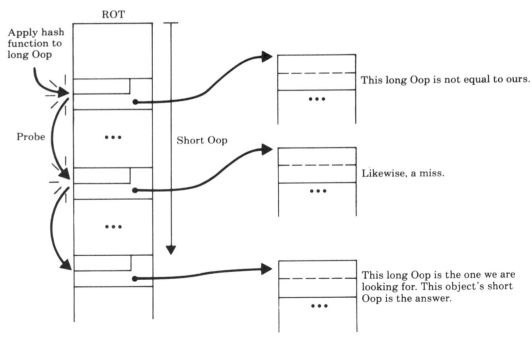

Figure 14.3

**How Objects in Primary and Secondary Memory
Refer to Other Objects.**

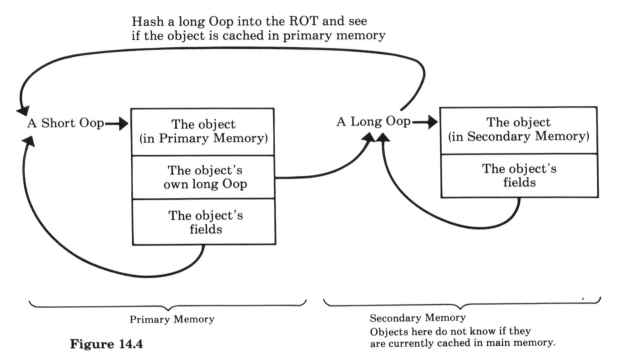

Figure 14.4

When an object on secondary storage is brought into main memory, its fields must be translated from the long form to short form. The object is assigned an appropriate short Oop (one to which its long Oop hashes), a block of memory is reserved for it, and all of its fields are translated from long Oops to short Oops. Those fields that point to objects already in main memory are given the short Oops of those objects; those that point to objects not in main memory are handled in one of two ways, with leaves or with lambdas.

☐ *Leaves* Leaves are pseudo-objects that represent an object on secondary storage. They have a short Oop hashed by that object's long Oop and a ROT entry, but their image in memory only contains a length word, disk address words, and the delta word. Their image contains no class word or fields, as shown in Fig. 14.5. Leaves therefore, only take up 4 words of memory, whereas the average object takes up 13. Leaves are created without looking at that object's image on secondary storage.

This is very important, since a major cost in virtual memories is the number of disk accesses. The short Oop of the leaf may be treated as if it were the short Oop of the object; it may be pushed and popped on the stack, stored into fields of other objects, without ever needing the actual contents of that object. Its reference count can be incremented and decremented (see p. 262).

A Leaf

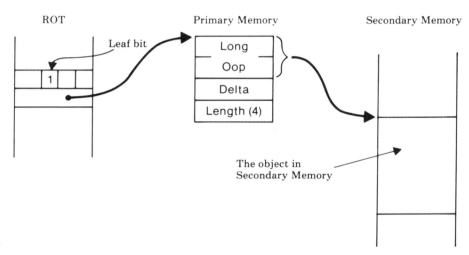

Figure 14.5

An object is always in one of three states. Either the entire object is in main memory, a leaf for the object is in main memory, or the object exists only on the disk. See Fig. 14.6. When the interpreter needs a field from an object which is represented by a leaf, the entire object with its fields must be brought into main memory from disk. Since the leaf contains the disk Oop, the body is easy to find. After the body is translated into main memory form, its core address is stored into the leaf's OT entry, and the leaf body is discarded. Short Oop references to the object remain the same, but now the full object is actually there. Since a leaf can be substituted for an object body and vice versa with no effect on pointers to the object, LOOM is always free to make more room in main memory by turning resident objects into leaves.

☐ *Lambdas* Lambdas are the second way to represent fields of resident objects that refer to objects on secondary storage. Lambda is a place holder for a pointer to an object which has not been assigned a short Oop. Its purpose is to reduce the number of leaves in the system. Lambda is a pseudo-Oop, a reserved short Oop (the Oop 0) which is not the name of any resident object. Consider an object which has a lambda in one of its fields. To discover the actual value of that field, LOOM must go back to the object's image on secondary storage, look in that

States of an Object in LOOM

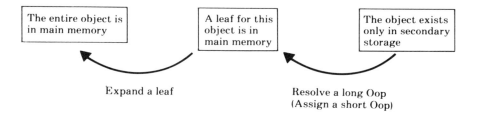

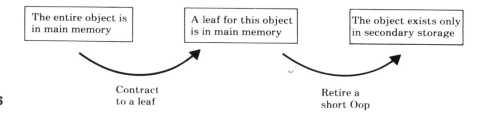

Figure 14.6

field for a long pointer, and create a leaf or resident object. This means that the cost of fetching a lambda field is an extra disk reference. However, unlike leaves, lambdas do not take up ROT entries (they all use the single pseudo-ROT entry at 0) and they do not take up any main memory storage. Since the number of ROT entries is limited to 2^{15}, and main memory is a somewhat scarce resource, this saving can be important. During an object's typical stay in main memory, some of its fields will not be referenced. If leaves are created for the values in those fields when the object is swapped in, and then destroyed again when the object is thrown out, much work is wasted. Putting lambdas into fields which will not be referenced during the object's current stay in primary memory saves both the space and the time needed to create and destroy many leaves.

Determining whether to make the fields of an object be leaves or lambdas when the object is brought into main memory is a tricky business. The choice of strategy strongly affects the performance of a LOOM system. Creating a leaf takes more time and uses up more memory and a ROT entry, but does not cause any extra disk accesses. A lambda will cause an extra disk access if the field it occupies happens to be referenced, but a lambda is faster to create. One way to make the decision between leaf and lambda is to rely on history; if a field was a lambda when this object was written to the disk one time, it is likely to remain a lambda during its next trip into main memory. Each pointer field of the disk contains a hint, the *noLambda* bit, and the object faulting code follows the advice of the hint.

The Translation Between Object Representations

Translating between the memory-resident and secondary-storage representations of an object is straightforward. For those fields that contain short Oops, the Oop refers to an object or a leaf. The corresponding long Oop can be found in the header of the object or leaf. If the field refers to an object which has not yet been assigned a long pointer, a long pointer is assigned to the object and a copy is installed in the field. For those fields that contain lambdas, the field is guaranteed not to be changed from the object's previous disk image. (The object's disk image is read before it is written). If the object being translated still has some short pointers to it (has a positive in-core reference count), then it must be converted to a leaf instead of being deleted completely from core.

When to Translate

We have already mentioned when the translation between representations must occur. When a field of an object being brought into main memory has the noLambda bit set, and that field refers to a non-resident object, then a leaf is created. A leaf is also created when a field of a resident object containing a lambda is accessed. When the interpreter needs to access a field in a leaf, the flow of control in LOOM begins (see Fig. 14.7). The leaf is expanded into a resident object; its fields are translated from long form to short form. This is called an *object fault* (because the similar situation in paging virtual memory systems, trying to access a page that is not resident, is called a *page fault*). The inverse operation, *contracting* an object into a leaf, may be done at any time. The final part of an object's journey into primary memory consists of destroying the leaf and reusing its short Oop and memory space. This can only be done when there are no longer any fields in any resident objects pointing to the leaf.

Lambdas may be resolved into leaves and leaves may be expanded into full objects before they are needed, and this is called a *prefetch*. The complementary operations of contraction and prefetch of objects can both be done in the background. The exact order and mix of objects to prefetch or contract can be adjusted at run-time to optimize the performance of secondary storage (disk head movement or network traffic).

LOOM Implementation Details

In this section, we provide some details of how LOOM may be implemented. In particular we discuss the discovery of object faults, reference-counting, and the assignment of the extra bits in the ROT entry and the delta word.

Object Faults

Object faults occur when the interpreter tries to access a field in a leaf or a field in an object whose value is lambda. By the time the interpreter scrutinizes them, all objects must be full resident objects. How can leaves and lambdas be discovered without greatly slowing the speed of the interpreter?

The Flow of Control in LOOM

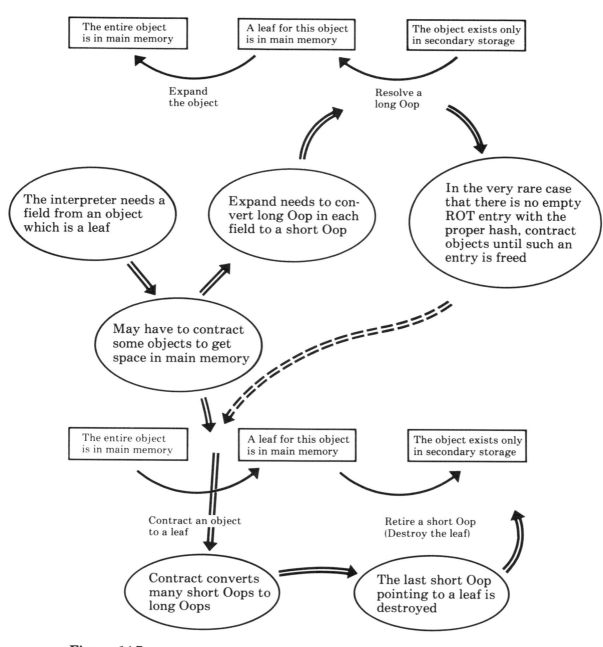

Figure 14.7

It has been our experience that implementations tend to have a single subroutine (or expanded macro) that takes an Oop and sets up some base register to point to the actual address of that object. We call this subroutine "Otmap." It corresponds roughly to the ot:bits: method of the memory manager in the formal specification of the Smalltalk-80 virtual machine, in *Smalltalk-80: The Language and its Implementation*[4]. Otmap is called if and only if you want to fetch or store a field of an object. Note that this is exactly the condition where you must test for the object being a leaf. (Otmap may sometimes be used for other purposes—for example a compaction routine may call Otmap to get the main memory address of the object in order to move it, but it wants to treat leaves and objects the same. These cases tend to be rare, so it is worth having a second subroutine for them.) We reserve one bit of the ROT entry to say whether the entry is for an object or a leaf. The Otmap subroutine tests this bit and calls the LOOM routines when the entry is a leaf. Since both words of the ROT entry are fetched anyway, this extra test usually only costs one or two extra instruction executions.

Testing for lambda however, must be done on *every* field reference. In the worst case, this would mean testing occurs every time a field is fetched from an object and every time an object is pushed onto the stack. To decrease the number of tests, we include one bit in each resident object called "holds lambda." It is set by the LOOM routines whenever that object has a field that is a lambda. The interpreter guarantees that the current context, the home context, the current method, and the receiver all have no lambdas in them. If any of them does contain a lambda, then the LOOM routines are called to make those fields into leaves. In this way, the most common fields fetched and all stack operations can work without testing for lambda. Note that these objects must be cleared of lambdas only when the active context changes. This occurs during message sends, returns, process switches, and during the execution of BlockContext value and value:.

It is useful to note that the LOOM design actually will work with leaves alone, and without lambdas. When the expand routine brings an object into main memory, it turns all the fields into leaves and never creates a lambda. This approach tends to use more short Oops and main memory than the full LOOM design, but could be an intermediate stage in the implementation; providing a working virtual memory system with only the modification to the Otmap subroutine.

Reference Counting

Although some Smalltalk-80 implementations use mark/sweeping garbage collection, most implementations so far, including ours, use reference counting to identify garbage. Therefore we will describe the reference-counting scheme as it applies to LOOM. Reference counting serves two different purposes. One purpose is to detect when the total count of any object goes to zero. The other is to detect when the last short pointer to any object disappears so that the short pointer may be reused. The resident Smalltalk-80 interpreter keeps reference counts of short pointers. This count is kept in the ROT. LOOM uses the ROT reference count to keep the number of short pointers to an object. In addition, every object on the disk contains a reference count which is the number of long pointers to the object. The total count is the sum of the number of short and long pointers to an object. Whenever a long Oop is converted to a short Oop and installed in a field in main memory, both counts for the object pointed at must change. To avoid a disk access to find and modify the long Oop count every time a field is converted, LOOM keeps a "delta" or running change in the long Oop reference count for each object in main memory. The true long pointer reference count of any object is the count found on the disk in the object's header plus the count found in the "delta" part of the object's delta word in main memory. Fig. 14.8 shows the ROT entry, object body, and disk image of an object. The object has three short Oops pointing at it. It used to have pointers from 6 long Oops, but two were destroyed recently (they were probably converted to short Oops). The total number of references to the object is seven.

There are three sources of reference-count changes. One pointer can be stored over another, a long pointer can be converted to a short pointer, and a short pointer can be converted back. Since the interpreter only deals with short Oops, every store consists of a short pointer replacing another short pointer. This high-bandwidth operation touches only the short pointer reference counts, so the existing code in the interpreter does not need modification. When a leaf expands to a normal object, pointers in its fields change from long Oops to short ones. The expand-a-leaf routine increments the short count of that object and decrements the delta of its long count. The inverse happens when the routine which shrinks objects into leaves converts short Oops to long ones.

Consider the case when the short Oop count of an object goes to zero. The reference-count routine then looks at the object's long Oop count to see if the total count of the object is zero. If it is zero, the object is truly free, and its storage can be recycled. If not, the object is still held by some long pointers. When the short Oop reference count goes to zero, and the delta reference count is zero, then the object's long Oop count on disk need not change. Thus if the ultimate long pointer count of a leaf can be guessed correctly when the leaf is created, the disk count and delta count can be adjusted so that the leaf disappears from main memory without further disk references.

*Other Data
LOOM Holds for
Each Object*

As a help to the LOOM system, two other bits are added to the ROT entry for any object—"clean" and "unTouched." Clean is cleared whenever a field of the object is changed; unTouched is cleared whenever a field of the object is read or changed. Clean tells the LOOM system that it need not rewrite the object's image on disk (unless of course, its true reference count changed). Clean is set when the object is newly created

The Three Types of Reference Counts

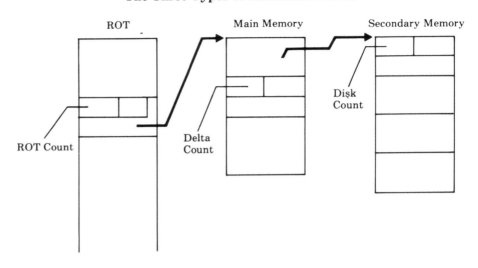

Example Reference Counts

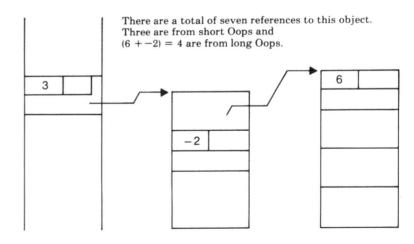

Figure 14.8

or swapped in. UnTouched is set by a routine that sweeps core whenever space is needed. Any object that the routine finds with unTouched still set has not been touched in an entire pass through memory, and is thus a candidate for being *contracted* (turned into a leaf).

The activity which is most likely to cause LOOM to thrash is the resolution of lambdas. When a lambda needs to be resolved (turned into a leaf or discovered to be an existing short Oop), LOOM must first look at the disk image of the parent object. If the pattern of computation is such that the noLambda hint does not correctly predict which fields are needed by the interpreter, lambdas would have to be resolved often. Even so, lambda resolution is likely to happen soon after the parent was expanded, so keeping the most recently fetched disk pages in a cache relieves the need to go to the disk. When a lambda needs to be resolved, the LOOM procedure looks first in the cache of pages that is called the *disk buffer*. If it finds the object in the buffer, it can directly retrieve the long Oop for the lambda, saving one disk access.

LOOM Implemented in the Smalltalk-80 Language

The LOOM design, though based on only a couple of simple principles, has a number of reasonably complex algorithms that require a substantial amount of code. We were faced with the problem of whether to implement LOOM's object swapping algorithms in a low-level language or a high-level language. Low-level implementations typically provide better performance at the cost of some flexibility.

We opted to implement the LOOM system in our favorite high-level system, the Smalltalk-80 system. A number of factors influenced this choice. The overriding factor was that for us, the Smalltalk-80 language was the most natural way to express and understand complex algorithms. We are implementing LOOM on the Xerox Dorado computer[5] (see also Chapter 7). We believe that the Dorado has sufficient performance and memory space so that the LOOM system will not be called very often. When LOOM is called, it will run with acceptable performance. Also, once the system is up and running, we will have a complete, debugged high-level description of the algorithms. Should we decide to reimplement LOOM on the Dorado or another machine in a lower-level language, only a translation of the code would be required. In addition, we designed LOOM not only as a working virtual memory system for our Smalltalk-80 work, but also as a test-bed for virtual memory techniques. Jim Stamos' master's thesis[6] is an example of one experimental technique based on simulation. We want further studies to use a real virtual memory system.

Deciding to implement LOOM in the Smalltalk-80 language itself led to problems that might not be encountered in a low-level language implementation. In particular, the amount of "machine state" that needs to be saved when switching between running the Smalltalk-80 interpreter for "user" and for LOOM was quite large. The amount is much larger than the amount of Smalltalk-80 virtual machine state that would have to be saved to run the LOOM code written in machine language. Also, to avoid a fault on the faulting code, all of the code and other objects which comprise the implementation of LOOM must be guaranteed to stay in main memory at all times.

We handled the first problem, saving state, by reworking our interpreter. It now obeys the convention that within the execution of a bytecode, an object fault is possible only before any "destructive" operations occur. In other words, before the interpreter writes into a field of any object or changes the reference count of any object, it reads fields from all objects needed by the current bytecode. In this way, the state we needed to save was only the "permanent" state that exists between bytecodes. Temporary state within a bytecode is not saved. In our system then, if an object fault occurs, we back up the Smalltalk program counter, switch the interpreter to the LOOM system, handle the fault, and then restart the bytecode.

The second problem, insuring that no object faults occur during the execution of the LOOM algorithms themselves, went through a couple of different designs. The first method we tried was to have the LOOM objects and the user's objects in the same Smalltalk-80 space, but to mark all the objects LOOM would ever need "unpurgable", and to guarantee that free space never went below a certain level. We made an almost-complete implementation of LOOM using this method on the Xerox Alto computer[7] before moving onto the Dorado. The problem with LOOM and the user sharing the same Smalltalk is retaining the marks on objects that LOOM needs. If the user adds many methods to class SmallInteger and its method dictionary grows, how does the new array in the dictionary get marked "unpurgable"? There are many similar cases.

The LOOM implementation on the Dorado has two separate Smalltalk-80 systems in the same machine: a full-size system for user's programs, and a smaller one for LOOM. The LOOM system has some primitives that enable it to manipulate the bits inside of objects in the user system. (Note that because they use the same interpreter, the user system has these primitives also. However, they make no sense in the user system, so are never used.) Because the LOOM system uses only a small subset of the Smalltalk-80 system, it can be much smaller, and can be guaranteed to fit entirely within its portion of main memory and never cause an object fault. Fig. 14.9 provides a view of the communication between the systems.

Alternative Smalltalk Virtual Memory Designs

The LOOM virtual memory design is only one of many ways to implement a virtual memory for a Smalltalk-80 system. The advantages of the LOOM design are:

1. It runs as fast as a resident Smalltalk-80 interpreter when the working set is in core,

Two Separate Smalltalks in the Same Machine

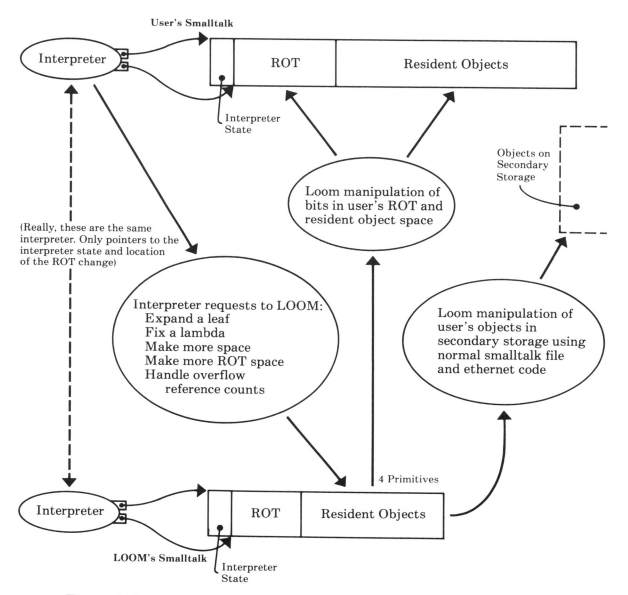

User's Smalltalk

Interpreter

ROT

Resident Objects

Interpreter
State

(Really, these are the same
interpreter. Only pointers to the
interpreter state and location
of the ROT change)

Loom manipulation of
bits in user's ROT and
resident object space

Objects on
Secondary
Storage

Interpreter requests to LOOM:
  Expand a leaf
  Fix a lambda
  Make more space
  Make more ROT space
  Handle overflow
    reference counts

Loom manipulation of
user's objects in
secondary storage using
normal smalltalk file
and ethernet code

4 Primitives

Interpreter

ROT

Resident Objects

LOOM's Smalltalk

Interpreter
State

Figure 14.9

2. It uses 16-bit fields in core to conserve space,

3. It allows the interpreter to avoid handling 32-bit Oops, which makes the interpreter smaller and faster on 16-bit machines,

4. It only uses memory for objects that are actually referenced, and

5. It provides a large, 32-bit virtual address space.

Its major disadvantages are:

1. It relies on fairly complicated algorithms to translate between the address spaces,

2. It takes no advantage of current hardware technology for memory fault detection, and

3. It must move objects between disk buffers and their place in memory.

There are alternatives to many of the design decisions within LOOM and to using the LOOM design itself.

LOOM was designed specifically to experiment with various methods of "grouping" objects on disk pages. If objects which are likely to be faulted on at the same time live on the same disk page, only the first fault actually has to wait for the disk. Static grouping restructures the arrangement of objects on disk pages while the system is quiescent. It reduces the number of disk accesses for both paged virtual memories and object swapping systems. Stamos extensively studied the advantages of static grouping and compared LOOM to paged virtual memories[8]. LOOM is also designed for experiments in dynamic grouping. We have several algorithms in mind for moving objects on the disk while Smalltalk is running. These algorithms will endeavor to reduce faulting by dynamically placing related objects on the same disk page.

We also mentioned that a LOOM system can be built that only uses leaves and not lambdas. Another alternative that we did not pursue is to use a marking garbage collection scheme for resident objects and reference counting for disk references. This should be possible using the delta reference-count scheme.

LOOM is currently intended for use over a local area network. The design could be extended to bring many users, many machines, and large quantities of immutable data into the same large address space. If 32-bit long Oops are not big enough, objects in secondary memory could be quad-word aligned, giving 2^{36} bytes of address space. The LOOM algorithms are parameterized for the width of long pointers, so that a change to 48-bit wide long Oops would not be difficult to do.

The LOOM design may be used for non-Smalltalk systems. In particular, we have proposed a LOOM-like design to extend the address space of Interlisp-D. The design adds another level of virtual memory to the existing Interlisp-D paging system by treating a page as a single object and an existing page address as a short pointer.

Learning from LOOM

Our LOOM virtual memory system is in its infancy. We are only beginning to make measurements on its performance. The design choices of the LOOM system are based on the belief that the way to design good virtual memory systems is to determine what happens most of the time, make it go fast, and hope it continues to happen most of the time. Many trade-offs were made to meet this goal. Some of the design choices we made apply to almost all Smalltalk-80 implementations and some were determined by our hardware/software environment. For example, the general idea that object swapping saves main memory over paging applies to all Smalltalk-80 systems, but the relative cost of object swapping versus paging can be heavily influenced by hardware support for one or the other. Since we know of no current hardware that supports object swapping, but we do know that a great deal of current hardware supports paging, paging has a tremendous advantage. Many of the costs of paging are hidden, such as the address computation on every memory reference, and the "built in" paging hardware on many machines. If those costs were brought into the open, and the same amount were spent on assisting object references, object oriented virtual memories might have better cost-performance than paging systems.

The LOOM design uses two levels of object addressing and translates between address spaces when necessary. Up to 2^{31} objects residing on secondary storage are represented by a cache of 2^{15} objects in main memory. These behave almost identically to resident Smalltalk-80 objects. When a reference from an object in main memory to one in secondary memory is made, an object fault occurs, the latter is brought into main memory, and processing continues. This design allows for a large virtual address space and a space- and speed-efficient resident space. Because the major algorithms in LOOM are written in Smalltalk itself, LOOM will be a major test-bed for new swapping algorithms and for new ways of reducing page faults by grouping objects in secondary storage.

Acknowledg-ments

The design of LOOM was a true group effort. Jim Althoff and Steve Weyer proposed an early version to improve the speed of their work on programmer directed object overlays. Peter Deutsch worked out a design for an early version of the dual name spaces (short and long Oops).

Dan Ingalls, Glenn, and Ted designed the three kinds of reference counts. Danny Bobrow said that leaves were not enough, and Larry Tesler suggested lambdas from the design of his operating system called Caravan. Ted, Dan, and Glenn worked out the final system design, and Ted and Diana Merry built a test version of the LOOM algorithms. Ted and Glenn did the Alto and Dorado implementations.

References

1. Denning, Peter J., "Virtual Memory", *Computing Surveys* vol. 2, no. 3, Sept. 1970.

2. Burton, Richard R., et al., (The Interlisp-D Group), Papers on Interlisp-D, Xerox PARC CIS-5, July 1981; (a revised version of Xerox PARC SSL-80-4).

3. Kaehler, Ted, "Virtual Memory for an Object-Oriented Language", *Byte* vol. 6, no. 8, Aug. 1981.

4. Goldberg, Adele, and Robson, David, *Smalltalk-80: The Language and Its Implementation*, Addison-Wesley, Reading, Mass., 1983.

5. Lampson, Butler W., and Pier, Kenneth A., "A Processor for a High-Peformance Personal Computer", Seventh International Symposium on Computer Architecture, SigArch/IEEE, La Baule, France, May 1980; (also in Xerox PARC CSL-81-1, Jan. 1981.)

6. Stamos, James W., "A Large Object-Oriented Virtual Memory: Grouping Strategies, Measurements, and Performance," Xerox PARC SCG-82-2, May 1982.

7. Thacker, C. P., et al., "Alto: A Personal Computer", in *Computer Structures: Readings and Examples*, 2nd Edition, Eds. Sieworek, Bell, and Newell, McGraw-Hill, New York, 1981; (also Xerox PARC CSL-79-11, Aug. 1979.

8. See reference 6.

15

Managing the Evolution of Smalltalk-80 Systems

Steve Putz
Software Concepts Group
Xerox Palo Alto Research Center
Palo Alto, California

Introduction

This paper describes a software system currently being used by the Software Concepts Group (SCG) to help facilitate and document our development of the Smalltalk-80 system. The central feature of this development support system is a remote database containing information about past and proposed changes to the Smalltalk-80 system, as well as bug reports and an informal library of application programs. We call the present program which maintains this database the Smalltalk-80 version handler.

Three kinds of documentation which we have found to be important in the development of the Smalltalk-80 system are:

1. Documentation of system changes and system release versions,

2. Documentation of known bugs and other problems, and

3. Maintenance of a software applications library.

A Research Programming Environment

The SCG Smalltalk-80 programming environment is used as an experimental basis for the development of new concepts in user interfaces, language, and system development tools. The system is modified in order to repair bugs, to enhance existing functions, and to introduce new functionality. New versions of the system are released for use within the group frequently. Since different people are often working on the system at the same time, it is important to coordinate and document changes to the system, so that inconsistencies are not introduced and new bugs are kept to a minimum. Since each user has their own copy of the system, those who are using the Smalltalk-80 system for creating independent applications also need to know about changes to the system, so they can maintain compatibility and take advantage of new features. Documentation of problems found by users of the system can help to warn other users, as well as serving as a list of "things to fix." It is therefore very desirable to have a well maintained bug list which is easy to update and access.

In addition to fixing and improving the Smalltalk-80 system itself, SCG and other users often create small software applications or enhancements which may be of interest to others. We call these programs and enhancements "goodies." It is useful to have easy availability and documentation for these goodies in the form of a software applications library. If popular, goodies may be incorporated into a later version of the system.

Past Practices

In the early development of the Smalltalk-80 system, as with its precursors, we had only some *ad hoc* and informal mechanisms for maintaining the three kinds of system documentation mentioned earlier. At any given time, our current Smalltalk system would be more or less stable depending on the current focus of activity. During a period of rapid change and development, many people are doing systems programming and new versions of the system may be created as often as several times a day. Eventually this is followed by a more stable period in which more people are doing applications and other independent experiments; new versions of the system, with minimal changes, are then released every few months or so.

During the periods of rapid system development, changes were frequently made directly to the current system image, which was then written out to become the new, current system. Although old versions were always maintained for reference and recovery, no systematic documentation was kept of the changes made, other than verbal communication and some notes (written by the programmer) kept within the system itself. Bugs were either communicated verbally or sometimes listed on a whiteboard until fixed.

During more stable periods, changes were collected in Smalltalk-80 code files and later applied to the system all at once. A more or less detailed message would be distributed (via electronic mail) outlining the changes in the new version. Problems and bugs were usually communicated verbally and not necessarily written down.

An informal applications ("goodie") library evolved where users placed Smalltalk-80 code files on a special file directory and announced the new goodie via electronic mail. Usually little or no documentation accompanied the announcement. The announcements were not systematically collected, so unfortunately there was not a satisfactory index of what was available.

These informal methods worked reasonably well due to the small number of people involved, and the relative simplicity of the changes being made. One of the disadvantages was that less urgent information, such as a small bug, was often forgotten. Another disadvantage was that no detailed record was kept of *why* a particular change or fix was made, and why it was done the way it was. Often the programmer is not even fully aware of his implicit design decisions. As a result, sometimes an important part of a change would be accidentally undone or interfered with by a later change.

An Interim Development Support Mechanism

During one period of especially frantic development, we decided that some more formal mechanisms for dealing with documentation and system software were required in order to better support our needs for communication about our changing Smalltalk-80 system. One reason for this is that the Smalltalk-80 system is significantly larger and more complex than earlier Smalltalk systems. Software tools for manipulating this information would be very helpful and would be much less tedious than the corresponding manual methods.

Although we planned to create software within the Smalltalk-80 system itself for system development support, we started with a simple mechanism consisting of a minimum of automation in order to gain some preliminary experience. Fig. 15.1 is a diagram of the components of the interim support system, outlining as an example the submission of a bug fix report.

Initially we used an electronic mail system that was not part of the Smalltalk-80 system in order to enter and collect messages about the Smalltalk-80 system. Standard forms were used to send messages to a special "mailbox" (called "Smalltalk80Support") regarding bug reports,

Managing the Evolution of Smalltalk-80 Systems

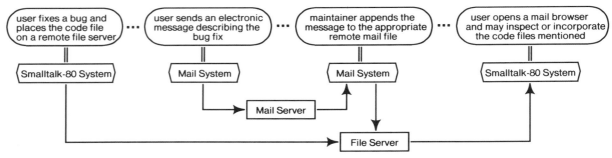

Figure 15.1

bug fixes, system changes, "goodies," or miscellaneous comments about the Smalltalk-80 system. Copies of these messages were also sent to a Smalltalk-80 users' group called "Smalltalk80Users." Fig. 15.2 shows the form used for submitting bug fixes. These messages were collected daily by a system maintainer in a number of mail files on a remote file server.

Subject: Smalltalk-80 Bug Fix: ***ShortDescription***
To: Smalltalk80Support.PA
cc: Smalltalk80Users↑.PA
Source-File: [Phylum] < Smalltalk80Support > ***FileName*** .st
From-Version: ***VersionDate***
Bug: ***DescriptionOfBug***
Fix: ***DescriptionOfFix***
Methods Affected:
            ListMethodsAffected
Figure 15.2   Reviewer: ***NameOfReviewer***

Messages regarding software submissions (e.g., bug fixes or goodies) contained the field *Source-File* indicating the name of a centrally-located file containing the source code. Periodically new versions of the system would be created based on the messages received. An electronic message would then be sent documenting the new version.

A simple user interface was created for browsing the message files from within the Smalltalk-80 system. The mail browser window shown in Fig. 15.3 has two parts. The top part is a menu containing the titles of the messages in the file. When the user selects a title, the corresponding message is displayed in the lower part, Fig. 15.4.

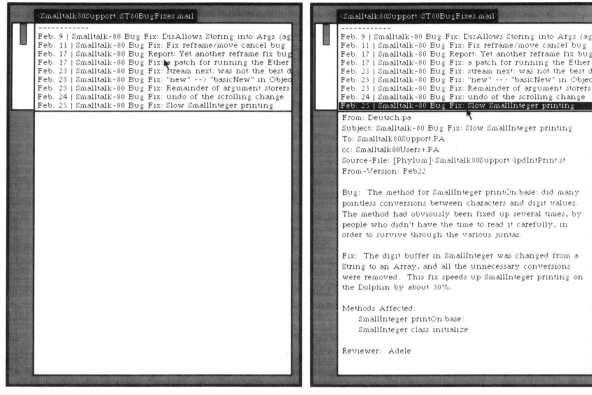

Figure 15.3   **Figure 15.4**

This user interface also allows the Smalltalk-80 source code referenced by a message to be inspected or incorporated into the user's Smalltalk-80 system via additional pop-up menu commands. Fig. 15.5 shows the user invoking the browseSource command for the bug fix entry being viewed; Fig. 15.6 shows the file window obtained as a result. The user is not allowed to modify the message text or the source code.

Detecting Conflicts Between Software Submissions

One of the problems encountered with this distributed approach to system development and maintenance is avoiding (or at least detecting) conflicts in work done by different people in parallel. The longer the time span between system releases, the more likely that incompatible conflicts will arise between system changes submitted by different

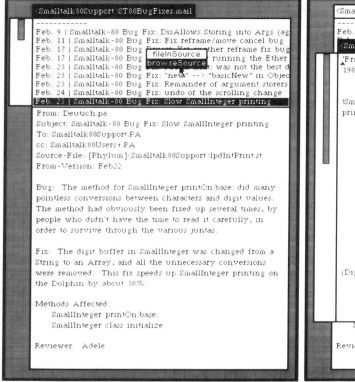

Figure 15.5

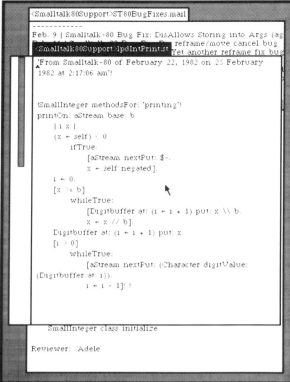

Figure 15.6

users. In the Smalltalk-80 system, this usually occurs when two programmers have modified the same Smalltalk method definition.

In order to help solve this problem, we developed a program for analyzing Smalltalk-80 code files and reporting the ways in which they conflict, i.e., by modifying the same method definition or other Smalltalk object. This approach works very well since most Smalltalk method definitions are very short and perform a very specific function. Whenever two or more submissions define the same method, all conflicting definitions are appended to a "conflict report" file. It is then up to the programmers involved to determine how to resolve the conflicts. Often one of the definitions can be chosen over the others. Otherwise a new method must be written which merges or resolves the functionality of the conflicting definitions. No automatic conflicts resolution was attempted.

Although this tool is fairly crude, it has proven very useful for detecting and resolving at least some conflicts which otherwise would have gone undetected or surfaced later as annoying bugs.

An On-Line System Development Database

After using the interim support mechanism for several months, we were ready to create a development support system within the Smalltalk-80 system itself. Since the Smalltalk-80 system did not then interface with the Xerox internal electronic mail system, one of the main disadvantages of the interim mechanism was that users were not able to submit reports directly from the Smalltalk-80 system. In addition to allowing users to submit bug reports and software submissions directly from within the Smalltalk-80 system, we wanted the new system to provide a Smalltalk-style user interface for browsing, adding to, and editing the system development database. Fig. 15.7 shows the components of the current support system involved in submitting a bug fix.

The new database, like the mail files of the interim system, resides in a number of data files on a remote file server, accessible to any running Smalltalk-80 system. Since the database is accessed by Smalltalk-80 systems rather than standard mail programs, we were able to automatically include additional information, such as cross references between related entries in the database.

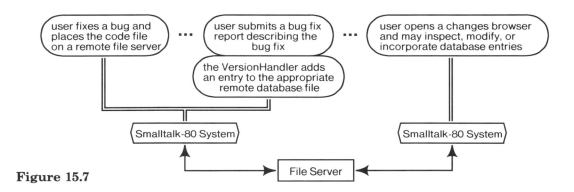

Figure 15.7

Structure of the Database

The current version handler database is patterned strongly after the mail files used in the interim system. The database contains three kinds of entries: *system versions*, *bug reports*, and *system changes* (including bug fixes and "goodies"). Each entry has a unique ID, and a user supplied title and message body describing the entry. The system adds fields specifying the date and the version of the Smalltalk-80 system from which the entry has been generated. Additional fields may contain various status conditions of the entry. Most fields are stored as text in the header portion of the message; some special fields (e.g., whether an entry is new or old or has been deleted) are hidden from the user.

System version entries also contain the ID's of the *system changes* which differentiate the version from its predecessor. Thus a new version can be generated from some previous version by automatically incorporating the appropriate changes into the user's Smalltalk-80 image. Version entries also contain the ID's of all *bug reports* which apply to that version.

In addition to containing a description of the bug, *bug report* entries contain the ID's of available *system changes* that fix the bug.

System change entries contain the names of one or more remote files containing Smalltalk-80 source code. If the change fixes a reported bug, the change entry also contains the ID of the corresponding bug report entry. No firm distinction is made between submissions which are actually changes or fixes to the Smalltalk-80 system and arbitrary user applications (i.e., goodies). Some changes get incorporated into later versions of the system while others simply remain in the database for optional retrieval.

The database is maintained by a special object, named VersionHandler, which is in every Smalltalk-80 system. The VersionHandler object acts as an interface to the actual database stored on a remote file server. It is responsible for reading and writing portions of the database and coordinating access among multiple Smalltalk-80 systems.

A Browser Style User Interface

The user creates Smalltalk windows for accessing the database by sending Smalltalk messages to the VersionHandler. The top level commands available to the user for accessing the database include:

• Open a version browser

- Submit a bug report

- Submit a bug fix

- Submit a software goodie

- Create a new system version

Fig. 15.8 shows a workspace containing the Smalltalk messages used to invoke these commands.

Figure 15.8

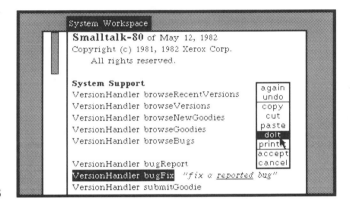

Each of these commands causes a new window to be created. There are three kinds of database browsers for the three kinds of database records: version browsers, change browsers and bug report browsers. These browsers differ only in their contents and the command menus they provide. Fig. 15.9 shows a version browser in which the user is selecting the browse changes command. Fig. 15.10 shows the changes browser created as a result of the selection.

Fig. 15.11 shows the command menus provided by each kind of browser. Selecting browse changes creates a browser on the changes which make up the version. The browse goodies command creates a browser on all changes which are *not* included in the current version. This is equivalent to searching an applications library of user programs and optional system enhancements. The retrieve version command is useful if the version of the Smalltalk-80 system one is running is not the most recent. By selecting retrieve version, the user can upgrade the system. The system then automatically retrieves all the required changes.

The browse source files and file in changes commands in the changes browser are similar to the special commands provided by the interim mail browser. File in changes allows a user to incorporate a bug fix or other change into the Smalltalk-80 system.

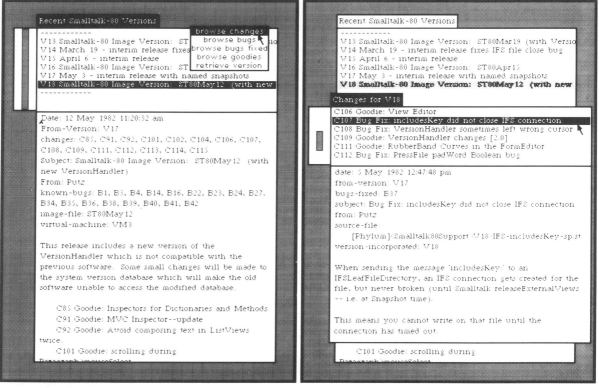

Figure 15.9   **Figure 15.10**

Fig. 15.12 shows the window obtained by selecting the browse bugs command. Unlike the interim mail browser, the text description associated with an entry may be modified by simply editing the text which appears in the database browser. Fig. 15.13 shows the user selecting the file in changes command in order to try out an experimental change to the Smalltalk-80 system. The goodie browser shown was obtained by selecting the browse goodies command in the version browser.

```
browse changes
browse bugs
browse bugs fixed
browse goodies
retrieve version
```

```
browse source files
browse bugs fixed
file in changes
```

```
browse fixes
```

Figure 15.11

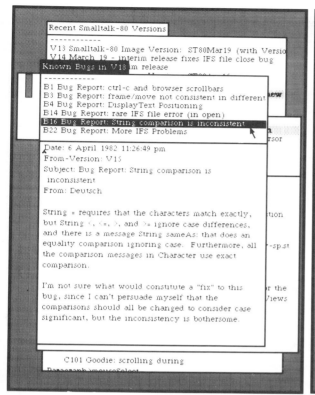

Figure 15.12

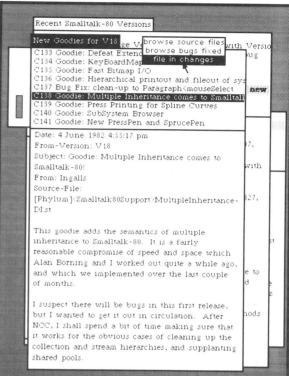

Figure 15.13

Creating Database Entries

There is also a special window used for creating each kind of database record. The user sends a Smalltalk message to the VersionHandler requesting to submit a bug report, bug fix, goodie or new system version. In response, a new window is created that contains a form for the user to fill in. The entry is added to the database when the user selects the accept command.

Figure 15.14 shows the window for creating a *system change* entry which fixes some known bug. The lower half of the window contains a bug report browser. The user selects the titles of the bug reports which he has fixed. Before selecting accept, the user also fills in a title, his name, and the name of the Smalltalk-80 code file he has already created.

The user can submit changes or goodies which are not bug fixes using a window which resembles just the top half of the bug fix window. Bug reports are also submitted using a similar window.

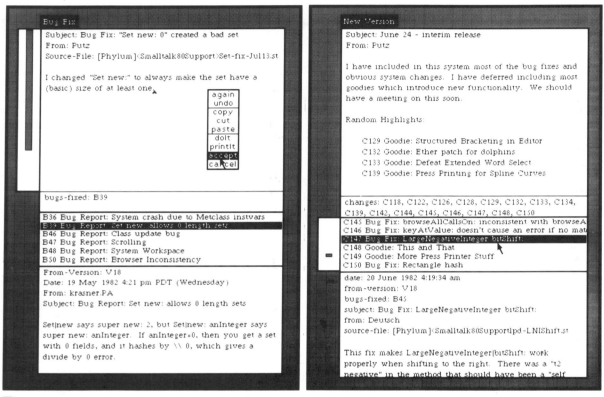

Figure 15.14   **Figure 15.15**

Fig. 15.15 shows a new system version being created. This is done by selecting from a menu of the *system changes* (goodies) submitted since the last version. A conflict detection program can then point out possible conflicts between the selected changes. (This is currently *not* done automatically.) The ID's of any bugs which have not been fixed by the selected changes are inherited and included in the new version. Whenever a new version is created, the source files involved are automatically copied to a new sub-directory on the file server to freeze and preserve the integrity of the new Smalltalk-80 system. The new system may be released as a new image file, or, due to the large overhead of generating an entire system, it may be left as an *interim release* which can be quickly generated from a previous image version each time it is used.

Fig. 15.16 is a diagram of a portion of the database. Bug reports are shown in the first column with lines connecting them with entries for corresponding fixes, if any. The second column shows the changes (including bug fixes) which have not yet been incorporated into any version; these make up the "goodies" application library. The third column shows changes entries connected by lines to the versions in which they have been incorporated. The rectangular boxes denote image versions, while the large ovals are interim release versions. The links between version entries and bug reports are not shown. When the next version, *V9*, is created, the changes *C21, C22,* and *C23* will no longer be considered "goodies."

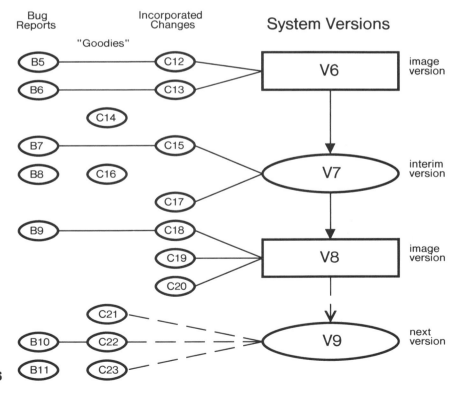

Figure 15.16

Conclusion

The system version database has proved to be a very useful software tool for managing and maintaining our Smalltalk-80 research system. It has provided us with a convenient mechanism for documenting versions of the Smalltalk-80 system. Each change made to the system has a corresponding entry in the database. This provides a complete history of the system's evolution. The most popular feature is that users may submit or browse bug reports directly from their Smalltalk-80 system. The database also provides a software applications library which may be easily accessed and augmented.

16

Implementing a Smalltalk-80 File System and the Smalltalk-80 System as a Programming Tool

*D. Jason Penney**
Tektronix, Inc.
Beaverton, Oregon

Abstract

The Smalltalk-80 system may be used without any file system, but a number of its features presuppose a working file system. Work must be done to effect a file system on a new Smalltalk-80 implementation. This paper describes the design and implementation of the file system for a Tektronix Smalltalk-80 implementation and concludes with some reflections on the use of Smalltalk-80 as a programming tool.

Background

The Smalltalk-80 system is designed to be host machine independent. The system uses files, but file systems tend to rely on the idiosyncrasies of a particular host. Thus the Smalltalk-80 virtual image can support files for a new implementation in an abstract manner. Higher-level methods in the system usually deal with files through FileStream, a subclass of ReadWriteStream. Files themselves have their functionality partially separated out into abstract classes File, FileDirectory, and FilePage. Fig. 16.1 shows the superclass relationships of these classes.

*Mr. Penney is currently employed by Servio Logic Corp., Portland, Oregon.

Object ()
 File ('fileDirectory' 'fileName' 'pageCache' 'serialNumber'
  'lastPageNumber' 'binary' 'readWrite' 'error')
  TekFile ('pageCacheOffset' 'lastPageAddress' 'creationDate'
  'creationTime' 'modificationDate' 'modificationTime'
  'firstPageMap')
Object ()
 FileDirectory ('directoryName' 'closed')
  TekFileDirectory ('nextSerialNumber' 'medium' 'freeListFile'
  'directoryFile' 'directoryStream')
Object ()
 FilePage ('file' 'page' 'binary')
  TekFilePage ('address')

Figure 16.1

The virtual image contains the details of one implementation in the "concrete" subclasses of File, FileDirectory, and FilePage; to wit, AltoFile, AltoFileDirectory, and AltoFilePage.

Implementors could implement the primitives these classes require, reimplement subclasses of the abstract classes, or start from scratch. The Alto classes presuppose a particular kind of disk and disk controller, as well as the existence of system utilities to manage the disk. Starting from scratch would require reimplementing FileStream, which is the interface class for all file manipulation in the system. We eventually chose the second approach, creating TekFile, TekFileDirectory, and TekFilePage.

Description of Chosen Problem

Class FileStream divides files into fixed-length chunks of bytes, called a FilePage. FilePage is intended to map directly to page-oriented media. A FilePage is associated with a File, and has additional state such as the page's pageNumber in the file, actual number of bytes used on the page, and a hardware-related address.

A File contains such things as where to find its FilePages and the String that represents the file's name. When the file is open, some of its state is cached in the File instance.

A FileDirectory contains the necessary information to access all the files within a given directory. It responds to some Stream messages such as reset and next (but not atEnd). A FileDirectory can iterate over all of its files (with do: but not reverseDo:). A FileDirectory keeps some of its state in object memory when it is open, hence it responds to state-caching messages (open, close, and flush).

*Alternate
Programming
Approaches*

At Tektronix we did not have the luxury of an existing file system on our Smalltalk-80 hardware. Thus it was not appropriate for us to try to emulate the Alto file system or to make another existing file system work on our hardware and map into the Smalltalk-80 FileStream class.

Since our virtual machine was originally implemented in Pascal, we briefly considered writing the file system itself in Pascal and providing a minimal interface in the Smalltalk-80 system. The disadvantage in this approach is that the resulting file system would be largely opaque to Smalltalk-80 inspectors and debuggers. Instead we chose to design, implement, and test the file system using Smalltalk and a small number of disk primitives.

Design Constraints

Our primary constraint was that the file system had to be simple, debuggable, and maintainable, so that we could use the file system in a short amount of time.

The Alto file system puts enough redundant information on file data pages so that a "scavenger" can recover significant amounts of a disk after a disk crash. We felt that this should be in our own file system.

Since the Smalltalk-80 source file system manipulates one very large file, it is necessary to be able to find the address of a specified page number in the file with relatively little effort. In other words, the file system should have reasonable performance for random access as well as sequential access.

Design Approach

Abstract class FilePage allows a chunk of data bytes to be sandwiched between a non-data header and trailer of a specified (possibly zero) length. We use a header in TekFilePage to describe the data bytes on the page. Since our disk driver does address checking and data checksumming, we did not include these in the page header. The page header does however, have redundant information (file serialNumber, file pageNumber, previous page's address, next page's address) as well as necessary state (size of data in bytes). Fig. 16.2 shows the organization of a TekFilePage.

Instances of a concrete subclass of File are suppose to "open" themselves when issued the message findLastPageNumber. Since the last page number (and the address of the last page) are quite useful for appending a new page to the end of a file and truncating a page from the end of an existing file, our concrete instances of TekFile have lastPageNumber and lastPageAddress as additional information for an open file.

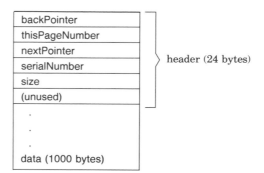

| backPointer |
| thisPageNumber |
| nextPointer |
| serialNumber |
| size |
| (unused) |

header (24 bytes)

data (1000 bytes)

Figure 16.2

*The Smalltalk-80
System's Role
in Initial
Design Effort*

Our first descriptions of file system design presupposed using Pascal. Pascal will handle certain types of data structures (such as 32-bit machine integers) more gracefully than the Smalltalk-80 system will. Pascal encourages fixed-length data typing. Sometimes this is acceptable, since FilePage pages are fixed length. On the other hand, a file name is merely a String of arbitrary length, which is not convenient at all with Pascal data structures. For this and other reasons, we chose to use Pascal for only the disk primitives.

Directory Design

Since we were free to design the directory in any way, we chose to implement it as a sequential file in the format shown in Fig. 16.3. This format allows the directory to be human readable as well as readable by Smalltalk-80 classes. Many Smalltalk-80 classes support a self-description facility through the selectors readFrom: and storeOn:. These selectors do their work on an accompanying Stream in a human-readable as well as Smalltalk-80-readable form. Since a FileDirectory is expected to deliver up a sequence of files in a Stream-like fashion, a Smalltalk-80 directory can be naturally envisioned as a FileStream that has a sequence of file definitions.

('Directory',1,1,12,2567462400,41166,2567462400,41166,11)
('FreeList',0,1188,1260,2567462400,41166,2567462400,41166,1)
('Smalltalk80.sources',2,1242,1259,2567462400,41242,2567462400,
    60378,13)
Items for each file are in order:
    1. fileName, a String
    2. serialNumber, an Integer
    3. lastPageNumber, an Integer
    4. firstPageMap, an Integer
    5. creationDate, seconds since 1 Jan 1901
    6. creationTime, seconds since midnight
    7. modificationDate, seconds since 1 Jan 1901
    8. modificationTime, seconds since midnight

Figure 16.3
    9. lastPageAddress, an integer

Design Details

Our hardware provides random access to a variable number of "sectors" 1024 bytes long. There is exactly one TekFileDirectory for a medium. The exact number of sectors available for each medium is available through a primitive.

Each "medium" may have bad sectors—i.e., ones that the device drivers will not handle without raising error conditions. One sector at a fixed address is presupposed to be good. This sector with its prespecified address is called a "leader"; it provides information about the medium as a whole.

Each sector on a medium (including the leader) is treated as a TekFilePage. A TekFilePage has a 24-byte "header" and 1000 bytes of data. "Data" refers to bytes that are handled by Stream messages next and nextPut:.

The header on a TekFilePage contains a back pointer to the previous TekFilePage within a file (or a nil-address if none), a pointer to the next TekFilePage within a file (or nil), the serial number of the page's file, the ordinal page number of this page in its file (i.e., "1" for the first page in a file), and the number of data bytes that are actually in use on this page (the size). All pages in a file except the last one are guaranteed to be full.

The header information in a TekFilePage is, strictly speaking, sufficient to completely recover files on a crashed disk. Exceptions to this are lost sectors containing file data and some information in the directory file such as creation/modification date and the String used for the file name. On the other hand this is not enough information to allow rapid nonhomogeneous access to a file, such as is required by the Smalltalk-80 browser. To accomplish this an extra data structure is written with each file in the system: pageMap pages. Fig. 16.4 shows the organization of secondary structures on a meduim.

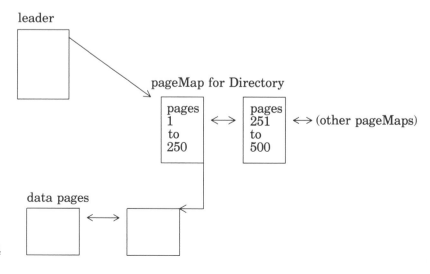

leader

pageMap for Directory

pages 1 to 250 ⟷ pages 251 to 500 ⟷ (other pageMaps)

data pages

Figure 16.4

The directory entry for a file specifies the address for the first pageMap for that file. A file always has at least one pageMap page. A pageMap is forward- and reverse-linked with other pageMaps. Its serialNumber is the same as the one used for the FreeList file, so that a disk scavenger will not confuse it with data. The pageNumber field of a pageMap page is not used in practice. A pageMap contains 250 4-byte addresses in its data section, each address corresponding to the appropriate page in a file. For instance, if one wished to read the 300th page in a file, one would read the first pageMap for the file, use the forward-link in that pageMap to read another pageMap, and read the 50th address in that pageMap to determine the correct address for the 300th page in the file.

As files are created on a given media, they must be given unique serialNumbers. The next available serialNumber is written on the leader page, using Integer storeOn:. The leader page's forward-link points to the first pageMap page of the file which is the Directory file.

The first two file definitions in a directory file are special: The first is the directory file itself (named "Directory") and the second is a relatively large file that occupies all the unused pages in the system (named "FreeList"). Both of these files are bona fide in the sense that they have a serialNumber and a complete set of pageMaps. The serialNumber of FreeList is zero, which signifies non-data. For the sake of consistency, FreeList's "data" pages are fully linked just like all other files in the system.

Implementation Approach

There is a bootstrap problem involved with implementing a file system. The source code for the new classes must be typed in by hand. The physical media must be formatted with a Directory and a FreeList. Once the file system is up and running, the very large file that contains the commented sources for the system must be converted to reside on the new format. Finally, one must recompile the file system methods, adding comments and regenerating variable names.

Typing in the new classes was irritating but not difficult on our implementation. If one's interpreter runs at 3500 bytecodes per second, keyboard echo requires three to five seconds. Our virtual image had a built-in performance problem that additionally delayed keyboard echo. Since there is no source code system, all the new and untested methods lack argument variable names, temporary variable names, and comments.

None of the file system could be tested until all necessary methods were typed in and initialization code written to properly initialize a new media. The debugging itself will be described later.

Converting the source code to the file system format turned out to be easy but time consuming. Our system already has software for saving and restoring memory images on our disk media. We split the source file into manageable chunks, converted the ASCII text to a downloadable image (as if the text were executable processor code), and saved the resulting memory-images on floppies using the existing non-file system format. A small bit of code in a workspace was necessary to read bytes off of a bogus TekFilePage onto a legitimate FileStream, and a very large amount of time was necessary for the conversion (about 11 hours).

Managing
Windows

Before implementing the file system, we were familiar with the Smalltalk-80 user interface, but we had only superficial experience with it. Each of us had his favorite snapshot with his windows placed just the way he liked it, but our interaction with the system was casual. We typically would execute selected examples to show to visitors or compose short methods to answer specific questions.

When we started the file system project, our placement of windows underwent metamorphosis. The old arrangements changed as new things came to light. For instance, the only kind of browser that we ever had at first was a full five-pane System Browser. These are useful because of their full generality. Unfortunately five panes take up a lot of room on our 512 x 512 display, which in turn means that less of each method ends up visible in the code pane. Since all of the code that we were entering belonged in a single class category, "Files-Tektronix," we quickly collapsed the System Browser and kept a Class Category Browser instead, which has proportionately more room in the code part of the browser.

Our typical display had a System Category Browser and a Workspace to do development work in. A System Transcript, a collapsed System Brower, and a collapsed System Workspace were kept off to the side. At first we did not overlap the Category Browser and the Workspace. After a little bit of use we reframed these two windows so that they did overlap substantially. Since we typically moved between the two windows, making changes in one window and testing the changes in the other, it was not necessary to see all of both windows at the same time. This was a significantly better use of display space on our system.

Using the Browser

The Browser worked pretty much as advertised. We added our classes without any difficulty, but when we finished, we discovered that we had misspelled an instance variable name. Several methods later in that class, we decided to change the class definition. Much to our surprise, when we changed the spelling of the instance variable, we did not get any syntax error messages while the class was being recompiled. If we had attempted to change the order of the instance variables, the actual roles of the instance variables would have reversed. This is because the decompiler used the new instance variable names rather than the old.

The method category pane of the browser, which provides categories of methods within a given class, was originally a nuisance. We chose to ignore it initially. An odd thing was that as long as we added methods to a new class, the selection in this pane read "no messages" but if we switched to another class and back, the selection would then change to "As yet unclassified".

Using the Editor

In general the text editor was a joy to use: all basic editing operations conform nicely with user intuition. Some features are not intuitive, but neither are they difficult to learn. For example, using control-F for "ifFalse:" or control-[for inserting "[ ]".

We used a full-ASCII keyboard on our implementation, which caused a special set of problems using the editor. Some of us were initially perplexed about how to type the back-arrow assignment symbol which is pervasive in Smalltalk-80 code: it turns out that this maps into the ASCII underscore character. A more serious problem was presented by the unencoded keyboard interface. Xerox uses an unencoded keyboard for their own Smalltalk-80 systems. An unencoded keyboard reports only key-up and key-down activity on the keyboard. An unencoded keyboard is closer functionally to a piano than a typewriter.

Whereas an unencoded typewriter keyboard provides greater flexibility than a conventional encoded-ASCII keyboard, they are less common. Our Smalltalk-80 hardware uses a readily available encoded-ASCII keyboard. The way Xerox has written InputSensor and InputState gave us a little grief. We were unable to force a user interrupt with the control-C character simply because no one at Xerox thought it would be possible for a keyboard to generate a control-C character without causing a control-key event. Thus when one types a control-C on an untuned Smalltalk-80 system with an encoded keyboard, one gets a garbage character instead of the expected Notifier. The unencoded keyboard also manifests itself as a problem with such things as control-0 through control-9 (used for changing fonts), and control-[(which is different from ASCII ESCAPE). Although the encoded keyboard was suitable for use with the Smalltalk-80 system, the control-C problem caused us grief when we were debugging the file system.

Using the Debugger

The debugger has done more to spoil us than any other single feature in the user interface. All aspects are fully integrated. It was never necessary for us to go to machine-level debuggers or anything else in order for us to fully debug the file system.

The interpreter simulator, invoked whenever one selects "step" or "send", runs about 1000 times slower than the machine interpreter. On our system this meant that the simulator ran at an effective 3 or 4 bytecodes per second. On at least one occasion we accidentally started the simulator only to determine afterward that we would have to wait longer than the MTBF of our hardware to allow the simulation to complete.

Typical Programming Problems

During the course of "accepting" methods into the system and testing our resulting code, we ran into a series of problems familiar to every programmer. In our estimation, this is the part of the Smalltalk-80 system that must distinguish itself: from a productivity standpoint, the amount of time that it takes to effect an application and the resulting reliability are paramount indices into a workbench's success.

Syntax Errors

Syntax errors on any system have a fairly limited number of causes, including user unfamiliarity and "cockpit errors". Those of us accustomed to higher level languages such as Pascal or Modula-II are familiar with a definite syntax phase when entering new program text. Such strongly typed languages attempt to limit certain kinds of errors by making a large number of static checks on the program text. The Smalltalk-80 compiler makes relatively few static checks. It does little or no semantic checking. Abnormal conditions are left to the objects involved during execution to report. This is all right in principle, but there are some semantic checks that the compiler does not do which could theoretically be done.

One syntax error that occurred early on is worth mentioning. When one writes a Smalltalk-80 conditional expression, it will look something like

```
3 frob ifTrue: [↑1]
        ifFalse: [↑2].
```

However, if one wishes to code a whileFalse:, one might be tempted to type

```
3 frob  " creates syntax error "
    whileFalse: [4 frob].
```

This latter construct gives a syntax error because the compiler requires the receiver of a whileFalse: to be a literal block. Thus the correct syntax for a whileFalse: using the previous example would be

```
[3 frob] whileFalse: [4 frob].
```

Once the novice user has discovered this, he may be tempted to write

```
[3 frob]  "gets by compiler but doesn't work"
    ifTrue: [↑1]
    ifFalse: [↑ 2].
```

The compiler will accept this without complaint because it makes no requirements on the receiver of an ifTrue:ifFalse:. However, when this method is executed the response is a mustBeBoolean notifier, because the receiver is a block instead of a boolean.

Off-by-One Errors

Programming languages that allow indexing data structures open themselves up to off-by-one errors. Smalltalk-80 is such a language. The first item in a Smalltalk-80 indexable collection is indexed by one instead of zero. Some of us have grown accustomed to programming with adjustable-offset indexes, which resulted in three off-by-one errors in our initial attempts.

Learning Curve

As with any problem, there is a "learning curve" involved with approaching a novel situation. In implementing the file system, we traversed learning curves involved with file systems, disk hardware, and the Smalltalk-80 system itself.

Familiarization with the abstract and concrete implementations of File took a significant amount of the time necessary to implement the file system. After that, there was a certain amount of raw familiarization that had to take place. For instance, is the correct selector to append an object to an OrderedCollection addLast: or lastAdd:? (The former is correct). Also, several times we discovered that we had made inefficient use of existing methods.

Once we discovered that although we could add and update files properly, we could not delete them from the directory. Closer examination revealed that close-ing a FileStream does not necessarily entail shorten-ing a FileStream. In other words, there were indeed occasions where hidden functionality of the supplied building blocks caused problems.

After we had corrected most of the rudimentary syntax and design errors, a peculiar snag came to light. The system returns self from a message in absence of some particular result that is expected. This is reminiscent of the difference between procedures and functions in more traditional languages. Unfortunately, unlike functions, a Smalltalk-80 method can rely on "self" being returned from a message. This caused a problem for us when the documentation for the abstract file classes specified no particular result for TekFile read:. It turns out that this selector is supposed to return the TekFilePage that it reads, not self. The error that resulted from this misunderstanding was a doesNot-Understand: message quite removed in time and execution from the actual source of the error.

Design Errors

After the first several hours of debugging, the remaining errors in the system were all in our design. There were such things as Disk (a TekFileDirectory) telling itself to close in the midst of closing itself. There were some problems involving managing the pageMaps, particularly on larger files.

Since problems in this category go directly back to the definition and solution of the actual problem to be solved, these problems must reflect the programmer/analyst more than the system itself. The impressive part of the Smalltalk-80 system's performance in this regard is that the turnaround from clerical, syntactic, and learning curve errors back to design errors occurred quickly, even though the system itself was slow.

Summary/ Conclusions

Design and implementation of concrete subclasses for the file system took 43 hours over the space of two and a half weeks. A large part of this time reflects the speed of our implementation as opposed to programmer time.

At the end of this time all of the higher file-related functions in the system worked perfectly. Most debugging problems were due to our incomplete understanding of the Smalltalk-80 system.

One measure of success of a workbench is the quality and applicability of the tools that it offers. Our experience with workbenches in general is that if a tool indeed exists for the problem at hand, its interface is poorly documented and its behavior erratic if not outright destructive. This is the first workbench we have ever used in which we are willing —albeit reluctantly—to use new and unfamiliar tools that are already available. The integration of tools in the system is so complete that the apparent reliability of higher level system components (such as browsers and debuggers) is enhanced.

Like any large software system, the Smalltalk-80 system has its share of bugs. By and large, bugs tend to remain isolated, although a bug in a widely used component will have significant repercussions throughout the system. To this extent the full integration of the system is a double-edged sword: although compactness and ultimate reliability are aided, one is also able to make changes that blow up the system. Then again, the system uses snapshots and transaction files to help a user regain his work in the event of a system crash.

Our final judgment is that yes, the Smalltalk-80 system is a good programming tool. It would be simplistic to cite a single reason for our decision, but one of the salient strengths of the system is its high reliability and useability.

17

Implementing a Smalltalk-80 System on the Intel 432: A Feasibility Study

Guy Almes
Alan Borning
Eli Messinger
Department of Computer Science
University of Washington
Seattle, Washington

Abstract

During autumn 1981, the authors carried out a feasibility study on the implementation of the Smalltalk-80 language on the Intel iAPX 432. This report presents the conclusions of that study, together with supporting technical material.

Briefly, a Smalltalk implementation on the 432 would result in several important advantages over Smalltalk on conventional computers. These advantages include support for multilingual systems and for parallelism, including parallel garbage collection. There are also however, some corresponding disadvantages that could prevent a Smalltalk implementation on the 432 from being competitive with implementations on conventional computers. These disadvantages include large storage overhead per object, very heavy loading of the parallel garbage collector, and the possibility of insufficient microcode space. These difficulties can probably be surmounted; some approaches to dealing with them are discussed below.

Introduction

This report describes an effort to study the feasibility of a Smalltalk-80 implementation on the Intel 432. The main body of the report is divided into three parts:

- The potential benefits of a Smalltalk-432 system.

- The principal threats to the feasibility of Smalltalk-432.

- A sketch of an implementation of Smalltalk-432.

A final section presents some conclusions and recommendations for further study.

Background

We assume that readers of this report are acquainted with the Smalltalk-80 system. However, not all readers will know about the Intel 432 processor, so in this section we give a brief description of the features of the 432 that are particularly relevant to the task at hand.

The Intel iAPX 432 is a 32-bit microprocessor. It is designed to be a processor for Ada; however, as we shall see, with suitable modifications it may be an effective Smalltalk engine as well. Physically, the 432 consists of a two-chip *general data processor* (GDP) and a single-chip *interface processor* (IP). Standard I/O functions are handled separately by one or more attached processors, which will typically be Intel 8086s. The basic clock rate is 8 MHz. The 432 chips include microcode in read-only memory; there is no user-modifiable microcode.

The 432 supports an object-oriented environment (although the meaning of "object" is not the same as in Smalltalk). A 432 object is a contiguous segment of memory, up to 64K bytes in length, containing data and addresses. There can be up to 2^{24} segments in a system. Each segment has a type, which determines the operations that can be performed on it. Addresses for these segments are called access descriptors, and are protected addresses very similar to capabilities on systems such as Hydra[1,2,3]. Two fields totaling 24 bits contain the unique identifier for the object, 1 bit indicates whether the 32 bits in fact constitute a valid access descriptor, and each of the remaining 7 bits indicates whether the owner of the access descriptor has a given right for the segment in question. These rights include "read rights" (can parts of the segment be examined?), "write rights" (can the segment be modified?), and "delete rights" (can the access descriptor be deleted or overwritten?). Every access to a segment is checked automatically to see that the possessor of the access descriptor has the required rights, and that the access is within the bounds of the segment. The hardware and microcode makes a distinction between data and access descriptors, so that it is not possible to inadvertently treat 32 bits of data as an access descriptor or vice versa.

The 432 is designed for multiprocessing. Many 432s can be connected to a common memory, the maximum being determined by electrical rather than logical characteristics. Within the common memory, *process objects* represent tasks requiring servicing, and *processor objects* are the representatives of the physical processors. This representation makes it easy to add new processors without the need for making software modifications.

Interprocess communication is handled by a *port* mechanism. A given process can send an access descriptor for a message segment to a port object, which can be received by any process with an access descriptor for that port.

Objects can be allocated from a global heap or on a local stack. Parallel garbage collection for heap-allocated objects is supported. Using Dijkstra's parallel garbage collection algorithm, objects are marked as "white" (possibly inaccessible), "black" (accessible and traversed), or "gray" (accessible but not traversed). The hardware supports parallel garbage collection by marking each white object as gray when a pointer to it is copied. A software garbage collector, running as a 432 process in parallel with other processes, handles the rest of the work.

Papers on the 432 architecture have recently appeared in the literature. These include papers describing the port system[4], the structured address space[5], and the structure of the operating system[6].

Approaches to Running Smalltalk on the 432

There are a number of possible ways to run Smalltalk on the 432. The best approach is probably to make a Smalltalk object be the same as a 432 object (in general), and to modify the microcode of the 432 to allow it to execute Smalltalk bytecodes directly. A system that used this chip would include both Smalltalk processors (STPs) and ordinary Ada GDPs.

In the remainder of this section, we describe some of the alternatives and indicate why the above approach was selected.

It would be very convenient to run Smalltalk on the 432 without modification to the chip. One way of doing this would be to allocate a set of 64K-byte 432 data segments to hold Smalltalk objects, and to handle Smalltalk object allocation and deallocation independently of the facilities provided by the 432. This may in fact be the best way to run Smalltalk on the 432 as it exists. However, if this is the case, then the 432 is just being used as a rather slow conventional processor, with no use being made of its special properties. If this is the best that can be done, it would be better to select another processor.

A more attractive alternative, still using an unmodified 432, would be to identify Smalltalk objects and 432 objects. There are two possibilities for storing Smalltalk code: writing an interpreter for the present bytecode set, or changing the Smalltalk compiler to emit mixed native 432 code and subroutine calls. We suspect that a software interpreter for the present bytecode set would be quite slow. Nevertheless, such an interpreter should be developed for at least two reasons:

- It might turn out to be acceptably fast.

- Even if it is too slow, it will yield valuable experience that will inform the eventual Smalltalk processor design. Specifically, it will show how well the Smalltalk object to 432 object mapping works.

Once this interpreter is built, its designers will be able to judge the extent to which such an implementation is competitive with other Smalltalk-80 systems.

Another alternative would be to mix native 432 code and subroutine calls. A severe disadvantage of doing this is that there will be an enormous expansion in code size, probably by 5 to 10 times. This expansion would be acceptable only if done for those methods most frequently executed. If a small set of very frequently executed methods can be identified, either statically or dynamically, then this set might be a candidate for such expansion.

We are thus led to consider producing an additional 432 processor type. In addition to the present Ada GDP and IP processors, there would be a new Smalltalk processor (STP) designed as a modification of the present Ada GDP processor. Our approach is to try to modify only one of the two chips, by making changes to the microcode stored in its ROM and in its PLAs. Again, we make Smalltalk objects and 432 objects be the same, since not doing so would lose whatever advantages the 432 has over a conventional chip. The advantage of this approach is that it is faster than other approaches; a disadvantage is that it does not allow its implementors to change the interpreter or bytecode format without replacing the processor chips.

Benefits of Smalltalk-432

The implementation of Smalltalk on a 432 would yield many benefits. Some of these benefits improve the performance of the system, while others make a Smalltalk system on the 432 qualitatively better than Smalltalk systems on conventional machines.

*Support for Large
Numbers of
Smalltalk Objects*

One of the most important benefits of implementing Smalltalk on the 432 would be its ability to handle systems of more than 32,000 objects. Most existing Smalltalk implementations use 16-bit words for pointers, and one bit is effectively lost in implementing Small Integers. It should also be pointed out that a 432 implementation would share this benefit with any other implementation with a large address space; an implementation on the Digital Equipment Corp. VAX, for example, can support similarly large numbers of objects.

Since the Smalltalk system moreover, is well suited for large advanced applications, this benefit could be crucial.

*Support for
Communication
with non-
Smalltalk
Programs*

The design of the 432 system seems to lend itself particularly well to the idea of a multi-lingual system. With Smalltalk and, for example, Ada processes agreeing on the "432 protocol," communication between them can be done.

A Smalltalk processor and a general Ada processor would have the same notion of what 432 objects and messages are. Thus processes running concurrently in different languages would be able to share memory, and send messages to each other through 432 ports. No existing Smalltalk implementations support such a multi-lingual system. The Dolphin and Dorado systems at Xerox PARC, for example, run either Smalltalk or Mesa, but never both within the same processor. This is due in part to conflicting technical requirements of Mesa and Smalltalk runtime environments.

*Support for
Parallelism*

One of the primary advantages of a 432-based Smalltalk system would be support for parallelism. As described in the introduction, the 432 environment includes process and processor objects. Instances of the Smalltalk class Process can be mapped in a straightforward way onto the 432 process objects, so that in a system with multiple STPs, Smalltalk processes could be executed in parallel.

There are a number of relatively simple ways of exploiting this parallelism:

- When filing in a class definition, each method is compiled separately. It would be easy to make each of these compilations a separate process, thus speeding up filing in considerably. The only synchronization needed would be a lock on the method dictionary when a new method was being inserted.

- There are a number of messages to dictionaries for doing searches for example, to find all classes that implement a method for some selector, to find all methods that invoke a given selector, to find all references to a symbol, and so forth. All these searches could profitably employ parallelism.

- Parallelism could also be used in graphics. When displaying a paned window, or updating several windows, each pane or window could have a separate process to display it. When displaying an elaborate image, the display method could divide the work among several processes. In general some synchronization between the subprocesses would be necessary, but in many cases (e.g., when the subimages were nonintersecting, or when they were or'd together to form the entire image) the subprocesses could proceed asynchronously.

There are other applications for which parallelism would be valuable, but its use would require more sophisticated synchronization techniques. In simulations for example, it is sometimes useful to have one process perform the simulation, and a separate viewing process to display snapshots of the simulation's state.

Support for Virtual Memory

Because a virtual memory scheme is in the design of the 432 system, it will automatically accrue as a benefit to the Smalltalk system. This will be especially important for applications with large numbers of objects. The quality of the iMax virtual memory mechanism will be very important for the quality of the Smalltalk implementation.

Support for Parallel Garbage Collection

Similarly the parallel garbage collector, which is to be part of the standard 432 system, will also benefit the 432 Smalltalk implementation.

Because a storage manager will not have to be written anew for the Smalltalk virtual machine, the task of implementation will be simplified. Also, because the garbage collector—as opposed to reference counting techniques—will be able to collect circular structures, Smalltalk users will not have to break loops explicitly to deallocate them. (An anomaly of the Smalltalk object representation called "soft fields" requires modification to the garbage collector. The soft field technique is used to add a pseudo field to instances of some class. Soft fields are implemented through the use of a global dictionary whose entries contain a pointer to an object, paired with that object's soft field. The problem then is that an object whose sole reference is from the soft field dictionary is in fact garbage. Given the large overhead per object already present, one might prefer to add a real field to Object to point to a list of backpointers. This would remove this special case in the garbage collector, at the cost of 4 more bytes per object.)

Support for Object Filing

A scheme is planned for iMax that would allow 432 objects to be filed away in an archival format, onto external memory[7]. Thus Smalltalk objects could be stored and later retrieved from secondary memory after an arbitrary amount of time. This scheme would allow Smalltalk programmers a more flexible facility than the saving of entire work-spaces.

Threats to Smalltalk-432

The Smalltalk-80 implementation on the 432 seems to be feasible, and due to the advantages cited above would result in a qualitatively better facility. There are several potential problems however, with the mapping of Smalltalk onto the 432 which could make the performance of the resulting implementation unacceptable. At this point we do not believe that any of these threats is fatal, but they do serve to focus our attention on the real issues in the rest of the study.

Storage Overhead

Release Three of the 432's architecture incurs an average storage overhead of approximately 24 bytes per object. This breaks down as 16 bytes for the object descriptor, and a minimum of 8 bytes for the "memory image." On the other hand, in the model implementation of the Smalltalk-80 system, there is only an 8-byte overhead per object; similarly, the LOOM implementation has 14 bytes of overhead per object (see Chapter 14).

Statistics show that the initial Xerox Smalltalk virtual memory contains approximately 20K objects (including 4K method objects), with a mean size of 20 bytes. However, since the 432 implementation would use 32-bit object pointers (as opposed to 16-bit pointers on the Xerox systems), the average object size would increase. At one extreme, where no Smalltalk object contains a pointer to another object (e.g., strings), the average size would remain at 20 bytes; at the other extreme, where all Smalltalk objects are composed solely of pointers to other objects, the average size would double to 40 bytes. Clearly the true average lies somewhere in between. For the basic Smalltalk system, Ballard (see Chapter 8) found that its size increased by 50% when going from 16 to 32 bit pointers, implying that the average object size increased to 30 bytes. For a big application program with more data than code, the average number of bytes per object might be somewhat larger.

Regardless of the average object size, the overhead remains 24 bytes per object. Thus a system of 20K objects would incur approximately 0.5 Mbytes of overhead for about 0.6 Mbytes of objects. (Assuming here an average object size of 30 bytes.) Also note that the 20K objects figure is only for the Smalltalk system itself. A reasonably large application, which takes advantage of the 432's ability to support more than 32K objects, might use upwards of 100K objects, thus making the overhead about 2.5 Mbytes for 3.0 Mbytes of objects.

It is thus clear that the Smalltalk-80 system on the 432 is practical only with a virtual memory system; otherwise the number of objects that could be used would be so restricted that one would lose all the advantages of moving from 16-bit to 32-bit pointers.

Also, even with virtual memory, the large per object storage overhead will increase the amount of real memory required to support a given working set of Smalltalk objects. This increases both the cost of a given hardware configuration and the amount of disk traffic due to swapping. The user should certainly not be forced into a constrained style of programming where she or he becomes wary of using too many objects; this would be very destructive of good Smalltalk programming style. Any way that is found to reduce the storage overhead of 432 object descriptors or memory images would certainly benefit Smalltalk. However, even if the 24 bytes/object overhead is regarded as a fixed parameter of the 432, there are other things that can be done to reduce the total overhead in a Smalltalk system.

One technique would be to represent some Smalltalk objects in other ways than as full-fledged 432 objects, for example, by embedding their representation in a pointer rather than storing it separately as a 432 object. Small integers are a prime candidate for such a representation, but other objects could be so represented as well. This topic is discussed on p. 316 below.

Insufficient Microcode Space

Experience with the Xerox Smalltalk system has shown the value of implementing a good portion of the Smalltalk virtual machine in the host system's micro-architecture. At a minimum, the bytecode interpreter, plus some critical primitives, must be implemented in microcode if reasonable performance is to be achieved on the 432.

Clearly the size of the 432's microcode store is much smaller than any of the Xerox systems. For example, the Xerox Alto has a 32-bit microinstruction, in comparison to the 432's 16-bit word. Further, the Alto has 1K of ROM and 3K of RAM available to the Smalltalk implementor; the 432 has much less. In speaking of the microcode requirements of the Smalltalk-80 system, Glenn Krasner[8] says:

> For the systems that we have implemented at Xerox, the Smalltalk-80 Virtual Image consists of about 300K bytes of objects. Our typical implementation of the Smalltalk-80 virtual machine is 6 to 12K bytes of assembly code, or 2K microcode instructions plus 10K bytes of assembly code. Of this, about 40% is in the storage manager, 20% in the interpreter, and 40% in the primitive subroutines.

The 432 has a total of 4K microwords, of which a certain amount will be left devoted to 432 system primitives (e.g., ports and object tables). A rough guess would estimate this at 2K, thus leaving 2K for the Smalltalk implementor. It is difficult to evaluate the extent to which the PLAs and special-purpose data paths of the 432 microengine will offset the smaller amount of microcode space.

There are several functions which should be implemented within the microcode of the 432 in order to achieve reasonable performance. We list them here in decreasing order of importance:

- The standard object table functions—necessary. In order for Smalltalk programs and Ada programs to be able to share the same memory space, it is necessary that both have the same notion of object table and access descriptor.

- The standard port functions—necessary. In order for Smalltalk programs and Ada programs to be able to engage in interprocess communication, it is necessary that both have the same notion of port and carrier.

- The standard process and processor functions—necessary. In order for Smalltalk processes to be dispatched in a uniform manner, it is necessary that Smalltalk processes share the same structure and dispatching functions as Ada processes. (Note that these three requirements, taken together, require that the Smalltalk processor support the standard 432 Carrier, Communication Segment, Descriptor Control, Object Table, Port, Process, Processor, Refinement Control, and Type Definition Objects. It is not however, necessary to support the standard 432 Context, Domain, Instruction, or Storage Resource Objects.)

- The bytecode interpreter—necessary. The bytecode set of the Smalltalk machine is a relatively simple set of instructions. Most of them are simple push, store, and jump instructions. The others are more complex instructions for sending a message to an object and returning from such a send; these functions are similar both in nature and complexity to the call-context and return instructions on the standard GDP.

- The Smalltalk primitives—varying. The Smalltalk bytecodes do not for example, include add or compare instructions per se. Rather these functions are handled by invoking special methods, called primitive methods, known to the Smalltalk virtual machine implementation. These methods are primitive for either of two reasons:

  1. Intrinsic. Some primitives would be impossible or at least very hard, to express as ordinary methods coded with ordinary bytecodes. Examples are the Process Resume and BitBlt methods for process synchronization and icon manipulation, respectively. Most of these primitives could be supported by sending a request message to an Ada program executing on a standard GDP, then receiving a reply from it.

  2. Performance. Some primitives are invoked so frequently that the system would be slower if they were handled by the standard message-sending scheme. Examples are the methods for stream operations next, nextPut:, and atEnd. (Note that these

two motivations for making a method primitive are not mutually exclusive. Consider, for example, the at: and at:put: methods for indexing into objects. They would be hard to implement as ordinary methods both for intrinsic and performance reasons. Those methods that are primitive only for intrinsic reasons can often be implemented by auxiliary processes running either on Ada GDPs or on attached processors. Those that are primitive only for mild performance reasons might best be implemented by means of standard Smalltalk methods or by auxiliary processes as above. Many however, will best be implemented directly in the microcode. Various techniques for implementing primitives other than directly in the microcode will be discussed on p. 317 below.)

- Object creation—optional. We may decide to have actual allocation of segments from Storage Resource objects be performed by an auxiliary Ada process. It should be put into microcode only if there is plenty of microcode to spare. Allocation of Smalltalk objects is discussed in more detail in the implementation sketch.

- Large integer and floating point—optional. The primitives for large integers and floating point numbers may also be handled by an auxiliary Ada process. Since the floating-point microcode in the standard 432 uses considerable space, there would be substantial benefit in performing floating-point arithmetic using an auxiliary Ada process.

Thus just what can be fit into microcode is bound to be a central issue. However, a partial solution can be effected by implementing some of the Smalltalk primitives "off board." Here, low-overhead linkage to primitives will be very important. Possible implementation techniques include using an attached processor (AP), an Ada co-process, or interprocessor communication (IPC). We would expect that some combination of these techniques would be used in an eventual system. These techniques are discussed in more detail in the implementation sketch.

Overloading of the Garbage Collector

A final major threat is the overloading of the garbage collector, since Smalltalk will put a much heavier load on it than does Ada. In the 432 implementation of Ada, contexts and local variables for procedure calls are not stored in the global heap, and so don't need to be reclaimed by the parallel garbage collector. However, in the book implementation of Smalltalk, all objects are allocated from a global heap.

If the garbage collector can keep up, then all is well. However, if Smalltalk processes spend a significant amount of time blocked, waiting for the garbage collector to free up some storage, or if the garbage collector consumes a large amount of processor or memory resources, then performance will be improved if ways can be found to reduce the number of objects that need to be garbage collected. This could be done either by reducing the number of real 432 objects created in the first place, or by reclaiming some objects by means other than the parallel garbage collector.

One place to look is contexts. In general, contexts must be allocated from the heap, since it is possible, for example, to obtain a pointer to the current context and store it into a global variable. However, in most cases, contexts will be allocated and deallocated in a stack-like fashion, and probably advantage could be taken of this fact. (The presence of block contexts, used for many control structures, complicates the situation. Each block context includes a pointer to its "home context", which will be some method context. When used to implement such standard control structures as iterations through the elements of a collection, the block context is only passed up the stack, and the method contexts still obey a stack discipline. However, there is no guarantee that a pointer to the block context won't be bound to an instance or global variable. Hence the presence of block contexts makes it more difficult to keep track of all the pointers into the stack.)

Another place to look is short-lived objects in general, that is objects that are created, bound to temporary variables, and used in the course of executing a method, but which are not returned or bound to an instance or global variable.

For Ada, the 432 uses "level numbers" to help with this situation. Each context object, along with that context's local variables/objects, contains a level number that is one greater than that of the calling context. Upon termination of a context (i.e., a return instruction), the run-time stack is popped by deallocating all objects whose level number matches that of the terminating context. We devoted some effort to studying whether modifications to the level-number scheme could be used with Smalltalk, for example, just using level numbers for method and block contexts. Unfortunately, none of the techniques we devised had satisfactory characteristics. Generally, these techniques suffered either from too much complexity, too little applicability, or too great an overhead. We believe however, that reasonable solutions to this problem can be found with additional work. For example, in Ballard's VAX implementation, which uses a garbage collector together with a limited reference count scheme, only about 5% of the contexts needed to be garbage collected (see Chapter 8).

This is an area that will require further investigation if in fact the garbage collector threat materializes. Intelligent responses to this threat will be based on detailed experience with running Smalltalk systems (for example, what is the rate of creation of method contexts, block contexts, and other objects, and how frequently do they exhibit stack-like behavior?) with the iMax Garbage Collector, and a detailed review of current garbage collection literature. (See for example, the October 1981 issue of *Computing Surveys*. This area is very active, partly due to work on various kinds of Lisp machines.) If this area is pursued, benefits will accrue not only to Smalltalk programmers, but also to Ada programmers who desire to use the heap heavily.

Implementation Sketch

This section presents approaches to several aspects of Smalltalk implementation. Areas discussed include the representation of Smalltalk objects, special system types for Smalltalk, allocation of Smalltalk objects, ways of reducing storage overhead, execution of primitive methods, communication between Smalltalk and Ada programs, and interfacing to the display.

Representation of Smalltalk Objects

Smalltalk objects would be represented directly as 432-objects, each with an object descriptor and a memory image. The object descriptor would include the object's length and its system type, if any. The few system types needed specifically for Smalltalk will be presented in a following section. The Smalltalk notion of class would be mapped directly onto the Release Three 432 extended type notion. Thus Smalltalk objects that are not of some system type would contain an access descriptor to a Type Definition Object, which would take the form of a Smalltalk Class object.

With the exception of Smalltalk methods, all Smalltalk objects are either pure data objects, e.g., strings, or pure access objects, e.g., dictionaries. In the case of pure data objects, they may be byte-addressed or (16-bit) word-addressed, depending on the characteristics of the Smalltalk class. In the case of pure access objects, they will use the release three notion of embedded values (see p. 316).

System Types for Smalltalk

The Smalltalk system makes heavy use of several system types. Ordinary Ada GDPs need only be able to access these types as generic objects, i.e., be able to access their fields, but not their peculiar operations.

☐ *Class* The first type is Class. Each object of this type describes some Smalltalk Class, and includes the following kinds of information:

- How to create a new object of this Class, and

- Methods to be executed when a message is sent to an instance of this Class.

The format of this type is shown in Fig. 17.1. The first pointer leads to another Class object, which is the Superclass of this Class. The second leads to a Message Dictionary, which contains the Methods for all messages defined directly on this Class. The third pointer is actually an embedded value, which includes:

- The number of fixed fields in an instance of this Class,

- Whether the instance's representation contains pointers or numeric data,

- If data, whether it is organized as bytes or words, and

- Whether the object is indexable.

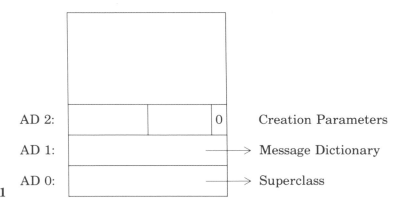

Figure 17.1

☐ *Message Dictionary* Just as in the model implementation, we require a Message Dictionary to be an array of pointers to Symbols with a parallel array of pointers to Methods. This Message Dictionary is used by the microcode which implements Message Send bytecodes.

☐ *Method* Another system-defined type is the Method, an analogue of the Ada Instruction Segment. This type is the only Smalltalk class to contain both data and pointers. The format of these objects is shown in Fig. 17.2. The byte-organized data, shown below the thick line, contain the bytecodes for the Method. (A nice property of the 432 implementation is that the initial instruction address is always zero!) All but the first pointers are literals, i.e., pointers to constants or global variable objects. The first pointer is the Method Header, packed within an embedded value. The representation for the Header is:

- Temporary Frame Size: 5 bits

- Argument Count: 5 bits

- IsPrimitive: 2 bits

- Context Size: 1 bit

- Primitive Index: 8 bits

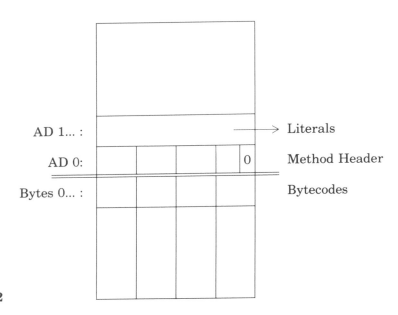

AD 1... :   → Literals

AD 0:   0   Method Header

Bytes 0... :   Bytecodes

Figure 17.2

The alignment of these data should be designed to simplify the microcoding of the Send bytecodes. The IsPrimitive field has the following four values:

00	Not a primitive Method.
01	The special primitive "return pointer to Self".
10	The special primitive "return a field from within Self". In this case the primitive index can be used to indicate which field.
11	An ordinary primitive. In this case the primitive index tells which one.

☐ *Contexts* The other two system-types are Method Context and Block Context. The Smalltalk Method Context is the activation record that results from a message being sent to a receiving object, and corresponds to the standard Ada Context object. Unlike the Ada Context object however, Smalltalk Method Contexts are allocated from a global heap and can persist after they return. The format of a Method Context is shown in Fig. 17.3.

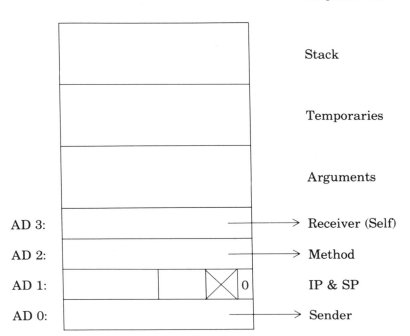

Figure 17.3

The fields in a Method Context are as follows:

- Pointer to the Sender, i.e., the Context that issued the Send instruction that caused this Context to be created. On the 432, this pointer would lack DeleteRights.

- The Instruction Pointer and Stack Pointer embedded in one pseudo-access descriptor. The IP is a byte offset into the Method's bytecode part. The SP is a pointer offset into the Context itself, and indicates the top of the stack region of the Method Context.

- Pointer to the Method of which this Context is an invocation. This pointer would also lack DeleteRights on the 432.

- Pointer to the receiving object (=Self). This pointer would also lack DeleteRights on the 432.

- Next come zero or more arguments. These are the values pushed on the stack by the sender prior to issuing the Send bytecode. The number of these is specified by the Method Header, Fig. 17.2.

- Next come zero or more Temporaries, or local variables. The number of these is also specified by the Method Header, Fig. 17.2.

- Finally, there is room for the expression stack for this context. This stack is initially empty, so the initial value of the SP must be determined from the size of the Argument and Temporary frames.

The Block Context system type is very much like the Method Context, and is used to implement control structures other than ordinary Message Sending. Like the Method Context and all other Smalltalk objects, it is logically allocated from a heap. The format of the Block Context is shown in Fig. 17.4.

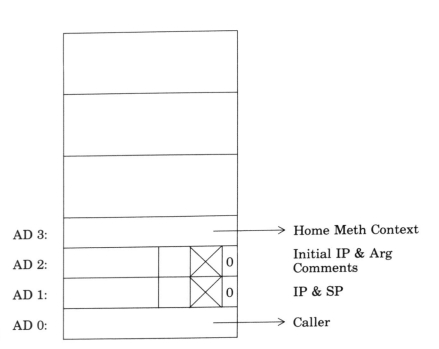

Figure 17.4

Three fields of the Block Context differ from those in the Method Context:

- The caller field of the Block Context points to the (Block or Method) Context that called this Block Context. Note that this may differ from the Context that created the Block Context.

- An embedded value storing the initial IP and argument count replaces the Method pointer of the Method Context. These values allow the interpreter to initialize the Block Context for a new call. (The Method can be found via the Home Method Context pointer.)

- The Home Method Context points to the Method Context that created the Block Context. It is used for locating the receiver and temporaries of the Method.

*Allocation/
Deallocation
of Objects*

The allocation and deallocation of Smalltalk objects poses several difficulties:

- Smalltalk objects are allocated from global heaps. Their deallocation cannot therefore, be performed simply because some method has executed a return instruction. As mentioned earlier, this threatens to overload the parallel garbage collector.

- Microcode space on the processor chip is at a premium. It would conserve microcode sp ace if object allocation, including maintenance of Storage Resource Objects and Object Tables, could be removed from the microcode.

One consequence of the first point is that any implementation of Smalltalk on the 432 (or any other machine) must pay serious attention to efficient garbage collection of Smalltalk objects. This topic is discussed fully on p. 308.

The allocation of objects, on the other hand, is easier and gives us an opportunity both to speed allocation and to save microcode space. We propose that an Ada auxiliary process be assigned to maintain a data structure that contains pointers to well-formed, unallocated segments. This data structure would take the form of an access segment, with one access descriptor for each of several commonly used sizes of segments. (Since most Smalltalk objects are small, and since object images in the 432 come in chunks of 8 bytes, the sizes 8, 16, 24, 32, 40, 48, 56, 64 would take care of the vast majority of cases.) Each access descriptor in this structure would be the head of a singly-linked list of unallocated segments of a certain size. If the Smalltalk processor wants to "create" a new Smalltalk object, it need only pull a segment of the right size off the appropriate list. No carving of storage from heap SROs or allocation of entries from object tables is needed. Also, the auxiliary process could ensure that the segments it places in the list are all zeroed out. The Smalltalk processor would only have to adjust the object descriptor to indicate the proper actual size and type, and would have to put the class access descriptor in the object.

This way of allocating objects should in fact be faster than doing the actual manipulation of SROs and object tables required of the Ada 432. In addition to entries in the list for each of the most common sizes, there should also be a port for use in making requests for odd sizes. (Handling this case by having a request-reply protocol via ports would not be very fast, but it is general and simple and would only be used rarely.) Another set of lists should be maintained specifically for the two sizes of method contexts; here there would not even be any need for setting the class/type in the object. One elegant possibility is to use ports as the heads of the linked lists—pulling a segment off a list then becomes the ordinary Receive Port primitive, synchronized access to the list is taken care of, and the auxiliary process could use surrogate sends to find out when certain sizes of segments are being used up. Furthermore, this auxiliary process could coordinate closely with the parallel garbage collector to effectively recycle objects, rather than going through the overhead deallocating objects by putting their storage back into an SRO and deallocating their object table entries.

Reducing Storage Overhead

As discussed on p. 305, one of the threats to a 432 Smalltalk implementation is excessive storage overhead per object.

□ *Embedded Values* One technique for reducing this overhead would be to represent some Smalltalk objects in other ways than as full-fledged 432 objects, for example, by embedding their representation in a pointer rather than storing it separately as a 432 object. Note that any object stored this way must be of an immutable class, since one isn't sharing pointers to a mutable piece of storage. (The model implementation uses this technique to represent small integers. Instead of small integers being represented as an object pointer to an integer object, the value of the integer is encoded directly into the object pointer.)

On the 432, if the "valid bit" of an access descriptor is turned off, that access descriptor is not regarded as referencing any 432 object, and the remaining 31 bits can be used to store the representation of some object. Since we would have more bits available than in 16-bit implementations, more things than just small integers can be encoded. A reasonable set of objects to be encoded in the access descriptor is as follows. (We assume that bits 29-30 are used to disambiguate the different sorts of objects so encoded, so that bits 0-28 are available for storing data. If it were important, another bit could be squeezed out for representing some of the classes by a more clever encoding.)

small integers	These are integers between -2^{28} and $2^{28}-1$. Note that this is much larger than the maximum small integer in the 16-bit implementations, and should mean that large integers would be used even less frequently.
the constants true, false, **and** nil	There would in fact be only a trivial space saving due to encoding these constants as embedded values, since there is only one instance of each. However, this will make life much simpler for the garbage collector, since it will be able to ignore these oft-encountered values.
characters	There are exactly 256 distinct instances of this class, representing the ASCII characters. As with the above constants, there would only be

a trivial space saving due to this encoding; the garbage collector would be the primary beneficiary.

In the current version of the Smalltalk-80 system, points are mutable objects. However, it would take a relatively small amount of work to make them immutable. If this were done, small points would be another good candidate for representation as embedded values. (Making points be immutable would also eliminate some annoying sorts of bugs arising from accidental sharing.) The x and y values of a small point could be stored in 2's complement in the low-order 28 bits of the access descriptor, 14 bits each. This is sufficient to hold points arising in nearly all graphics applications, save perhaps the generation of very high resolution hardcopy images. There would also be a class LargePoint to hold points with floating point values or large integer values, in analogy with the Smalltalk classes LargePositiveInteger and LargeNegativeInteger.

Floating point numbers are another possible candidate for this representation. They are stored in 32-bit fields on the 432, so if one is willing to give up 2 bits of precision, they could be represented as embedded values. However, as described on p. 306, it is likely that floating point arithmetic will be handled by an auxiliarly Ada process running on another chip, rather than on the Smalltalk chip. In this case, it would be better to let floating point numbers be ordinary 432 objects, making it easier to send them to the Ada process.

☐ *Other Techniques for Reducing Storage Overhead*   Another—more problematic—possibility for reducing the number of objects is to merge some collections of objects into a single object. This sort of merging should be used in only a few critical places, if at all; certainly the average programmer shouldn't need to think about it. As an example of this technique, rather than maintaining each method object as a separate segment, all the methods for a given class could be stored in a single object, with 432 refinements being used to refer to individual methods. There are about 4000 methods in the Smalltalk virtual image, so this would reduce the number of objects by close to 4000, since most classes have many methods. Making this modification might also improve swapping behavior, but would have the disadvantage that all the code for a given class would need to be in main memory at one time, rather than just the methods being used.

Techniques for Executing Primitives

As discussed on p. 306, several time-critical primitives will be directly executed on the processor chip. Other primitives are best executed off the chip. This section discusses several different ways of executing these primitives.

☐ *Execution of Primitives on an Attached Processor*   One alternative is to send requests for primitives to a port served by an attached processor. In the 432, this is the natural technique to use for i/o primitives. It may also be important for non-i/o primitives handled better by an attached processor than by another 432 GDP. If BitBlt is not implemented on the Smalltalk processor, it may be an example of this.

☐ *Execution of Primitives by an Ada Process*   Here we devote an Ada process to be a Smalltalk primitive server. Then, using inter-process communication (i.e., ports), the Smalltalk system sends requests to the Ada co-process to execute primitives. Again, this is a natural technique to use on the 432, and if it works well, is the method of choice for most non-i/o primitives handled off-board. The speed, and therefore the value, of this idea will hinge on both the execution speed of Ada programs, and the speed of inter-process communications. Preliminary statistics give an overhead of approximately 300 microseconds for such inter-process communications.

One advantage of this technique is that the primitives will be coded in Ada; this should simplify the implementation. Also, with this technique, the Ada co-process is not locked onto a particular GDP as it is with the inter-processor communication technique discussed below.

Note that in both of these first two techniques, a message is sent to a port, and a reply is received on another port. This means that the implementors of Smalltalk can postpone or change the decision as to whether a given primitive is implemented by an attached processor or by an Ada process, and that no change to the microcode would be required. This flexibility would be achieved by having an access segment, indexed by the primitive index, that mapped a primitive to a port. This would make the first two techniques indistinguishable at the microcode level.

☐ *Execution of Primitives by a Dedicated GDP*   This technique devotes one GDP exclusively to the Ada primitive handler. Thus when Smalltalk needs an off-board primitive executed, it sends a wake-up signal to the GDP and then sends its request. When the GDP is finished handling the request, it sends itself a stop processor signal. Thus the GDP is either working for the Smalltalk system, or it is blocked, waiting for a wake-up signal from Smalltalk. The Intel 432 Architecture Group suggested implementing this approach via the Lock instruction on the standard GDP.

The advantage here is that we make use of the faster inter-processor communications facilities of the 432. The disadvantage is that the system becomes less general, since the Ada process must be resident on the GDP whenever the Smalltalk processor is active. This alternative is attractive only if the improved overhead is worth the reduced generality and dedicated processor.

As described in the introduction, one of the potential benefits of a 432 implementation of Smalltalk would be support for multi-lingual systems. In this section we outline how communication between Smalltalk and Ada programs might take place.

Within the Smalltalk image, there would be "local representatives" of Ada tasks with which the Smalltalk program could communicate. These would be full-fledged Smalltalk objects to which one would send messages in the usual way. Internally, these representatives would have an access descriptor for a 432 port. The Smalltalk invocation messages would thus run methods that would in turn send 432 messages to the Ada task. There should be a Smalltalk class AdaTask that holds this general sort of information, with subclasses of AdaTask used to represent particular Ada tasks.

Smalltalk and Ada will have different ideas about how data is to be represented. For example, Smalltalk integers will be represented either as embedded values or as large integers; Ada integers will be stored simply as 32-bit quantities. To convert between these representations, the class AdaTask should have a set of conversion messages that accept certain Smalltalk objects as arguments and encode them on a byte stream for eventual transmission to the Ada task. For example, the message encodeInteger would take a (Smalltalk) integer argument and a stream of bytes, and put out the 4 bytes representing the integer as a 32-bit quantity. An analogous set of messages would be used to convert values returned by the Ada task back to Smalltalk objects.

A critical factor in the performance of a Smalltalk system, particularly the user's perception of its performance, is the speed of the graphics. There are a number of plausible ways in which the display can be connected to the processor, as discussed below. In regard to the production of a new version of the 432, the relevant question is whether BitBlt should be supported on the chip; other decisions regarding the display can be made independently. We conclude that to ensure flexibility, BitBlt should indeed be supported on the 432, unless there is a severe shortage of microcode space. While the 432 hardware doesn't have any special facilities to support BitBlt, its performance would still be quite adequate if it were implemented in microcode.

One way of connecting the bitmap display to the processor, used in the Xerox machines, is to make the memory for the bitmap display be simply part of the machine's main memory. This approach gives maximum flexibility. An unfortunate problem is that the maximum size of a 432 object is just short of what would be needed to represent the bitmap as a single 432 object. The maximum size of a 432 object is 64K bytes. A 600x800 display would just fit, but a more generous size (1000x1000) would not; such a limitation shouldn't be built into the system. With some additional software complexity, the problem can be overcome by mapping the display memory onto several 432 objects. The 432 would write some data into these objects, which would be reflected on the display. This approach clearly requires that BitBlt be implemented on the 432.

Another approach is to have the display memory be separate from the machine's main memory, and to send messages to a separate display processor to make changes to it. For this approach to have acceptable performance, there should be some high-level requests that can be made of the display processor, for example, to display a paragraph or to replicate a bit pattern along a given path. For flexibility and completeness, low-level BitBlt requests should be supported as well. There would need to be facilities for swapping fonts and the like into display memory. Even with this approach, there may well be occasions on which BitBlt on the 432 itself would be valuable. For example, the programmer might create an image in main memory—not displayed at all—and only later show this image on the display.

Thus for maximum flexibility, we recommend that BitBlt be included in the primitives supported by the 432 microcode, unless there is a severe shortage of microcode space.

Conclusions

Our study of Smalltalk and the 432 leads us to conclude that the implementation we have described here is feasible. We have pointed to what we believe to be the three chief technical threats, but we believe them to be surmountable. The potential qualitative advantages of Smalltalk on the 432 present real motivations to attempt its implementation.

References

1. Wulf, William A., Cohen, Ellis; Corwin, William, Jones, Anita, Levin, Roy, Pierson, Charles, and Pollack, Frederick, "Hydra: The Kernel of a Multiprocessor Operating System", *Comm. of the Assoc. for Computing Machinery* vol. 17, no. 6, pp. 337–345, June 1974.

2. Wulf, William A., Levin, Roy, and Pierson, Charles, "Overview of the Hydra Operating System Development", in *Proceedings of the Fifth Symposium on Operating Principles,* Assoc. for Computing Machinery, pp. 122–131, Austin, TX, Nov. 1975.

3. Wulf, William A., Levin, Roy, and Harbison, Samuel P., Hydra/C.mmp: An Experimental Computer System, McGraw-Hill, New York, 1980.

4. Cox, George W., Corwin, William M., Lai, Konrad K., and Pollack, Fred J., "A Unified Model and Implementation for Interprocess Communication in a Multiprocessor Environment", Presented at the Eighth ACM Symposium on Operating Systems Principles, 1981; (to be published).

5. Pollack, Fred J., Cox, George W., Hammerstram, Dan W., Kahn, Kevin C., Lai, Konrad K., and Rattner, Justin R., "Supporting Ada Memory Management in the iAPX-432", in *Proceedings of the Symposium on Architectural Support for Programming Languages and Operating Systems*, Assoc. for Comp. Machinery, pp. 117–131, March 1982; (also distributed as *SigArch Computer Architecture News* vol. 10, no. 2, and as *SigPlan Notices* vol. 17, no. 4).

6. Kahn, Kevin C., Corwin, William M., Dennis, T. Don, D'Hooge, Herman, Hubka, David E., Hutchins, Linda A., Montague, John T., and Pollack, Fred J., "iMAX: A Multiprocessor Operating System for an Object-Based Computer", in *Proceedings of the Eighth Symposium on Operating Systems Principles*, Assoc. for Comp. Machinery, pp. 127–136, Dec. 1981; (also distributed as *SigOps Review* vol. 15, no. 5).

7. Pollack, Fred J., Kahn, Kevin C., and Wilkinson, Roy M., "The iMAX-432 Object Filing System", in *Proceedings of the Eighth Symposium on Operating Systems Principles*, Assoc. for Comp. Machinery, pp. 137–147, Dec. 1981; (also *SigOps Review* vol. 15, no. 5).

8. Krasner, Glenn, "The Smalltalk-80 Virtual Machine", *Byte* vol. 6, no. 8, pp. 300–320, Aug. 1981.

18

Preferred Classes: A Proposal for Faster Smalltalk-80 Execution

Robert Hagmann
Computer Science Division
Department of Electrical Engineering and
Computer Sciences
University of California, Berkeley

Abstract

A straightforward implementation of a Smalltalk-80 interpreter has two main bottlenecks: memory management and message send/return overhead. In addition, since Smalltalk-80 is a typeless language, it is harder to compile than to interpret. This proposal addresses both the send/return bottleneck and the difficulty of compilation by introducing an optional limited typing mechanism for the Smalltalk-80 language. The typing mechanism does not change the Smalltalk-80 semantics in any way. Its sole purpose is to allow for a more efficient execution.

Introduction

This proposal is for a Smalltalk-80 implementation strategy[1] that is different from conventional interpreters. Where existing implementations typically try to gain performance through caching and special casing of high probability cases (see Chapter 11), this proposal explores the gains made possible by using compiler technology. This strategy has not been implemented, nor have all of the performance data needed to validate the effectiveness of this proposal been collected. This paper presents only one way to apply compiler technology to Smalltalk-80 implementations. The author hopes that by illustrating one technique that other researchers will be motivated to explore alternate strategies.

Briefly, the idea is to "fix" the class of arguments and variables to selected Smalltalk-80 methods by explicit declaration. By making the "fixed" classes be only hints, the semantics would not change. Several benefits could then occur. First, the target methods of some sends could be identified at compile time. Second, translation to machine code instead of bytecodes would be made easier since the class of all objects used in some methods would be known at compile time. Finally, some methods could be compiled in-line.

The proposals in this paper have some similarity to those of Borning and Ingalls[2]. Where their proposal deals with compile time type checking, this proposal addresses the issue of performance.

Assumptions

There are three assumptions that are necessary for this technique to be efficient in speeding up Smalltalk-80 execution.

1. The overhead associated with the send and return bytecodes is high.

2. A Smalltalk-80 application spends a large fraction of its time at or near the leaves of the message-send tree: that is, in methods that send no other messages other than to primitive methods.

3. A significant portion of methods executed dynamically do not exploit the polymorphic nature of the Smalltalk-80 language: that is, the classes of the arguments and variables used by the method remain nearly constant over some relatively long time period.

The assumption that message sends and returns are a bottleneck was confirmed by measuring several implementations. The percentage of execution time attributable to send/return, excluding memory management, for the Dorado and Dolphin are 38% and 34%[3]. For Berkeley Smalltalk, the same statistic is about 30%[4]. Since memory management during message send/return is also a bottleneck for the Dorado and Dolphin[5], for these implementations about half of the execution time is directly attributable to message-send and return bytecodes.

The second assumption has also been verified. In measurements of a Smalltalk-80 interpreter[6], it was found that 55% of all non-primitive message sends go to methods that do no further non-primitive sends. That is, 55% of all methods executed dynamically are at the leaves of the message send tree. A second interesting result is that the leaf nodes tend to be extremely short: 70% of the leaf nodes executed 5 or fewer bytecodes before returning. The conclusion is that most methods execute at the leaves of the message-send tree and they tend to be small.

The final assumption is that a significant portion of the methods do not exploit the polymorphic nature of the Smalltalk-80 language. In particular, a large fraction of methods are executed with "fixed" classes for the arguments and variables. That is, for many methods, the classes of the arguments and variables nearly always are the same from call to call. No direct evidence has been collected to verify this assumption. However, one measurement has been made that makes this seem plausible. As measured dynamically, for a given send bytecode in a given method, the probability is 95% that the receiver is of the same class as the last time this particular bytecode was executed[7]. This indicates a strong lack of polymorphism for a large part of the system.

Of course, this measurement does not directly validate the third assumption. Even though the class of the receiver was often the same, the classes of the arguments and variables (if any) were not measured. However, it is unlikely that the 5% of variability in receiver is distributed evenly over the system. Probably, many sends almost always have the same receiver as the last time. It is also likely that similar results hold for arguments and variables in methods.

For this final assumption to be true, there must be dynamically a significant number of methods that are almost always presented with the same classes for the arguments and variables as the last time. While the number of methods for which this holds is unknown, it is certainly true for some methods. For example, some graphics methods most certainly expect only to be passed an instance of class Point.

The Technique

The proposal is to augment the Smalltalk-80 language with an optional declaration of the class of arguments, instance variables and class variables. In addition, some methods would have optional declarations of the class of the value returned from the method and/or the class of the receiver. These declarations would define the *preferred class* of the argument, variable, return value, or receiver. This preferred class is the class expected to match the actual class used in the method in the vast majority of activations of the method. The receiver and arguments are not forced to match: if at run time the actual class did not match the preferred class, then the method would be executed by a conventional interpreter. If however, the preferred classes match the actual classes for all arguments and variables, then a more efficient method of execution could be performed.

At least two other techniques for introducing the notion of types to Smalltalk languages have been documented. One[8] uses type inferencing, and the other[9] uses type declarations. This proposal is somewhat different from either of these.

For the purpose of this paper, the use of pool dictionaries or the Smalltalk-80 dictionary in a method would make it ineligible for this technique. The problems involved in incorporating these dictionaries appear not to be insurmountable, but they confuse the concept being presented here.

Since the system would always interpret bytecodes when the actual and preferred classes did not match, the Smalltalk-80 semantics would not change. The only effect of the preferred classes would be that some methods would run more efficiently.

The idea behind all of this is that the upper portions (near the root) of the message-send tree are likely to be polymorphic. However, to perform some low level function, only a small locus of methods is used. Many sends and much looping occur inside of this locus. If the boundary of this locus can be identified and the classes passing over this boundary checked, then the class of objects inside the locus might be predicted. This would lead to faster execution of this small part of the computation. The rule of thumb in conventional programming languages is that 10% of the code accounts for 90% of the execution. Typically most of this 90% is found in inner loops. If this conjecture is also accepted for the Smalltalk-80 language, then this technique could effect the vast majority of execution.

There is a danger in this approach: by having two execution strategies for methods, the more efficient one with preferred classes might tend to encourage programmers not to exploit the polymorphic nature of the language. Programmers might tend to use the more restrictive but more efficient style of programming rather than the fuller and more powerful nature of the Smalltalk-80 language. If however, the addition of preferred classes to a collection of methods is viewed as an optimization step performed by the applications programmer after initial system test, then the polymorphic nature of the Smalltalk-80 language will be effectively preserved.

Implementation

The implementation technique is to compile methods to machine code as much as possible. For methods where the preferred classes are declared, two types of compiled methods are produced: the existing compiled method and a new machine code compiled method. It is assumed that a conventional interpreter is available to execute methods where there are no preferred classes and for use when the preferred classes do not match the actual classes.

For methods where the preferred classes of all arguments, instance variables, and class variables are declared, a variant of the message dictionary will be used. This will be set up at compile time. The message dictionary entry will be flagged to indicate machine code is to be executed. The machine code for the method will be divided into two sections. The first section, called the *prologue*, will validate the class of the arguments and variables. To do so, only a few instructions are executed for each argument and variable. Variables will only be checked if they are used in the method (unused instance and class variables need not be checked). If the method explicitly uses self, the class of the receiver will also be checked. If any of these tests fail, the method will be run by the standard interpreter. If all these tests succeed, the second part of the machine code, called the *body*, will be executed. The body is the machine code program to perform the method. The body would be all that would be executed from other machine code methods when the classes matched. That is, there will really be two entries to the machine code: a checked (prologue) and an unchecked (body) entry. The first is used when the classes of the arguments and variables cannot be predicted at compile time. The second will be used when this prediction is possible.

More optimizations could occur during compilation. If the class of the receiver of a send can be predicted at compile time and the target method is short, then it could be compiled in-line. If the target method is not short and the classes match, the send could be bound to the unchecked entry. Finally, if the target method can be predicted, a hard pointer to this method can be used instead of a lookup at execution time. Primitives are prime candidates for these optimizations.

Additional information must be kept to allow the debugger to operate as usual. In case of an error, it must be possible to map from machine code and expanded in-line machine code to a more conventional representation. This could be done with an auxiliary table for each machine code method that would set up the correspondence of program counter values between the two types of methods. Code would be generated such that at each potential error point, the execution would cleanly map into the conventional representation. Dependency lists could be kept to detect what methods need to be recompiled after another method is changed[10].

Sometimes during the execution of a method in machine code, the class of the value returned by some message might not match the preferred class. In this case, the machine code form of the execution would also need to be converted to interpreter form (i.e., compute the effective program counter for the interpreter). The interpreter would then start executing as usual.

For example, suppose the + primitive when called with a receiver and argument of class SmallInteger, returns either a SmallInteger or LargeInteger. The normal case is for a SmallInteger to be returned. If a LargeInteger is to be returned (possibly detected by testing the overflow bit in machine code), the system would invoke full fault recovery to convert the executing machine code form to the normal interpreter format. Once this is done, the interpreter would continue to execute the method. It is hoped that this type of fault is a low probability event, so that it would not add significant overhead.

By insuring the class of the receiver, arguments, and variables at method entry, the class of all objects relevant to the computation at the start of the method are known at compile time. By checking the class of all objects returned by message sends where needed, the class of all objects would be known at compile time for the whole method.

The checking of the preferred class at method entry need not be too time consuming. For class variables, checking could occur when they are changed. If the setting did not match the preferred class, then the object table could be flagged to not execute the machine code for those methods that depend on this class variable. Conversely, the setting of a class variable to the preferred class would re-enable the execution of machine code. By doing the checking of class variables when they are set, normal method execution would do no class variable checking. This would be faster since it is presumed that variables are read more often than they are written. The instance variables would have to be checked, but this could also be reduced to checking a flag in the object if the setting of the instance variables by the standard interpreter also caused a check of the preferred class. Note that changing an instance or class variable might involve converting existing suspended methods from the machine to the bytecode form of execution. Finally, the arguments would have to be checked. Since dynamically, most methods have few arguments (an average of 1.3 has been reported[11]), this would take only a few instructions. The number of machine instructions to check the classes might be about six. This would make the checking be about three times faster than executing a single bytecode in a conventional interpreter. If the tests succeeded in the clear majority of the cases, then this overhead would be acceptable.

The final question is that of execution efficiency. Will anything be gained or lost by the use of this technique? Certainly there will be added complexity during compilation, debugging, and error handling. Additional space will be consumed with machine instructions, mappings from bytecodes to machine instructions, and dependency lists. Additional overhead will be incurred when sending messages to methods with preferred classes when the actual classes do not match the preferred classes. The interpreter must also do extra work when setting instance and class variables that have preferred classes. But what savings can be obtained from running part of the system in machine code instead of using a standard bytecode interpreter? If we assume:

1. Executing machine instructions is five times faster than interpretation,

2. Half of all executed bytecodes are compiled to machine mode, and

3. Half of all messages sends are eliminated by compilation in-line or direct calls without method lookup,

then the savings would be that half the execution would run five times as fast, while the other half would run at nearly the same speed. This means that a savings of about 40% could be obtained. Of course this number is approximate and depends on the selection of the preferred classes to be nearly correct. However, this shows that there is potentially a large gain possible by using techniques like the one proposed here.

Conclusions

A technique to augment a conventional Smalltalk-80 interpreter has been proposed. This technique uses the concept of a preferred class to gain efficiency in those methods that do not use the polymorphic nature of the Smalltalk-80 language. This technique allows for more efficient compilation to machine code. Since the receiver class can sometimes be identified at compile time, either the method lookup can be done at compile time, or the method can be expanded in-line.

With the assumptions stated in the body of this paper, it seems possible that some form of optimizing compiler techniques can be used to gain efficiency. Although only one technique was presented here (explicit declaration), many variations on this theme are possible. Type deduction, where the type is inferred from dynamic usage, seems equally viable but requires more compiler sophistication[12].

Acknowledgments

Professor David Patterson provided overall motivation, help, and guidance for this work. Hewlett-Packard allowed Berkeley to run an early version of their interpreter that was helpful in understanding Smalltalk-80 implementations and allowed certain statistics to be acquired. Xerox granted Berkeley access to documentation as well as many personal discussions. In particular, L. Peter Deutsch was most helpful in providing statistics and discussing alternate implementation strategies. L. Peter Deutsch, Adele Goldberg, Glenn Krasner, and D. Jason Penny also served as reviewers for this paper. Their comments were most helpful and greatly improved the quality of this paper.

References

1. Goldberg, Adele, and Robson, David, *Smalltalk-80: The Language and Its Implementation*, Addison-Wesley, Reading, Mass., 1983.

2. Borning, Alan H., and Ingalls, Daniel H. H., "A Type Declaration and Inference System for Smalltalk"; Ninth Symposium on Principles of Programming Languages, pp. 133–141, Albuquerque, NM, 1982.

3. Deutsch, L. Peter, Berkeley Computer Systems Seminar, Fall 1981.

4. Ungar, David M., Private Communication, 1982.

5. See reference 3.

6. Hagmann, Robert, "Some Smalltalk Performance Measurements Emphasizing Compiler Performance and/or Context Windows", Unpublished Class Paper for CS292R, Computer Science Div., Dept. of E.E.C.S., Univ. of California, Berkeley, Fall 1981.

7. Deutsch, L. Peter, Private Communication, 1982.

8. Suzuki, Nori, "Inferring Types in Smalltalk", Eighth Symposium on Principles of Programming Languages, pp. 187–199, Williamsburg, VA, 1981.

9. See reference 2.

10. Mitchell, James A., "The Design and Construction of Flexible and Efficient Interactive Programming Systems", Garland, N.Y., 1979; (A Monograph of Mitchell's 1970 thesis at Carnegie-Mellon University).

11. See reference 7.

12. See reference 10.

19

Low-Overhead Storage Reclamation in the Smalltalk-80 Virtual Machine

Scott B. Baden
Computer Science Division
Department of Electrical Engineering and
Computer Sciences
University of California, Berkeley

Abstract

Measurements of the Smalltalk-80 virtual machine indicate that 20% to 30% of the time is spent managing storage. Following the work of Deutsch, Bobrow, and Snyder[1,2,3,4], we introduce a strategy that reduces the overhead of storage reclamation by more than 80%. We also discuss the design of simple hardware to support this strategy, and compare our approach to one using only software. We conclude by suggesting directions for future research.

Introduction

Last fall, Smalltalk came to Berkeley. Under the direction of Professor David Patterson, students in the Computer Science department ported the Smalltalk-80 virtual machine (SVM), generously provided by Hewlett-Packard Laboratories, to a research VAX-11/780, and analyzed several aspects of its performance[5,6,7].

As a result of these studies, we discovered that a large percentage of SVM execution time was spent managing storage—20% to 30%[8,9]. Most of this overhead is due to management of activation contexts. According to our statistics, context objects account for 82% of all object allocations and deallocations, and references from the evaluation stack and from local variables (both of which are contained by contexts) cause 91% of all reference-count operations.

These findings are encouraging: if the SVM could treat context objects as special objects, then it would save considerable time managing them. Consistent with this reasoning we show how to reduce storage reclamation overhead by a factor of five.

Assumptions

Our assumptions deal with changes to the SVM, both to its specification and implementation, and to the processor that executes it.

SVM Changes

An invariant of the SVM specification states that "the reference count of an object must equal the number of references to that object"[10]. In our implementation we will relax this invariant; the reference count of an object will usually not include the references made from the n most recent context activations. We call those contexts whose fields are not reference counted *volatile* contexts[11].

Owing to the presence of volatile contexts, an object might not be free when its reference count reaches zero. This condition prevents the SVM from reclaiming storage incrementally. Instead it reclaims storage periodically, accounting for all the volatile references before freeing any storage (we must ensure that the Smalltalk-80 virtual machine never runs out of storage between reclamation phases).

In addition to relaxing the reference-count invariant we also relax one other: that "all objects must be assigned an Oop"[12]. Usually, the proposed SVM does not assign Oops to method contexts nor does it allocate space in the object memory for them. Instead, the system stores the contexts in FIFO order from a fixed region of physical memory.

Occasionally, nonlinearities in the context nesting sequence or other exceptions will arise, causing the system to momentarily enforce previously relaxed invariants. Later, we will show that these conditions arise infrequently enough so that they do not degrade performance significantly.

Hardware

Although volatile contexts can be stored in main memory, they are used like registers in a conventional CPU, so we provide a small register cache, called the *context cache*.

Two registers, the *Top Window Pointer* and the *Bottom Window Pointer*, mark the physical memory bounds of the volatile contexts. The system uses these pointers, as in RISC-I[13], to resolve references to contexts (e.g., is the context volatile—in the registers—or not?). All the contexts between the two markers are volatile, while all the contexts below the Bottom Window Pointer are *stable* (i.e., their fields are reference countable). In our implementation, the storePointer operation will not do any reference counting if the destination field is volatile. To simplify the cache design we assume that all contexts are 32 words deep.

To speed up storage reclamation, we provide a special memory, called the Zero Count Table (ZCT), that indicates all the objects with a zero reference count. The ZCT has 32K entries and is 1 bit wide (the depth of the ZCT will always equal the number of possible Oops in the system). It is capable of operating in both random access and content associative modes. The system accesses the ZCT over its memory data and address busses, using a special request line to distinguish the ZCT from the object memory. The ZCT will behave like a Content Associative Memory (CAM) when the system searches it for free objects—this behavior speeds up the search time considerably (compare with queues elsewhere[14,15,16]). At all other times it behaves like a RAM. When an object's reference count reaches zero the CPU sends the object's Oop over the memory address bus and tells the ZCT to mark the appropriate entry (owing to possible volatile references to the object, it might not be free).

Reclamation

The CPU suspends normal execution during the storage reclamation phase. First, it accounts for the volatile references—a process we call *stabilization*[17]. To stabilize a register, the CPU increments the reference count of its contents (a *refI* operation). During the stabilization phase, a reference count may get incremented from zero to one—we call such a zero reference count a *spurious zero reference count*. To prevent the Smalltalk-80 virtual machine from freeing an object that had a spurious zero count, the CPU clears the ZCT entry on a zero to one reference count transition.

After stabilizing the registers, the CPU frees any object marked in the ZCT. During the reclamation phase further storage may become free and so new ZCT entries will be set. When reclamation finishes, the system *volatilizes* the registers by decrementing the reference count of their contents (we call a reference-count decrement a *refD*).

The difference between our scheme and that of its predecessors lies in the structure of the ZCT (Others used a queue.). Our implementation of the ZCT is preferable to a queue for two reasons:

1. The table will not overflow.

2. The search time will depend on the number of free objects, and not on the number of possible objects (i.e., there is no need to examine spurious zero counts).

Overhead

There are three potential causes of overhead in a volatilizing system:

1. Window underflows and overflows.

2. Periodic stabilizations and revolatilizations.

3. Special case treatment of volatile contexts.

Since the depth of the stack is bounded, some sends will cause a window overflow and some returns will cause a window underflow. The system must stabilize the bottom window in the cache on an overflow and volatilize the top window in memory on an underflow. For an 8 deep context cache, we found that only 3% of all message sends and returns caused an overflow or an underflow; these conditions result in negligible overhead[18].

There are certain cases where improper treatment of volatile contexts could cause the system to fail: non-linearities in the context nesting sequence, caused by blocks (e.g., a message may return a block as a result), and sending messages to contexts (e.g., sending a thisContext message). We assume that these activities have a negligible cost. We have observed that only 6% of all activations are due to blocks[19], and it is well known that messages to contexts happen much less frequently than method activations and messages to other types of objects[20].

Although we have provided a fixed region of memory devoted to contexts, this does not mean that we have imposed a hardwired limit on the maximum context nesting depth. When the system overflows the fixed region, it migrates least-recently used contexts into the object memory[21]. We believe that this exceptional case can be ignored—we have observed a maximum context nesting depth of only 40 contexts in an execution trace of 559K bytecodes[22]. Assuming that the sample is representative, it would be reasonable to allocate a fixed region of, say, 64 contexts.

Experiments and Their Interpretation

Experimental evidence shows that our scheme improves storage reclamation overhead by at least 80%. First we will discuss our general method for gathering statistics; next, the experiments; and finally, our conclusions.

General Method

We monitored a session involving the execution of system code and application code—browsing, compiling, and execution of simple messages—a total of 559K bytecodes were executed. To collect a more representative sample we started the measurements after system initialization had completed.

The H-P code was written exactly as specified in the Smalltalk specification[23], hence it was highly modular and easy to change. We modified the code by inserting non-invasive calls to special auditing routines. Appropriate Oops, method headers, and other data were written onto disk. Owing to its size (17 megabytes), the audit file was copied onto magnetic tape. A context cache simulator was written and ran directly from the magnetic tape audit files. Complete documentation for the audit tape format appears in our previous work[24].

Several activities were audited:

1. Bytecode Execution

2. Reference Counting

3. Deallocations and Allocations

4. Method Lookups

5. Context Activations and Returns

6. Primitive Successes and Failures

The Experiment

We measured the effects of volatilization in a non-volatilizing system. There are two experimental variables: stabilization period (in bytecodes) and context stack depth (in 32-word windows). First we introduce a set of criteria for assessing the validity of our approach. Then we present the numbers to support our claims.

We had to adjust our figures to account for four optimizations not present in the Smalltalk-80 specification, that reduce reference-counting activity by 50%[25,26,27]. These optimizations include: nilling the top of stack on a pop, not reference counting explicit use of distinguished values (nil, true, false) in the push and return bytecodes, and not reference counting when moving Oops (e.g., return top of stack).

Since we did not have access to a volatilizing Smalltalk-80 system, we could not measure certain fine-grained activities such as spurious zero counts, or overflowed queues. Hence, we could not quantify our choice of ZCT implementation over that in the literature. However, we can justify our choice from an analytic standpoint since it allows us to place an upper bound on the cost of scanning for free objects. Resolution of this issue is a topic for future research.

Figures of Merit

We evaluate our results by reporting the net savings in:

1. Reference Counting,

2. Allocation Activities, and

3. Deallocation Activities.

The savings in 2 and 3 equal the number of allocated and deallocated method contexts. We do not include block contexts owing to the difficulties with handling blocks (see p. 332). This omission will not affect our results significantly because we observed that only 7% of all contexts *allocated* are block contexts (in contrast to 6% of all *activated* contexts). The savings in 1 equals the number of reference counts of cached method context fields (e.g., in active and deactivated contexts, also in initialized, but inactive, contexts) minus a small overhead.

The Smalltalk-80 system has three types of reference-count operations, listed here in order of increasing time complexity:

1. Reference-count requests that cannot be satisfied (the object cannot be reference counted).

2. Reference-count increment (*refI*).

3. Reference-count decrement (*refD*).

1 is decided by a simple check of the object table. 2 or 3 occur depending on the outcome of the check in 1, and 3 is accompanied by a check for zero, since the object might be free.

Experimental Results—The Effects of Volatilization

We simplify the analysis of reference-count savings by ignoring references from block contexts (they account for only 5% of all references[28]) and by assuming a minimum cache depth of two windows. This latter simplification forces most references contained by method contexts to always be in the cache:

1. The home context.

2. The sender (the caller context for blocks) context.

3. A newly created context.

Only two of these three contexts need be cached at one time since the SVM disposes of the sender context when activating a new one. To determine the savings owing to volatilization we maintained separate tallies for reference-count operations of volatile fields (as mentioned in 1 through 3 above) and nonvolatile fields. The tallies were broken down further into refI's and refD's. Table 19.1 summarizes these data—it shows that volatilization of contexts reduces reference counting by 91%.

Table 19.1 Savings Owing to Volatilization

Object	refI's	refD's	Totals
Volatile Contexts	492890	847979	1340869
Other Objects	65747	66789	132536
Savings (%)	**88**	**93**	**91**

Two events reduce these savings:

1. Window underflows and overflows.

2. Periodic stabilization.

To measure these reductions we simulate a register cache. The simulator stacks the active contexts (in memory and in the registers) and maintains the bounds of the cached contexts to keep track of underflows and overflows.

On an overflow the SVM writes out part of the bottom window to memory: the stack, header, and temporaries. When done writing it also reference counts these fields. Owing to linear context nesting the SVM can infer the sender from the top of stack pointer so the context header is shortened to four fields.

On an underflow the SVM restores the top window in memory into the registers and then it refD's the cached fields. The cost of an underflow is the same as an overflow. Table 19.2 shows that for an 8 window cache, the additional reference-count operations caused by underflows and overflows offsets the gains (of 91%) by no more than 2%.

Table 19.2 Cost of Overflows and Underflows

Activity	Cache Depth (# of Windows)		
	4	8	16
% overflows	19	3.0	0.0
% underflows	20	3.0	0.0
% degradation	6	2.0	1.4

During reclamation the Smalltalk-80 virtual machine accounts for all *reference-countable* cached references, so it does not reference count the ip and sp fields of volatile contexts. When done it revolatilizes these fields. Table 19.3 shows that this overhead degrades the savings (by causing extra reference-count operations) by less than 1%.

Table 19.3 Losses Owing to Periodic Stabilization and Volatilization

	Cache Depth					
	4 Windows		8 Windows		16 Windows	
Period	*Loss*	*Loss*	*Loss*	*Loss*	*Loss*	*Loss*
(Bytecodes)	*(Ops)*	*(%)*	*(Ops)*	*(%)*	*(Ops)*	*(%)*
8000	3354	0.2	6707	0.4	13414	0.8
16,000	1676	0.1	3354	0.2	6707	0.4
32,000	838	0.1	1676	0.1	3354	0.2
64,000	419	0.0	838	0.1	1676	0.1
128,000	210	0.0	419	0.0	838	0.1

Besides register examination, reclamation includes pointer chasing (number of recursive refD's done), exclusive of those done to method contexts, plus object deallocations. Since this work is also done incrementally in a non-volatilizing system it does not affect reference-counting activity but it does affect reclamation latency time. To calculate the reclamation latency we assume that the SVM executes 128K bytecodes/second and that it takes 400ns to execute an instruction or to locate a free object in the ZCT. The Appendix shows that it takes $2.8\mu s$ to free an object and $2.7\mu s$, on average, to "chase a pointer". Table 19.4 shows the latency period for different combinations of the experimental variables. The latency time is always less than 41ms (the time spent stabilizing and volatilizing the cache is insignificant compared to the time spent reclaiming[29]), so it does not slow down the system's response time appreciably. Table 19.4 provides the information needed by an implementor to adjust the reclamation period to suit any response time constraints.

Table 19.4 Reclamation Latency Time

Reclamation Period (K BC)	*Execution Time (ms)*	*Frees*	*Fields Chased*	*Reclamation Time (ms)*
8	63	136	811	3
16	125	271	1622	5
32	250	543	3245	10
64	500	1085	6489	21
128	1000	2170	12978	41

Evaluation

For interactive use, we recommend 128K bytecode reclamation periods. At this interval the accumulation of unusable storage is reasonable, 10K words[30], and the latency time is short, 41ms. We recommend an 8 window cache. Eight windows are far superior to four, but we appear to reach a diminishing rate of return at 8; 16 windows do not improve performance (i.e. overflow and underflow rates) significantly.

Our scheme reduces storage reclamation time by at least 80% — it rarely allocates method contexts, avoiding 82% of the object allocations and deallocations, and does 89% fewer reference-count operations than a non-volatilizing implementation. Reclamation overhead is reduced to 4% to 5%, and generally, the SVM performance is improved by 22%-27%[31].

Although we have not considered the speedup due to the caching of contexts in fast registers, we feel that it will be significant. We base our choice of fast registers over slower memory on current trends which favor the inclusion of more processor registers[32].

Our results were based on a 400ns processor cycle time. If a faster or slower one is available, then an implementor will adjust the reclamation period to suit any response time requirements.

Conclusions

A Smalltalk-80 system can save considerable time managing dynamic storage if it treats context objects as special objects. The hardware is inexpensive and a 20% general improvement in performance is realizable. The savings could be as high as 30%, depending on the implementation[33].

Although the strategy looks attractive, we must caution the reader that we have not dealt with two significant issues: how to reclaim cyclic garbage, and how to handle the special cases mentioned on p. 332. In the first case, we must resort to garbage collection or develop a scheme to keep track of cycles[34]. In the second case, the system implementor must weigh the technique's benefits against its complexity. The special cases are not straightforward and their complexity may make our scheme appear less attractive, i.e., we may want to replace the reference-count technique by garbage collection. No clear-cut answer has been found.

Acknowledgments

I'd like to thank my colleagues here at Berkeley: Ricki Blau, Clem Cole, John Foderaro, Robert Hagmann, Peter Kessler, Ed Pelegri, Richard Probst, Russell Wayman, and especially David Ungar, with whom I spent many enjoyable evenings discussing Smalltalk. At Xerox: Adele Goldberg, Dan Ingalls, Ted Kaehler, Glenn Krasner; also Peter Deutsch, who has shared with me and my colleagues a good deal of his insight into the Smalltalk-80 system. At Hewlett-Packard, I'd like to thank Bob Ballance, Ted Laliotis, and Jim Stinger. Without their help this work would never have been possible.

Two faculty members have been instrumental in the execution of this project: Yale Patt and my advisor David Patterson. Yale kindly offered his time as second reader. Dave made Smalltalk a reality at Berkeley. He provided a good deal of moral support—I am grateful for his time and for his consideration throughout the project.

Appendix— Analysis of Storage Reclamation Times

Reclamation consists of two activities: marking the entry as "free" in the object table, and chasing its pointers. We present both algorithms, assuming one 400ns machine instruction per step. We include branching probabilites at all decision steps (they are enclosed in square brackets, e.g. "[0.24]"). These probabilities were reported in[35].

The freeing algorithm involves seven steps totaling $2.8\mu s$:

1. Read and clear a ZCT entry.

2. Shift the Oop (to remove the tag bit).

3. Read the OT entry.

4. Set the "free" bit.

5. Write the OT entry back.

6. Thread the free object (in the object memory) into the free list.

7. Update the head-of-free-list pointer.

The pointer chasing algorithm involves 12 steps totaling $2.7\mu s$:

1. Read the field.

2. Nil the field.

3. Was the field a SmallInteger? If so, exit [0.10].

4. Shift the Oop to remove the tag bit.

5. Read the OT entry.

6. Extract the Permanent bit.

7. Is the object Permanent? If so, exit [0.80].

8. Read the reference count.

9. Decrement the count.

10. Write back the count.

11. Is the count zero? If not, exit [0.97].

12. Toggle the ZCT entry.

References

1. Deutsch, L. Peter, and Bobrow, Daniel G., "An Efficient Incremental Automatic Garbage Collector", *Communications of the ACM* vol. 19, no. 9, pp. 522–526, Sept. 1976.

2. Deutsch, L. Peter, Lecture given to the Berkeley Smalltalk Seminar, Feb. 5, 1982.

3. _____, Private Communication, 1982.

4. Snyder, Alan, "A Machine Architecture to Support an Object-Oriented Language", Ph.D. Dissertation, MIT Laboratory for Computer Science, MIT/LCS/TR-209, March 1979.

5. Baden, Scott, "Architectural Enhancements for an Object-Based Memory System", CS292R Class Report, Computer Science Div., Dept. of E.E.C.S., Univ. of California, Berkeley, CA, Fall 1981.

6. Cole, Clement T., Pelegri-Llopart, Eduardo, Ungar, David M., and Wayman, Russell J., "Limits to Speed: A Case Study of a Smalltalk Implementation under VM/UNIX", CS-292R Class Report, Computer Science Div., Dept. of E.E.C.S., Univ. of California, Berkeley, CA, Fall 1981.

7. Hagmann, Robert, "Some Smalltalk Performance Measurements Emphasizing Compiler Performance and/or Context Windows", Unpublished Class Paper for CS292R, Computer Science Div., Dept. of E.E.C.S., Univ. of California, Berkeley, Fall 1981.

8. Cole, Clement T., Pelegri-Llopart, Eduardo, Ungar, David M., Wayman, Russell J., "Limits to Speed: A Case Study of a Smalltalk Implementation Under VM/UNIX", CS-292R Class Report, Computer Science Div., Dept. of E.E.C.S., Univ. of California, Berkeley, Fall 1981.

9. See reference 2.

10. *Ibid.*

11. *Ibid.*

12. *Ibid.*

13. Patterson, David A., Sequin, Carlo H., "RISC I: A Restricted Instruction Set VLSI Computer", Eighth Symposium on Computer Architecture, Minneapolis, Minn., May 1981.

14. See reference 1.

15. See reference 4.

16. See reference 2.

17. *Ibid.*

18. Baden, Scott, "High Performance Storage Reclamation in an Object-Based Memory System", Master's Report, Computer Science Div., Dept. of E.E.C.S., Univ. of California, Berkeley, June 9, 1982.

19. *Ibid.*

20. See reference 3.

21. *Ibid.*

22. See reference 18.

23. Goldberg, Adele, and Robson, David, *Smalltalk-80: The Language and Its Implementation*, Addison-Wesley, Reading, Mass., 1983.

24. See reference 18.

25. See reference 3.

26. Ungar, David, Private Communication, 1982.

27. See reference 18.

28. *Ibid.*

29. *Ibid.*

30. *Ibid.*

31. *Ibid.*

32. See reference 13.

33. See reference 18.

34. See reference 3.

35. See reference 18.

Index